D0850687

ATLANTIC STUDIES ON SOCIETY IN CHANGE

NO. 90

Editor in Chief, Béla K. Király
Associate Editor in Chief, Peter Pastor

A Joint Publication with the
Committee for Danubian Research, Inc.

Jákosnak sok szeretettel,

Andris

Bp., 1997. június 16.

War and Society in East Central Europe
Volume XXXIV

PAX BRITANNICA

Wartime Foreign Office Documents Regarding Plans for a Postbellum East Central Europe

Edited with an Introduction by
András D. Bán

Social Science Monographs, Boulder, Colorado
Atlantic Research and Publications, Inc.
Highland Lakes, New Jersey

Distributed by Columbia University Press, New York
1997

EAST EUROPEAN MONOGRAPHS, NO. CDLXXV

The publication of this volume was made possible by grants from
Postabank és Takarékpénztár [Postal and Savings Bank], Budapest
and *Nemzeti Kulturális Alap* [National Cultural Foundation].

Originally published as *Pax Britannica,*
© 1996 Osiris Kiadó, Budapest

Library of Congress Catalog Card Number 96–61479
ISBN 0–88033–372–3

Printed in the United States of America

Contents

Contents

Contents

Preface to Series

The present volume is a component of a series that, when completed will constitute a comprehensive survey of the many aspects of East Central European society.

The books in the series deal with the peoples whose homelands lie between the Germans to the west, the Russians to the east and the Mediterranean and Adriatic Seas to the south. They constitute a particular civilization, one that is at once an integral part of Europe, yet substantially different from the West. The area is characterized by a rich variety in language, religion, and government. The study of this complex area demands a multidisciplinary approach and, accordingly, our contributors to the series represent several academic disciplines. They have been drawn from the universities and other scholarly institutions in the United States and Western Europe, as well as East Central Europe. The editor of this publication is researcher at the Institute on Central Europe, Budapest.

The Editor in Chief, of course, takes full responsibility for ensuring the comprehensiveness, cohesion, internal balance, and scholarly quality of the series. He cheerfully accepts this responsibility and intends this work to be neither a justification nor condemnation of the policies, attitudes, and activities of any persons involved. At the same time, because the contributors to the series represent so many different disciplines, interpretations, and schools of thought, his policy in this, as in the past and future volumes, is to present their contributions without major modifications.

Béla K. Király

Acknowledgments

When during the summer of 1994 I did research in London, on a grant from the Soros Foundation, I chanced upon these documents in the Public Record Office. These came from the Foreign Research and Press Service.

I put the documents together in Budapest, but wrote the introductory study in Palo Alto. I did this because of an American research trip that was already in progress. The book appeared in Hungarian in February 1996, made possible by the financial support of the National Sociology Research Fund. It was published by Osiris Publishers in Budapest.

In the American edition, I would like to express my thanks to those who have aided my work with their advice and observations. First of all, Professor Ignác Romsics who has given me continuous professional help. I am also grateful to Professors Béla K. Király and Peter Pastor, of Atlantic Research and Publications, Inc., to Sándor Taraszovics, the president of the Committee for Danubian Research, for their support. I must thank Nicholas Kolumban for the translation of the text preceding the original English language documents. In addition, I wish to express my gratitude to Professor John Lukacs who directed my attention to certain aspects of the European policies of Great Britain; he has followed my career for ten years. Needless to say, I can always rely on his professional advice. While I was in the United Sates, my colleague Zoltán Fejős took care of the daily matters concerning my manuscript. I would like to thank him for his efforts. I am also indebted to Zsuzsanna Dömök who keyboarded the documents. Last but not least, I would like remember Laszló Antal, the former editor of Európa Publishers in Budapest who died a few days ago. His critical comments on my writings helped me a great deal. I am not alone who will miss his advice on style and contents. I am also much obliged to several friends who contributed directly or indirectly to the American publication of this book. They shared my efforts to insure that this volume appears not only in the Hungarian.

Budapest, Hungary
20 May 1996

András D. Bán

Preface

The Foreign Research and Press Service was established in 1939 mainly as an advisory body to the Foreign Office and later it became one of its departments. Presumably this body prepared several thousand papers during its short life. The eight documents I selected for this volume constitute one unit and it can be found in the archives under the call number FO 371/35 261. (I am referring to seven memorandums and several entries attached to the first one from the desk of the official in charge.) These documents originated at the end of 1942 and at the beginning of 1943. The material has been available for research purposes since 1972. The memorandum entitled *Confederations in Eastern Europe* stands out from among the others in its size and importance. It can be considered a certain kind of basic document because in later documents references are made to it. In addition, certain problems that are only alluded to in the basic document are discussed in detail in some further papers. The group of documents marked *Minutes* contain remarks of a lower official and the under secretary, and are included with the *Confederations in Eastern Europe* document. Among these the first was dated three weeks before the basic document. The explanation for this is that the first version of the memorandum, annotated by J. D. Mabbott, was done by that time or even before. It is quite obvious that Foreign Office officials requested the revision of certain details but there could not have been substantial differences between the first version and that of 1 September 1942, which is presented here. Most entries that are presented in the *Minutes* responded to the paper written on 1 September, which could be considered the final draft.

The aim of this volume is to show what kind of ideas the British foreign experts held of the new East Central European order that were to come about at the end World War II. What were the views of the British specialists concerning the national alliances in the area and how did they come about? What did they think about borders, the national minorities and the location of the future confederations in the evolving political situation?

At the shaping of the documents it was apparent that one had to make allowance for the Soviet Union's great power status and its primary area after World War II. A special memorandum summarized the possible Soviet reaction to the British proposals. (See the document entitled *Attitude of the USSR*.) Indeed, the experts were so aware of future Russian influence that almost every document makes references to a potential response by the Soviet Union if the British designs are realized. The publication of these documents serves an additional purpose. It further refines the mental picture the reader may have formed or the impressions he or she had about Britain's East European foreign policy. This picture is quite diverse even among the experts. These memorandums possibly aid us in our quest to comprehend what intentions moved British foreign policy in that period of World War II when it was almost certain that the Allied Powers would defeat Germany. Conceivably, this will throw further light upon what happened (and why it happened) between Churchill and Stalin in Moscow at the end of 1944 when they finally agreed on the spheres of influence in East Central Europe. This was recorded on a scrap of paper, reflecting even the percentages of the influence. We present the documents in the same order as they occur in the archival files. This means that they don't follow a chronological order. They are separated by Roman numerals. We printed the documents in the *Minutes*, because we knew who the authors were in the case of the eight notations. At the end of the other memorandums there are no signatures because there were several individuals who authored them. The only exception to this is the basic document, but here J. D. Mabbott annotated the document. The publication is literal, only the obvious typographical errors were corrected. The words or phrases printed in italics were printed the same way in the original text. In a few documents one can find references to maps and papers that I was unable to locate at the Public Record Office. It is conceivable that they can be found in Oxford since the Foreign Research and

Press Service only moved to London in April 1943. The maps we added aim to clarify the boundary questions of interwar Eastern Europe.

Budapest, Hungary and Palo Alto, California
April-May 1995

András D. Bán

Introduction

The Foreign Research and Press Service was set up at the outbreak of World War II for doing political and economic analyzes for the British government about various regions of the world and certain countries. First of all, it furnished the theoretical background for the steps undertaken in British foreign policy and sometimes in military and economic policies as well. The nucleus of the organization came from the reputable Royal Institute of International Affairs. This academic research center was established in 1920 and was known as Chatham House. The Service, which was most often designated with the initials FRPS in English foreign policy papers, performed its advisory function first at Balliol College, Oxford. The shapers of British foreign policy many times recognized its useful contributions. Financial support for the Service came from the operating budgets of Chatham House, and Oxford University. Public founds were also used and these amounted to fifty-two thousand pounds in 1941. The organization, heeding Foreign Secretary Anthony Eden's proposal, moved toLondon on 1 April 1943 and became one of the departments of the British foreign ministry, the Foreign Office. It merged with the PID (Political Intelligence Department), and it changed its name to Foreign Office Research Department.

The materials prepared by the Foreign Research and Press Service can be grouped basically into three categories:

1. Weekly reviews of the foreign press. The presses of the countries allied to Great Britain and those of the neutral countries were reviewed separately from those of hostile countries or those of the occupied territories. The assembled press review abstracts often served as basis for the memorandums sent to the Foreign Office. Final drafts were sent regularly to the U.S. Department of State with whose corresponding divisions the FRPS established cooperation.

2. Reports on mixed topics. Generally, these had an ad hoc character and were prepared in response to requests by various British government officials.

3. Auxiliary materials, which were put together for use in manuals or reference books. These research papers included lengthy analyzes, dealing mainly with politics and economic policy, encompassed almost every region of the earth, from the Atlantic to the Arab world through East Central Europe.

The prominent historian Arnold Toynbee led the FRPS until 1946 when the organization ceased to exist. There were several dozen experts, even college professors working under his guidance. Research was divided into geographic areas. Naturally, those countries that were most important for British foreign policy were handled separately, besides the great powers one other example should suffice: Poland. Being of secondary importance for Britain, Hungary was included within the context of relations to the Southeastern European region. (It did occasionally happen that the Foreign Office requested an analysis from the FRPS concerning matters that were specifically Hungarian or problems that were mainly Hungarian in nature but this was not the usual practice.) In the case of Hungary, one could most often read at the end of the documents the names of Carlile Aylmer Macartney or Robert William Seton-Watson who frequently argued with each other and depicted a vastly different picture of the country. Macartney viewed the aspirations of Hungarian foreign policy and the development of German-Hungarian relationship with more understanding than Seton-Watson who did not belong to the FRPS. However, Seton-Watson's opinions were sought after by British government circles because he was a knowledgeable expert on topics such as the nationalities of East Central Europe and the problems originating from the mixed ethnic backgrounds of the prospective countries. The Foreign Research and Press Service started its own pamphlet series; the first one appeared in June 1941 under the title *The Arab Federation*. In addition, it started its own journal, *The Foreign Research and Press Service Review*.

What happened to the materials prepared by the FRPS was the following: these were sent to persons who had ordered their preparation, mainly Foreign Office officials. They read it thoroughly, discussed the contents among themselves and sent these papers on to the assistant under secretaries. Then these materials became sources for decisions. Sometimes it happened that a revision was asked for if one of the under secretaries or someone in charge of a desk found something questionable in the memorandum. Thus, an analysis was sometimes reworked several times. This is what happened to *Confederations in Eastern Europe*. This study can be considered the basic document, incidentally the longest of its kind, since it was the point of departure for deliberations on such general questions as the drawing of borders or the placement of the national minorities within the confines of a future confederation. In addition, there were other considerations: the anticipated political and economic advantages and disadvantages from the point of view of the individual countries within the confederation. The remaining memorandums discussed in detail those questions that the basic document raised or possibly just touched upon.

After the birth of the order based on the Treaty of Versailles (1919), British foreign policy was not particularly interested in the countries of East Central Europe. In this respect Great Britain did not show as much desire for action as France whose presence in the region was expressed in its mutual pacts with Czechoslovakia, Romania and Yugoslavia called the Little Entente. The British had their own internal problems: they experienced economic difficulties since Great Britain by that time was not the influential economic and political world power that it had been at the end of the nineteenth century. There were other factors why English foreign policy exhibited such indifference toward East Central Europe. A sizable portion of British public opinion felt a certain guilt about the Peace Treaty of Versailles. Many thought that Germany was punished too severely. This may have been a contributing factor to the Foreign Office's lukewarm concern about the affairs of Eastern Europe. Incidentally, Great Britain, because of its geographical position, was not as directly affected by the continental problems as France was. Naturally, there were some exceptions to this limited concern. Namely, British banks played an important role in the strengthening of the Hungarian economy in the 1920s. This interest later declined and by 1929 at the beginning of the worldwide depression it had waned.[1]

Since 1933, when Adolf Hitler came to power, Great Britain had no choice but to pay closer attention to Eastern Europe. From this time on, German influence in Eastern Europe increased along with the economic and cultural influences of the English and the French. The British attitude between 1938–1939 was that Germany may accomplish whatever it desires in Europe as long as it does it through peaceful means. The fate of Eastern Europe was not of such concern to the leaders of British foreign policy that their country would become entangled in an armed conflict with Germany. In June 1933 Germany, France, Great Britain and Italy entered into an agreement in Rome which stipulated that "The High Contracting Parties will consult together as regard all questions which appertain to them. They undertake to make every effort to propose within the framework of the League of Nations, a policy of effective cooperation between all Powers with a view of maintenance of peace."[2] The Four Power Pact offered a ray of hope to the Hungarians that with the support of great powers there could be the re-attachment to Hungary of those areas along the border where there was a Hungarian majority.[3] Two years later there was another sign that British foreign policy strove for peaceful consensus in every area: in London the British-German naval accord was signed.

After Germany annexed Austria and after it declared its claim on the territory of Czechoslovakia where there were Sudeten Germans, London simply had to realize that British foreign policy had to be altered, and its interests had to be represented more forcefully. However, the partisans of appeasement, the supporters of Neville Chamberlain, believed even after September 1938, after the signing of the Munich Agreement, that all the German demands had been met and, thus, an armed conflict had been averted. Whenever the East European problems and at the same time Hungary's revisionist demands were pushed to the foreground, the British political establishment's official response touched on generalities or employed delaying tactics.

We are not going to analyze here the British decision-making process as it applies to foreign policy; it suffices to mention, however, that the prime minister and the leaders of the Foreign Office held divergent views. This turn of affairs was noticed and exploited by György Barcza who represented Hungary in London between 1938 and 1941. With the assistance of various channels, he bombarded Chamberlain with numerous memorandums. It is reasonable to assume that Barcza also became aware of the fact that Foreign Secretary Anthony Eden, who was in office until 1938 and then again from the end of 1940, felt a strong aversion toward revisionist Hungary. While Eden was out of power, the partisans of appeasement in London received the news of the First Vienna Award decision of 2 November 1938 with joy and relief. From their point of view a relatively insignificant East European conflict had been resolved without the involvement of Great Britain. With this aforementioned decision, Germany and Italy were instrumental in returning from Czechoslovakia to Hungary approximately 12,400 square kilometer territory with 1.1 million people, most of them with Hungarian as their mother tongue.

Barcza recalled in his memoirs that both Foreign Secretary Lord Halifax and Permanent Under Secretary Sir Alexander Cadogan were very satisfied with the decision of the arbitrators. In the House of Commons Chamberlain maintained during questioning that the Vienna Award was a part of the Munich Agreement and that England interpreted the results as being legal and valid. There was nothing more said about the matter and Barcza asked the Hungarian foreign minister in vain to request from the Foreign Office a written confirmation of the government's position.[4] Indeed it is certain that in the light of later events such a declaration would have had little more than moral significance.

Concurrently with the aggressive foreign political measures of Nazi Germany, there were numerous obstinate foes of British appeasement policy in Great Britain. Thus, when German Ambassador Joachim von Ribbentrop declared in 1937 in London during a private discussion with Member of Parliament Winston Churchill, that Germany only wanted a free hand in Eastern Europe, the future prime minister rejected the whole idea. When Ribbentrop painted the specter of war, Churchill warned him: "When you talk of war, which no doubt, would be a general war, you must not underrate England. She is a curious country, and few foreigners can understand her mind. Do not judge by the attitude of the present Administration. Once a great cause is presented to the people, all kinds of unexpected actions might be taken by this very Government and by the British nation."[5]

Serious changes occurred in English politics and public opinion when Hitler did not live up to his Munich promise; and went back on his word that: "We have no more territorial claims in Europe." In his speech of 17 March 1939 in Birmingham, Chamberlain responded to the German occupation of Prague. He declared the end of appeasement policy and warned that since Great Britain was not indifferent to the problems of South Eastern Europe, it will henceforth oppose further German provocations. Consequently, for the first time Great Britain gave one-sided guarantees to protect the independence of Poland, Romania and Greece. With these pledges the British attempted to frighten off Hitler from grabbing further territory. Hitler hoped until the last moment, or even beyond, that he could reach an accommodation with England since British-German discussions continued through diplomatic and other channels. These parleys broke down because of the English intransigence.

When Germany attacked Poland the British guarantees brought Britain (and France) into the war, although this did not save the Poles. As World War II unfolded and British war aims were formulated, these were designed to prevent the errors made at the peace conference after World War I. More and more officials busied themselves with Eastern Europe and its future in the various departments of the Foreign Office, as well as in the FRPS and in foreign advisory boards, although this did not mean that the region had suddenly become vastly important in British eyes. The ones who were shaping British foreign policy, however, did recognize that in the long run it would be more desirable to have one or two federations or confederations rather than several economically and militarily weak East or Central European small states with inability to resist aggression and with penchant for bickering and for seeking advantages from great power rivalries. It was assumed that only through cooperation will those countries be able to frustrate German (and in the long run Russian) hegemonic aspirations.

* * *

On 4 June 1942 at a meeting in the Foreign Office, Sir Orme Sargent, assistant under secretary, who had been the head of the Central European Department of the Foreign Ministry for a long time, stated the ideas of those who shaped British plans for the postwar reorganization of East Central Europe after World War II. The experts from FRPS were present. Quite understandably, the leaders of British diplomacy between 1942–1943 focused their attention primarily on Germany. The countries of East Central Europe along the Baltic and Aegean axis were only considered to be important if their relationship with Germany was seen as being significant for British foreign policy. By East Central Europe they meant Germany, Russia, and also the countries between the Baltic and the Aegean Seas. There was an exception to this concept: it was the case of Greece with which Great Britain cultivated a traditionally good relationship on account of its maritime interests. Indeed, preferential treatment did exist; the possibility of resuscitating Poland or Czechoslovakia seemed to be a weightier matter than the Anglophile foreign policy projects of the Hungarian Count Pál Teleki.

In 1942 the Foreign Office was deeply involved in planning the new postwar borders of East Central Europe. The goal was to eliminate German political, military and economic influence. This was the cornerstone of the British reorganization plans for the region. The British experts of foreign policy were quite aware of the fact that for the small countries of the region Germany would remain potentially the outlet, the first channel for trade; thus, German economic influence could not be stifled permanently. They also had to be aware that, Europe's eastern part would fall irretrievably under Russian influence. This did not mean at the time the acknowledgment that Eastern Europe will remain unequivocally and forever in the sphere of influence of the Russians. The concession was made that the Soviet Union will enjoy a primary role in the reconstruction of the region.

Churchill's words to Charles de Gaulle in November 1944 imply this: "Russia now was a hungry wolf in the midst of sheep. 'But after the meal comes the digestion period?' "[6] What the British prime minister meant by this was that in the long run the Russians will be unable to dominate the East European countries. Beyond the thwarting of the reemergence of the German influence, British foreign policy, favored the establishment of two groups of confederated countries instead of one with a large contiguous territory. This desiratum, however, does not mean that there were no high officials in the Foreign Office who opted for the idea of a single confederation among countries (see *Minutes*).

The formation of the two confederations was based on the assumption that this might allay the deep suspicions of the Soviets who sensed, not without reason, in the establishment of any kind of East Central European coalition a danger to their aspirations as a great power. The experts at FRPS were asked to work on and complete the basic document, keeping in mind the aforementioned considerations. The Greek-Yugoslav and the Czechoslovak-Polish pacts of January 1942 served as possible models for the attainment of the planned northern and southern confederations. The plan for the Polish-Czechoslovak confederation had been maturing for a considerable time; in the agreement that was signed on 19 November 1941 the means of the actual cooperation were only loosely outlined. The Polish-Czechoslovak pact was signed a year later on 23 January, eight days later than the Greek-Yugoslav one. As far as the former one is concerned, the representatives of the two countries asserted that they will establish a confederation after the war with the understanding that a third country may join. Within the confines of this confederation, the foreign and economic policies and the security considerations of each country would be coordinated; on the other hand, taxation, the matters of customs and the general staff would be in common. According to the plan of Władisław Sikorski, the leader of the Polish government-in-exile in London, only one confederation were to be established encompassing all the countries located between the Baltic states and the Adriatic Sea. On the other hand, Eduard Beneš, the leader of the Czechoslovak government-in-exile, preferred two confederations that were based on in the Polish-Czech and Greek-Yugoslav pact.[7]

Indeed, the concept of a confederation was quite fashionable during World War II; it occurred even to those influential politicians from the East European countries who did not hold governmental posts anymore. In 1940, Count István Bethlen, who was at the helm of the Hungarian government between 1921 and 1931, expanded on his ideas in a memorandum sent to the Ministry of Foreign Affairs. In it he wrote about "a union between Hungary, Romania and an independent Transylvania, this time with the addition of Poland."[8] At the beginning of 1944 he wrote another memorandum about a Danubian confederation.[9]

There are other examples to emphasize the popularity of the concept of a confederation. Otto von Habsburg weighed the idea of such a Danubian confederation that would encompass the territory of the former Austro-Hungarian Monarchy, with a member of the Habsburg dynasty at its helm.[10] One does not need much imagination to gather that he was thinking of himself. There was a further plan that was somewhat different from the previous ones and was authored by the politician Tibor Eckhardt and the diplomat János Pelényi. After receiving directives from Regent Miklós Horthy and Prime Minister Teleki, Eckhardt journeyed to the United States in March 1941 in order to plan for the creation of a Hungarian government-in-exile. The Eckhardt-Pelényi plan stipulated the establishment of a loosely-linked alliance of three blocs: a Balkan, a Polish-Baltic confederation, and the Danubian union. The union was to include Hungary, Austria, the Czech Republic, Slovakia, Transylvania and possibly Croatia among its members.

In 1942 Oszkár Jászi, who lived in America in exile, returned to his "Eastern Switzerland concept" about which he had already written a book and several articles. At this time, diverging from his earlier ideas, he attempted to place the Danubian confederation within the framework of a larger, more looser European confederation.[11] The Greek-Yugoslav and the Polish-Czechoslo-vak accords of January 1942 had many unforeseeable difficulties. These pacts were, namely, negotiated by emigre governments and it was by no means a certainty that after the war these would be leading their countries. In addition, there were many ambiguous and inaccurate words and phrases; these appeared to be possible sources further difficulties. Despite all the misgivings, when Foreign Secretary Eden, was questioned in the Parliament about the intentions of the government to support the establishment of confederations such as a Danubian union that would bring together Austria, Hungary, Czechoslovakia and Poland, he answered in the affirmative.[12] According to the British concept, besides Poland and Czechoslovakia, Hungary and perhaps Austria would have belonged to the northern confederation; in the southern one Greece, Yugoslavia, Romania and Bulgaria would have been the members.

The status of Albania, Slovakia, Croatia, Slovenia, Macedonia and Ruthenia generated complications. The British experts held divergent views on whether Romania should belong to the southern confederation and how would this turn of events influence the future of Transylvania. They argued that the Romanian way of life resembled that of the people in the Balkans; however, their economic connections tied them more to the states of the future northern confederation. The experts at the FRPS knew that the borders effecting ethnic minorities had not been taken into account in 1919–1920, and, therefore, they believed it to be quite feasible that there could be some modifications of the borders, favoring Hungary and Bulgaria. However, they had to take into consideration alongside ethnic principles those of economics and military strategy. The historical and emotional factors were also crucial in the lives of the people in the East European region, as were the differences in traditions, religion, cultures and ways of life. It would have been an impossible endeavor to draw borders that were equitable to all parties.

It appeared that most problems were generated by the possible participation of both Hungary and Romania in a confederation. As the experts in the FRPS explained it, these two countries were more closely tied to Germany than the others; thus, they had little interest in joining other unions. The arguments of these FRPS experts projected momentary conditions into the future, and they often failed to make room for the possibility that the international political situation could change after the war. Also, there was no attention was paid, among others, that the Hungarian governments of 1939 and of 1943 did not have the same foreign policy. It is striking that when these memorandums were prepared at the end of 1942 and at the beginning of 1943 Miklós Kállay's government had been in power in Hungary for six months. Its increasingly Anglo-American orientation caused much concern among those who were in charge of German foreign policy. Yet, the British experts' confederative concepts did not focus on Hungary. Instead, they felt it was more crucial which group or confederation will Austria call its own. Judging from geographical or economic considerations, it would have obviously belonged to the northern one but what could have been brought up against such an arrangement was that, by joining, six and a half million of "fifth columnists" would have strengthened the two or three million Germans who would have remained within the borders of Czechoslovakia.

Although the cornerstone of the British design was the obstruction of German influence after the war, the experts of the FRPS were cautious enough to take into account Germany's inevitable position as a great power in the not too distant future. This manifested itself in the study they undertook about the possible effects on the foreign policy of Germany, of the separation of Austria from the Reich and its entrance into the northern confederation. They phrased it this way: "Germany would probably resent her severance from Austria in any case and if Austria were included in the confederation against her wishes or without a plebiscite to discover them, the fifth column danger would be increased and supplemented by resentment in Germany both against the Confederation and against the Western Powers for such a violation of the declared principles" (p. 43). In these memorandums idealistic statements intermingled in a peculiar fashion with the considerations involving political realism. There are several examples of both, especially related to the laying out the future borders of East Central Europe.

In the basic document, as the Western borders of the confederation were examined, the Polish-German border appeared as a top priority. Especially, the proper affiliation for East Prussia, Upper Silesia and Danzig (Gdańsk) was found to be important on account of their strategic and economic roles. The German control of the territories in question meant a constant threat to the Poles; this was the reason why the FRPS experts were of the opinion that these could not be excluded from Poland proper.

The high percentage of the German population in the disputed areas caused new British and, Polish concerns. The solution of the Sudeten problem, through the Munich Agreement that preceded the dissolution of Czechoslovakia was still fresh in the minds of the experts. Therefore, the published documents mentioned the issue of relocating national minorities as a solution that would appease every interested party. It is another question how feasible the resettlement of close to four million Germans from the Polish territories would have been and how it could have been carried out, not to mention the issue of other minorities whose resettlement from one state to another would have been on the order of magnitude of one million. We have to add though that the shapers of British foreign policy were not much concerned about the fate of the minorities.

Frank K. Roberts, the assistant department head of the Foreign Office's Central European Division, who accepted with patience and understanding even those measures taken by Hungary that were disliked by the political establishment in London, wrote in his notes of 13 September 1942: "Irreconcilable minorities should be transferred and, in the case of those who remain, the aim should surely be not to give them minority rights and thus perpetuate difficult problems but to insist upon the integration of the minorities within the states to which they belong" (see *Minutes*, pp. 101–102).

Needless to say, the British had considerable insight into the problem of integration, due to their colonial experience. Not only the drawing of the Polish-German border, but also the new Czech-German and the Austrian-Italian borders brought to light similar issues. Even Moravia, with its territories where Germans lived, and South Tyrol were problematical. The FRPS was equally concerned about the common borders between the member states of individual confederations. In the cases of Slovakia, Croatia, Slovenia, Ruthenia and Macedonia, which the basic document designated as special areas, they were examining whether these would form a confederative unit by themselves or whether these should integrate instead into some other union.

The already mentioned religious differences and divergent traditions among the nations of East Central Europe contained the danger of several potential conflicts. Such problems did occur as far as the Serbs and the Croats, the Czechs and the Slovaks, the Ruthenians and Hungarians were concerned. The researchers at FRPS thought it was natural to apply the principles of ethnicity while drawing up the contested borders. They maintained that the deviation from the ethnic principles was caused not only by history and by the turning to violence but also by the primacy of economic and strategic factors. They argued that, within the confines of confederations, it would be possible to draw the borders according to ethnic principles because common or at least coordinated economic and strategic policies would have been generated. If tariffs and custom duties were abolished, there would be no need for strong borders.

In the Foreign Office and in other bodies where the experts worked, they were quite aware of the easily stirred-up emotions in the region and also of East European nationalism. Yet, they depicted a future based on a supposed sobriety of the people living there who were seen as being understanding, and considerate. This is how they wished to determine the borders. There was no reason why one could not speculate on the natural evening out of the number of the minorities, but it was somewhat doubtful that the reorganization of East Central Europe could have been based on it. In the same way, the arbitration of some great powers could only postpone the solution of the contested border problems.

On 30 August 1940 the British government rejected the Second Vienna Award, which divided Romanian Transylvania between Hungary and Romania. This action attests to the fact that Churchill lived up to Chamberlain's Birmingham promise. The Foreign Office warned Barcza that the British government would not accept any territorial changes that took place in Europe since the outbreak of World War II. Yet, even in 1942–1943, the Foreign Office found the 1938 Hungarian-

Slovak border drawn by German and Italian arbitrators as being ethnically fair. The most they wished to do was certain minor alterations in favor of Slovakia.

* * *

The most difficult concern in the proposals that had to do with the East European confederations was induced by the situation of Transylvania. In a special memorandum, the FRPS analyzed the problems of Transylvania in detail. The basic document outlined only four possibilities:

1. Romania would receive all areas with a Romanian majority and the ones in the southeast with a Hungarian majority. This would resemble the border of 1919.

2. To partition Transylvania into two parts along the frontier that runs through the axis of the Bihar (Bihorului) mountain range. This way, the areas with Romanian majority given to Hungary would have counterbalanced the Székely territory.

3. To organize Transylvania as an independent unit according to cantons, taking Switzerland as a model.

4. To establish a sovereign buffer state between two future confederations.

Naturally, at that time numerous Hungarian analyzes and drafts were also prepared about the future of Transylvania. The Political Science Institute in Budapest that was established by Pál Teleki in 1926 held, as the starting point of for their analysis, the assumption that "the Transylvanian question" cannot be solved on the basis of ethnicity alone. Among the assignments of the Institute was to collect statistical data, maps, journals and the texts of laws and regulations about the successor states that were established in the area formerly belonging to the Austro-Hungarian Monarchy. Prior to the Second Vienna Award, the Institute worked on choices that were similar in part to those of the FRPS. They examined how the equal rights and autonomy of the Romanian and other populations could be assured if the entire territory of Transylvania would join Hungary; conversely, they studied how Hungarian home rule would work if Transylvania would remain under Romanian jurisdiction. The researchers were also aware of the possibility that Transylvania could be partitioned; for such an eventuality, they drew various lines of division, taking into consideration the economic and cultural situation. When they weighed the independent status of Transylvania, they tried to find an answer to such questions: what kind of constitution should Transylvania aspire to and what should be its internal structure. They prepared two cantonal models, taking into consideration the data of the Hungarian census of 1910 and the Romanian census of 1930. Finally, the Institute considered the possibility of territorial division combined with a population exchange, knowing full well that this version had been rejected by official Hungarian policy.[13]

The immediate precedent to the Second Vienna Award was the Soviet Union's successful June 1940 ultimatum demanding that Romania hand over Bessarabia and Northern Bukovina. Romania was also forced to return Southern Dobrudja to Bulgaria. After these events, the Hungarian-Romanian negotiations began in Turnu-Severin in August 1940. Because the representatives of the two countries could not reach an agreement, and because in his plans Hitler assigned important economic and militarily strategic roles to both Romania and Hungary, again a court of German and Italian arbitrators had to decide. According to the decision, Hungary received North Transylvania and Eastern Transylvania—the so called Székely territory— that amounted to an area of approximately 43,000 square kilometers. There were one million Hungarians and about the same number of Romanians living there. In his speech of 5 September in the House of Commons, Churchill declared that Great Britain cannot accept this decision because it was the result of a dictate. He also added, however, that he personally never had been pleased with the way Hungary was shortchanged after World War I.

From the late fall of 1940, Hungary was unfavorably regarded in Great Britain and by British foreign policy. After the German troops marched across Hungary into Romania, and after Hungary joined the Tripartite Pact of Germany, Italy, and Japan, Cadogan warned Barcza that the transit of German troops through Hungary, to a country allied to Great Britain would bring about the breaking-off of diplomatic relations.

Furthermore, if Hungary would attack such a country, than this would be taken as casus belli and Britain will declare war. When Hungary joined in the German attack Yugoslavia in April 1941, the British government kept its word and broke diplomatic relations. The declaration of war, however, came only at the end of the year, thanks primarily to the adroit diplomatic maneuvering by Barcza.

As Hungary's enemy, it was Britain's chore to deal with the Transylvanian question, which was first resolved to no one's satisfaction by the friends of Hungary and Romania—Germany and Italy.

In the memorandum of 21 December 1942 entitled *The Problem of Transylvania*, the FRPS took into consideration the pros and cons of several options:

1. If Hungary were to receive the whole of Transylvania, three and a half million Romanians would find themselves on the other side of the border. Obviously this would be that this would be unacceptable to Romania. This version was seen as realizable only if Romania were to disintegrate.

2. The borders of 1919 should not be restored because it would return to Romania the more than one million strong Hungarian population that was handed back to Hungary by the Second Vienna Award. Some areas in the Partium should be returned to Hungary. The Partium was the area located between the Hungarian kingdom and the sovereign Principality of Transylvania of the seventeenth century. This territory belonged sometimes to the former and sometimes to the latter.

3. From the Partium adjustment of the borders should be extended southward, in the direction of the Danube. They stated that it would not be necessary to follow exactly the borderline of historic Transylvania. According to the memorandum, "A line could be drawn which would be geographically, economically and strategically reasonable and would restore to Hungary (as compared with the frontier of 1919–1940) a substantial number—some half-million—of Magyars. With these it would place under Hungarian rule an even larger number of Roumanians and Germans—perhaps at the maximum 700,000 of the former and 300,000 of the latter—but these could be set off against the Magyars remaining in Transylvania whose numbers would be

quite as great" (p. 161).

Based on the experiences of the years between the two world wars, those experts who drew up the document were aware that in reality the protection of minorities guaranteed in international agreements means little. Population exchange as an alternative solution was seen as creating new problems not only because of the size of the population effected, but also because hundreds of thousands of people would have found themselves in unaccustomed geographical and economic circumstances, which would have hindered their adjustment.

4. It would aid the pacification of Hungary, if in addition to border adjustments of the Partium, Eastern Transylvania, the territory of the Székelys, would receive autonomy. This means that from a geographical point of view the borders between Transylvania and the Partium could be drawn in such a way that about the same number of Romanians would remain in Hungary as Hungarians would remain in Romania outside the Székely enclave.

5. According to another version, Hungary was to be compensated not only with the Partium but also with Eastern Transylvania, the territory of the Székelys. The latter was to be joined with Hungary through a corridor and this corridor would stay under Hungarian jurisdiction. These ideas were close to the frontier modifications of 1940 but were also essentially different from it because the areas to the north of the corridor were to be returned to Romania. This area was heavily populated with Romanians. Thus, the number of the Romanians living in Hungary were to be reduced by 600,000. It was also recognized, on the other hand, that this division will disrupt the economic unity of Transylvania.

6. In theory, a sovereign Transylvanian state, was seen as the best solution. When they studied its feasibility, they drew on the analogy of the Swiss model but found that this model should only be followed as far as the regulations about the languages are concerned. They believed that the traditions of Transylvania and those of Switzerland were too divergent. They thought that in the law-making and in the administrative spheres the usage of the three languages (Romanian, Hungarian and German) should enjoy equal status. The smaller administrative units

should be developed, preferably, on a national basis. According to the document, the realization of an independent Transylvania would be impossible as Hungary and Romania would rather possess it than see it as a viable sovereign state. The reinvention of the historical Transylvanian principality —in any form—seemed quite unrealistic. One of the reasons for this was that, whenever the idea of autonomous Transylvania was discussed, it became charged with emotions both in Hungary and in Romania. The other reason was that one of the prerequisites for the idea of autonomy appeared to be the continuity of constitutional traditions. But this continuity was lacking. The existence of an independent Transylvanian state would not have been a matter of sheer speculation only in the case where Romania and Hungary would have been the members of the same confederation. In the final analysis, the FRPS's confederative ideas, the different alternatives, pivoted around this point: what kind of political, strategic and economic effects would the projected participation of the East European countries in the two confederations bring about in the region?

The British experts examined the feasibility of the above alternatives according to the thought of whether Romania and Hungary would become members of the same or different confederations. They were of the opinion that the most equitable proposal would be the one that would give autonomy to the Székely territory beyond the border adjustments in the Partium. Meanwhile the rest of Transylvania would remain under the jurisdiction of Romania. If Romania and Hungary were not members of the same confederations, then the Székely territory would belong to Romania; if they appear in the same confederation than Hungary could claim the Székely enclave as its own. The experts were convinced that this solution would be acceptable to both parties since Hungary would be delighted, and, at the same time, this solution would not be disadvantageous to Romania.

* * *

The future of Austria did not cause any concern even in a relative sense. They assumed at the FRPS that this small country "will drop out" of the Reich after the military defeat of Germany; the state machinery would fall apart because since the Anschluss of 1938 the Nazis were at the helm. In *The Future of Austria* they put forth the following alternatives: the country would become either independent or would belong to one of the confederations. Undoubtedly, they meant the northern confederation. Several arguments were offered for either proposal. Austria had enjoyed a rich past as a great power; this former position offered many advantages with which the other East or Central European countries could not compete or could only compete to a limited degree. The level of civilization and refined culture stood on a higher plane in Austria than was the case with its southern or eastern neighbors, not to mention the people living in the Balkan states. Although Austria cannot be viewed as a model of democracy in the period between the two world wars, still, if we take into consideration the country's experiences as a great power, enriched by the refined cultural traditions and Western orientation of the population, a case could be made that this country was practically predestined to be the defining member of a future alliance among states or even its actual leader. It is reasonable to assume that only the Czechs and the Hungarians would have agreed with such configuration, hoping that, similarly to the extinct Austro-Hungarian Monarchy, they could have had primary roles alongside that of the Austrians. Even this was not unambiguous because, for example, the strong Austrian industry could have meant serious competition for that of the Czechs in a future confederation.

Austria's dominant role would have been vigorously challenged by the successor states because they would have been guarding the precious freedom they had attained after 1918. In the early stages of World War II, there were a few supporters in the influential foreign policy establishment for the idea of a possible Habsburg restoration. In 1940 the Foreign Office brought several times to Barcza's attention that Great Britain would view the following developments with sympathy and understanding: the possibility that Austria, Czechoslovakia, Poland and Hungary would become members of a democratic monarchy. They thought that Otto von Habsburg would be the best qualified for the role of monarch. It was not by chance that some promoted this idea since Germany would have been weakened with this solution, and, at the same time, a confederation of states would have been established that would have sympathized with the Anglo-Americans. These experts had no doubt that the majority of people living in this region were pro-British and would have been closer to the British way of thinking than that of the German. These assumptions were not completely true. Moreover, as time went on, it was no longer worth reflecting on the sympathies of the population because the supporters of the concept of restoration must have sensed that they could not act in Eastern Europe without Russian consent.

The idea behind the plans for confederations was the economic consideration that with their realization, the differences in standards of living among the East Central European countries could be equalized. Thus, the underdeveloped member states could catch up with the leaders. The free movement of the labor force would be made possible. The FRPS did perceive, however, that, taking into consideration only the above mentioned viewpoints, it was not in the interest of Austria to join any confederation. But if the country would become isolated than the danger would arise that it could again fall under the influence of an increasingly strong Germany. This potentiality was opposed by the British because the mainspring of their concept was the obstruction of the rebirth of a German hegemony that would have been expressed by economic and military means.

In the memorandum that concerned itself with Austria, the thought surfaced that dealt with the development of some kind of East European common market as an alternative to the formation of confederations. (The authors were thinking within the confines of international organizations that were established by the allied powers.) However, the idea of a common market was dismissed: "since perfection cannot be expected in an imperfect world, the substitution of a confederation for a collection of independent sovereign states would be of value as a means of eliminating friction which the international authority could not otherwise overcome and Austria would benefit from inclusion in it" (p. 150). This wording unites in a unique way the frequent duality of the following FRPS concept: the outlining of the future East Central European political and economic situation was based simultaneously on idealism and political realism. Since the suprarational body was actually unsuitable to organize the economies of the region, there was no guarantee that the confederal form of government would be able to do the same. On the other hand, it is true that the economies of the East European countries did complement each other; still, this was not enough to bring about substantial cooperation.

* * *

As far as the Balkans were concerned, the same problems surfaced as were present when the future confederal participation and the independent status of Austria were examined. In the Balkans these problems were somewhat more intense and effected things with greater force. This was natural because the Yugoslav question was several layers deep. (The FRPS, having found no better title, entitled its 5 November 1942 memorandum on Yugoslavia, *The Problem of Yugoslavia.*) The most important one appeared to be how the Serbian-Croatian, the Croatian-Slovene and the Serbian-Croatian-Bosnian relationships would develop. These relationships not only projected the inner concerns of a possible Yugoslav federation, but they also inferred their dealings with neighboring countries and, thus, they had a bearing on their confederative plans. In the Serbian-Croatian-Bosnian state that had been established after 1918, there were peoples living side-by-side who had divergent religions, mentalities, cultures and economies (which were either less or more developed); they emphasized their separateness, their divergent natures, instead of their willingness to cooperative. In the FRPS they identified "the South-Slav sentiment" (p. 180). as an existing reality by which they meant a certain similarity between the languages and the ways of living, but they still acknowledged that its content "is of variable and not easily calculable" (p. 180). How could it have been! There were very few supporters of a unified Yugoslavia. The Slovenes stood above the Croats in culture and education; the Croats placed themselves in these two aspects above the Serbs. Similarly, the membership in the Balkan union did not please either the Slovenes or the Croats. In addition, here the Serbs enjoyed a predominance in number. Partially because of this, the experts of the FRPS were considering the establishment of a Danubian union where they counted on—beside the participation of Austria, Hungary and Czechoslovakia—an autonomous Croatia and Slovenia, with the possible inclusion of Poland, Serbia and Romania. The Danubian union, about which a separate memorandum was written, was a special crossbreed between the planned northern and southern confederations. They also brought up the idea of the establishment of a Croatian-Slovene commonwealth, a so-called "South Slavia" (p. 176).

While working on its implementation, the authors of the memorandum expressed a certain skepticism because it became obvious that the disagreements between the Serbs and the Croats during World War II would have come to the forefront again with the difference that the Croats, because of their superiority in number, would have taken over the role of the Serbs. The gaining excess to the Adriatic Sea, the possession of Trieste and Rijeka (Fiume) necessitated the development of another alternative plan. Here the British point of view was the following: if Trieste would belong to Slovenia or be under international jurisdiction, then it would not be in Slovenia's interest to form a common state with Croatia nor to participate separately in a Danubian union. If the case is reversed—if Slovenia is not allowed to possess Trieste—it would have no other choice but to share Rijeka with the Croats. According to the first version, the Croat-Slovene borders needed no modifications. Not so in the second version: if Rijeka would belong simultaneously to the Croats and the Slovenes, then the Slovene border would have to continue along the Ljubljana railroad line until it reaches Rijeka, so the stretch that is located west from the city could remain in Slovene hands. However, if Italy could not keep a part of Istria that has a Croat population, and it would belong under Croat jurisdiction, then this arrangement would have further consequences. This way the Slovene railroad line would be located on Croat soil. If there were a state called "South Slavia" or membership in the same confederation, this situation would not present a problem. Any other configuration would present a problem. There were four possibilities facing Serbia in the design of the FRPS:

1. membership in the Danubian union along with "South-Slavia"
2. independence
3. participation in the Balkan union
4. merging with the Soviet Union if Bulgaria and Romania decide to do the same.

The first alternative would have undoubtedly promoted the development of the Serbian economy. Independence had a strong legacy, especially in the army which greatly influenced those who had political power. Yet the status of independence would not have assured those economic advantages that would have been brought about with the acceptance of membership in the Danubian union. A plan for the Balkan union, similarly to the Danubian one, was prepared in two versions: in a broader sense FRPS experts included the Serbs, Bulgarians, Greeks, Turks, Albanians and possibly the Romanians. It is worthy of note that Greece was also thought of as being part of the group although it always enjoyed special privileges in the eyes of the English foreign-policy makers as compared to the other East European countries.

The economic strength of the Balkan union was not seen as being on par with that of the Danubian union; the former one did not have economies that complemented each other. However, economic considerations were not behind the plan for a looser Balkan union. Rather, the FRPS was concerned about possible aggression that could be committed in the Balkans by non-Balkan countries. It named Germany, Italy, the Soviet Union and the Danubian union (obviously, the experts here thought of a configuration that would have excluded Serbia and Romania and perhaps Slovenia and Croatia) as the possible aggressors. The most realistic threat was a potential Russian attack for which the the United Nations was more of a deterrent than that of the alliances of the Balkan states.

The FRPS also made allowance for the establishment of a smaller union with the participation of Serbia, Bulgaria and Macedonia. A peculiar situation developed for the Bulgarians for whom it would have been advantageous if Croatia and Slovenia, which show no interest, would have been included in the union. This way there was a chance to avoid Serbian supremacy. It is noteworthy that Bulgaria's interests were not counter to letting Croatia and Slovenia stay out of the union because Serbia alone did not represent such an economic and military threat as a federation rounded out by Croatia and Slovenia.

In the FRPS memorandum, as the alternatives facing Serbia were discussed, the consequences of an annexation by the Soviet Union were analyzed the most clearly: "Serbia's inclusion in the USSR would presumably only take place in the event of Communist revolutions in at least Bulgaria and Serbia. The extension of the Soviet power into the Balkans would have effects, not easy to estimate beyond that area. It might so draw together the Danubian States, including Slovenia and Croatia, as to unite in a closer union; or might result in the Russian absorption of the whole Danubian area" (p. 178). Except for this last possibility, the need for an accurate delimitation of the Croatian-Serbian border was part of all other scenarios. Undoubtedly, the drawing up of ethnically equitable borders would have run into the greatest obstacles in the case of Bosnia and Herzegovina where the Serbs, Croats and the Bosnians intermingled profusely. Finally, in the document the principles for a federation of Yugoslavia were also outlined; these were based on the aforementioned "South-Slav sentiment." According to the specialists its coming into being would have hinged primarily on the further development of the Serbian-Croatian relationship. It was critical how the majority of the Serbs viewed Yugoslavia: did they see it as an enlarged Serbia where every other nationality would only be subject to a subservient role? On the other hand, the Croats and the Slovenes—even if they showed any willingness toward a unified Yugoslavia—would have only agreed to it by obtaining an extensive autonomy.

* * *

Similarly to the other ones, the memorandum about the Danubian confederation contained a multitude of choices for those countries that were involved. Just as in the basic document, the experts started with the assumption, that the countries located between Germany and the Soviet Union are by themselves militarily weak; therefore, they could only insure their security if they would unite, thereby promoting the security of the region. By their cooperation within the confines of a union, the strength of their economies would be greatly enhanced. At the same time, the fate of the national minorities—at least in those countries involved—was not a matter to be ignored. The FRPS realized that the countries on both sides of the Danube had ethnically mixed areas and it was impossible to drew borders along ethnic boundaries. It was also clear that the treaties of the League of Nations concerning the protection of minorities could not be relied on. This served as an additional argument for bringing into existence the Danubian confederation. It would be another matter to consider whether the assumption that a tightly structured confederation of states would limit the domination of the majority nationality over the minorities. The experts at FRPS brought up the example of the Austro-Hungarian Monarchy when they were of the opinion that divergent peoples following similar social norms and customs, when brought together in union, would effectively cooperate in the long run. Actually, the plan for a Danubian confederation was an alternative or rather a type of the northern confederation that was outlined in the basic document. The following states were considered: Czechoslovakia, Hungary, Austria and Romania. (Thus, in relation to the northern one, Poland was left out; Romania, on the other hand, was included whose membership in either one was the subject of much debate among the British experts. They could not decide where Romania belonged. We must also add that in the case of Poland the contentions were more on the uncertain side.)

Czechoslovakia with its pre-1938 borders was designated as the pivotal state in the Danubian union. That is, both Slovakia and Ruthenia (the experts called it Sub-Carpathian Ruthenia /p. 186/) would still have been considered participants although they were not on the same level with Czech lands economically or in other aspects. The British viewed their membership as desirable even if the Czech compliance would have had the price tag of a wide-ranging autonomy. About Hungary they all agreed: "Because of Hungary's central position her exclusion from a Danubian union would leave it in every respect—geographic, economic, political and strategic—a collection of limbs with no body" (p. 187). They maintained that Czechoslovakia's future security can only be strengthened by Hungary being the union's equal member; they viewed Hungary's participation as advantageous to its own interests because it could then hope for a fair-minded treatment during the peace negotiations.

At this point almost naive notions took over, defeating the logic of political realism. It should be mentioned that it is reasonable to assume that the peace negotiations would have preceded the formation of any kind of confederation and the course of the negotiations could not have been influenced by future confederative plans. One could also question the logic behind the support for Romanian membership. The experts repeated what they wrote in *Confederations in Eastern Europe*, that is, the country's traditions belong more to that of the Balkans than to the Danubian area (or rather to Central Europe), but they argued for its inclusion, because through Romania another region exhibiting a different culture could become part of the confederation.

It did not sound more convincing when the experts asserted that the Romanians like to call themselves people of the Danube rather than folks of the Balkans because then, based on this, all the East European nations could have requested their inclusion. There was no debate about Austria. Its entry seemed to be advantageous—especially for the union. Not only would it have broadened the possibilities for the confederation's industry, commerce, transportation, but also it would have, to some extent, restricted German economic expansion in Eastern Europe. At least, the FRPS nourished such hopes. In addition, the presence of Vienna as a cultural center of the region had the potential of attracting other countries to the confederation.

A few months earlier the problems concerning the future of Yugoslavia had been already discussed; here they just mentioned that the country should under no pretenses become a member of the Danubian union because this step would have questioned the Balkan confederation's right to exist. Although the interests of Slovenia and Croatia were focused elsewhere than that of Serbia, still, it was quite obvious that in a unified

Yugoslavia things could not be achieved that opposed the wishes of the Serbs. But their religion, culture, and economic ties made the Serbs somewhat alien to the Danubian nations. The experts wrote that if Slovenia and Croatia became independent after the end of the war, their participation in a confederation would quite naturally have positive effects on its functioning.

The smooth functioning of the Danubian union presumed the close relationship of member states via centralized direction and control. The memorandum never described the organs that would have communicated the regulations from the top. The memorandum mentioned, however, that if the states of the union would be able to function and cooperate in a not strictly hierarchical form, than it would be worthwhile to reflect on the feasibility of one confederation that would stretch from the Baltic to the Aegean. This should be done because its establishment would offer greater security for its member countries than either the Danubian or the Balkan confederation. Yet the cooperation of the Danubian states had the obvious advantage that it would be easier to sustain and operate a union that is based on four or five member countries than one that consisted of nine or ten members. They did not refer to four or five countries by accident. Namely, the fifth would have been Poland whose joining the experts insisted on because of its military strength. This argument did not hold water because in September 1939 the Polish army had collapsed within a few days under the pressure of a joint German and Russian assault.

The memorandum did a more realistic job when it weighed the economic advantages of gathering the Danubian nations into one group. The harmonious development of united markets, the increased exchange of goods, transportation, industry, agriculture held out promise for the prosperity of the region. Let us add though that all these measures required local and central organizations with a precisely defined scope of authority. The text did not discuss this. In the practical implementation of the confederation, the experts insisted on the fundamental principle of equal treatment. This meant that in judging the value of the future member states, one could not start with its behavior in the last war nor with its political past because, to their way of thinking, both kinds of countries played a role— those that were allied with Great Britain and those that were in the opposite camp.

The FRPS found it necessary to hold preliminary talks with countries that were represented by emigre governments (such as Poland and Czechoslovakia) though it knew full well that there was no certainty that these governments would be in position of power in their own countries after the war. With the others that had no governments that were functioning in exile (for example, Hungary) there was no opportunity to confer.

The FRPS attempted to bridge these difficulties by declaring that there was no reason to wait until the end of World War II because with the passing of time the chances for establishing a confederation would be clearer. The experts emphasized that the plan for the Danubian union had to be first agreed upon, and verified by the allies of Great Britain such as the United States and, especially, the Soviet Union. The Soviets received any ideas on confederations with suspicion because their basic interest was that the East European countries do not form unions, in fact, that they are left fending for themselves.

In order to allay the suspicion of the Russians, the British believed that it would suffice to let them participate in the negotiations and the future execution of the plans. Although this view may have contained a certain amount of naivete, it did not mean that the experts at FRPS did not perceive the true character and nature of Russian hegemonic policies. Indeed, they were aware of a possible Soviet presence in Eastern Europe. This was apparent from the extremely prudent wording of the following: should Great Britain and the United States negotiate with all the governments that are being formed in the region or only with those that "are held by their neighbors or the USSR to be 'non-Fascist' in character" (p. 199).

According to the experts' reasoning, a conference should be held after the end of the negotiations with the countries that are effected, where the Allies would offer them the federative plans and they would be called on to join. But, if all these talks would occur in the last stage, what could they have negotiated in the earlier stages? They did not clarify either what would happen with the borders before the final conference makes its decisions. Should they be drawn on a temporary basis or should they be outlined for good? The first alternative reflected the troubles and worries of the occupation by the Allied Powers, at least from the viewpoint of the British. We indeed cannot be certain whether the Russians would have had such worries about the occupation of Eastern Europe.

One memorandum finally dealt with the northern and southern neighbors of the Danubian confederation. From the north, Poland—if it did not join—would have formed the boundary of the confederation and from the south the states of the Balkan confederation. The FRPS did not know what to do with Poland. There were as many arguments for as against its joining a union. In favor of its joining one could mention the already discussed Polish military power, the traditional Polish-Hungarian friendship which would have mitigated the bad blood between the Czechs and the Hungarians, and its almost exclusive attachment to Catholicism. Against it one could argue that Poland had a sizable population if compared with those of other Danubian countries and, because of this, a more solid future prospect for its economy. Then, again, an argument against Poland's place in a confederation was the presence of the Soviet Union which would have preferred along its borders a Poland that was left to fend for itself, rather than a confederation that included thirty million Poles.

As far as the circle of those states that were to border the Danubian union on the south is concerned, there were a few unclear points. If Romania or the whole of Yugoslavia—possibly only Croatia and Slovenia—could have belonged to the Danubian confederation, instead of that of the Balkan one, than the latter would have been confined to Bulgarian, Turkish, Greek and maybe Serbian and Albanian participation. Out of these countries, Albania was looked upon as the weakest. Actually, the British did not find the idea farfetched that if Albania would not receive any substantial economic aid from the Western allies, than its neighbors may divide it up among themselves.

Since the FRPS experts treated Greece as a special case they interjected that: "If she were left in a position of isolation, she would have to be included in a Mediterranean security system organized by the United Nations" (p. 206). This way it was difficult to give a raison d'être for a Balkan confederation since, with the possible absence out of Greece and Albania, one could only count on three potential members: Bulgaria, Serbia and Turkey. However, in this alignment there was a hint of the possible establishment of a Serb-Bulgarian alliance which would have been under strong Soviet influence. The experts of FRPS had to admit that the concept of a Danubian confederation was imbued with too many uncertainties compared to the originally planned northern and southern confederations. This version was the least attractive both for Eastern Europe and for British foreign policy. Still, they did not dismiss the idea of the Danubian union off hand; they made an allowance for it as a long-run possibility after the war.

* * *

The future role of the Soviet Union was touched upon in the proposals of the experts. Naturally, this did not exclude the idea that as a kind of conclusion to the previous six memorandums, the authors should discuss separately the problems that could have been generated by possible Russian reactions. *The Attitude of the USSR* was not only logically but also almost chronologically the last one. The FRPS divided into three subheadings the interests of the Soviet Union: strategic, economic and political. The first two did not seem essential. The specialists ignored the strategic factor because they took for granted that the Soviet Union would demand bases and territories from the East European countries and it would take possession of them whether these countries were members of a confederation or not. They also ignored the economic factor because the region appeared not to be too important for the Soviet Union from the point of view of the supply of raw materials and markets. The Soviet Union seemed to be a huge country that was headed toward isolation and was capable of existing as an autarky. (The experts did not deal with the qualitative aspect of such an economy.)

The political interests of the Soviet Union required a closer, more detailed analysis. It was apparent from the British analysis that the Russians would play a double game: they would simultaneously make an effort to discourage the states of East

Central Europe from accepting either German or Anglo-American influence. The experts were of the opinion that the German influence could be stifled if the allied forces disarmed and occupied Germany; thus, the Russians will follow, with the customary suspicion, the steps taken by Great Britain and the United States.

The FRPS people had no difficulty understanding the Russian worries since behind their fears there were two risk factors: one real and one not so real. The concern that the Western powers with the help of their acquired economic position in the region would aspire to defeat the Soviet system was unrealistic. The reasons were manifold—the size of the country, vast sources of raw materials and a huge army. The experts found the Russian suspicions relatively well-founded in the case of the other scenario: East Central Europe would be reconstructed through its own strength but with Anglo-American support. This latter notion was in the realm of possibilities because the British and the Americans possessed material resources, economic know-how and experience. The possibility of having an economically viable, later highly-developed confederation along the Soviet border could rekindle one of the strongest fears of the Soviet leadership. According to the FRPS, "...an area, revived and flourishing through Western aid, just across the Soviet border, would bring the Soviet people into too close proximity to an effective non-communist economy, and thus cause internal a unrest in the Union itself even though this was no part of the aim of the Western Powers" (p. 213). After reviewing the material above, the British experts gave the following prognosis:

1. The East Central European countries would unite in one or two confederations; thus, the dangers of German influence would diminish for a long time. This latter coincides with Soviet interests, no matter how much the Soviet leadership opposes the idea of confederations.

2. The Russians would establish their own sphere of influence in the region, and they would bind the respective states to them by means of political and military institutions and alliances.

This situation could develop with the passage of time into a dangerous weapon because it could divide the nations of East

Central Europe into two blocs, those that are friendly toward the Russians (they ranked here the Serbs, the Bulgarians and the Czechs) and those opposing the Russians (Hungarians, Poles, Romanians, Croats, and Slovenes).

The reasoning of the FRPS was logical. The British were taking the long view: if one would think with a sense of perspective, one would unambiguously count on the Soviet Union not wanting nor tolerating any Anglo-American or German influence in the proximity of its border. Although the feasibility of a German sphere of influence was negligible after World War II, this was definitely not the case with an English-American one. This is why a way had to be found to dispel or at least to soothe the uneasiness of the Soviets about the plans involving confederations. The most direct means for this was provided by preliminary discussions and meetings for the verification of the composition of future confederations and their planned operations. Their importance was again and again emphasized by the British. In conjunction with the matters above, it was quite apparent that the Soviet Union not only wanted to take part in the discussions about future confederations, but it would also support some alternatives and veto others. This last consideration spoke against the establishment of one large confederation. The plans about two confederations appeared to have a better chance to be realized in either variety—the northern and the southern ones or the Danubian and the Balkan ones. This held true especially if Poland would have been excluded from all confederations since Stalin was the least tolerant toward it. Yet it could not be expected that the majority of the population in either the northern or in the Danubian unions would immediately embrace the Russians—the absence of Poland did not guarantee this.

On the other hand, there was a better chance that the Russians would find themselves in a more advantageous position as far as the Balkan union is concerned; because of their close-knit relationships with the Serbs and the Bulgarians, they would become more influential and most likely effect the operations of this union. Although the FRPS memorandum did not spell it out, one could detect reading between the lines, the idea of partitioning Eastern Europe into the spheres of influence: the northern (Danubian) confederation would be under Anglo-American influence, and the southern (Balkan) confederation would be under Russian control. Nevertheless, this did not mean that according to British logic the mutual interests would be separated in a precise and well-defined way since they were counting on the cooperation of the three great powers even after the war. And with good reason because it was apparent that the Soviet Union would be economically exhausted by the end of the hostilities and, therefore, it would need the aid of the Western powers as much as the East European small countries did.

The authors of the memorandum recommended paying close attention to a very important consideration: it was advisable to accomplish the assistance in such a way as not to hurt the Russians' traditional sensitivity. This was a sharp insight that was observed by only a few of the leaders of those countries that formulated global policy both at the time immediately after the war and ever since. The majority of these leaders did not see that the humiliation of the Russians could have unforeseen consequences. The document stated that any economic aid to the Soviet Union should be offered after due consideration because then the Russians would not oppose a similar assistance to Eastern Europe. Even with the numerous arguments for or against a position, the British viewpoint was unambiguous. One should attempt to win over the Soviet leadership and, what is more essential, its participation.

Already in 1942–1943, as far as this was concerned, the shapers of British foreign policy had no illusions. (This outlook could be contrasted with that of the Hungarians which hoped until the end of the war, actually until the last moment, that the country would be occupied by Anglo-American forces.) As the end of the war approached, the East Central European policy of England was more and more determined by its relations with the Russians. This was reflected in the two notes Churchill wrote to Eden on 4 May 1944: "I cannot say there is much in Italy, but broadly speaking the issue is: are we going to acquiesce in the communisation of the Balkans and perhaps of Italy?...Evidently we are approaching a showdown with the Russians about their communist intrigues in Italy, Yugoslavia and Greece. I think their attitude becomes more difficult every day."[14]

A very serious phrase of this contest of strength was the destruction of Warsaw. The Warsaw uprising began on 1 August 1944. The Soviet troops not only did not support it, but also they did not permit the British and American planes that dropped supplies to the resistance to use the Soviet airfields. Churchill intervened several times in theses matters; he had discussions with Stalin. Yet the Russian troops did not move until 10 September although they had been stationed on Warsaw's outskirts since the end of July.

A resolution to the rift was found in October 1944. The conference of foreign ministers in Moscow accepted Churchill's proposal: the countries of East Central Europe were divided into Russian and English spheres of influence. This was done through the so-called Percentages Agreement. Figures were set down on a piece of paper on which the British prime minister wrote: Russia in Romania 90%, the rest 10%; Great Britain in Greece 90%, Russia 10%; Yugoslavia 50%–50%; Hungary 50%–50%; Russia in Bulgaria 75%, the rest 25%. Stalin checked the list. The ratio of percentages were later modified to the disadvantage of Great Britain: in Hungary and Bulgaria the ratio changed 80%–20% in favor of the Soviet Union.[15] At first Stalin respected the agreement in deed, since in December 1944, at the time of the attempted putsch of the Greek communists, he overlooked the British intervention. We also have to add that Stalin did not support plans for power grab by the communist parties in Italy, France and Belgium; in all three countries these parties were strong after World War II. On the other hand, he did not permit interference in Bulgaria and Romania where communist regimes were victorious. Churchill reconciled himself to the realities in Eastern Europe: the formation of pro-Russian non-communist regimes. He was able to see such governments in Czechoslovakia and Hungary for a short while. The two conferences in Yalta and Potsdam were basically a conclusion, an ending to the agreements that were made openly or tacitly about the fate of the East European countries. As John Lukacs noted: "At Potsdam, Stalin, who was probably baffled about British non-committalness about Hungary, asked Churchill a point-blank question about that country. Churchill was unprepared for answer."[16] The United States was represented by President Henry S. Truman during the Potsdam Conference. During the second part of the conference, Churchill was succeeded by Clement Attlee who had won the British elections. These changes had significance: Stalin profited from them because the new leaders were unable to develop the kind of cooperation Churchill and Roosevelt had.

Between 1939 and 1945, but, especially from the year 1943, British foreign policy was more assertive, enforcing its claims toward Eastern Europe with more energy than that of the American. After the war this situation was reversed: Great Britain was financially exhausted; it could not raise its voice and debate the United States on essential matters. In retrospect —from the perspective of fifty years—we could possibly smile a little at the FRPS's concepts concerning confederations, but it would be unwise to dismiss them with a gesture of the hand. Attempts at regional cooperation in today's East Central Europe indicate that the documents prepared in 1942–1943 were not completely Utopian solutions to the economic and other woes of Europe's Eastern half. The reader should not expect these dated proposals to be valid solutions for the future. These should be seen as thoughtful constructs whose parts could be considered as proposals to achieve East Central European integration.

DOCUMENTS

[U 420/61/72]

DOCUMENT 1

Confederations in Eastern Europe

Introduction

1. The following assumptions (paras. 2-6) were laid down at an interview at the Foreign Office on 4th June 1942 between Sir Orme Sargent[1] and F.R.P.S. representatives. Our terms of reference were to work out their implications under the main heads included in the present memorandum.

2. In the settlement of the region between Germany and Italy on the one hand and the USSR and Turkey on the other, it will be a paramount British interest to prevent the return of German occupation or control—military, political or economic.

3. To be effective any arrangements made for this purpose must include (a) some linking together of the States in this region, (b) some outside support, above all from the USSR, for these new and larger political units.

4. It is not possible to envisage a single large unit covering the whole area. Two units will emerge, springing from the Polish-Czech and Greek-Yugoslav Confederations. The former will include Hungary, the latter Roumania and Bulgaria. Hungary and Bulgaria will probably be, at any rate to begin with, unwilling members of their respective confederations.

5. Neither of these two new units can be expected to start with any form of union closer than a confederation. Discussion of their structure must begin from such arrangements as they have already announced or are known to have under consideration.

6. The USSR will have territorial interests in this region extending at least as far as the territories she held on the eve of the German attack in June 1941. She will probably seek to recompense Poland and Rumania for the territory they would thus

lose by offering them territorial compensation at the expense of Germany and Hungary respectively.

Note 1. Attitudes of the Eastern European Peoples

7. The attitudes of the Eastern European Peoples towards their Great Power neighbours and towards each other may be expected to be as follows:

(i) The peoples now under Axis domination will hate and fear Germany in different degrees; in the highest degree, Poles, Czechs, Slovenes, Serbs, Greeks; in the second degree, Rumanians, Albanians, Magyars, Croats, Slovaks, Bulgars. Few of them will have these feelings about Italy.

(ii) The USSR will be hated and feared by Poles, Magyars, Rumanians, and perhaps also (for religious rather than political motives) by Croats, Slovenes and Slovaks. On the other hand, the USSR would be welcomed as a leader and protector by many Czechs, Serbs and Bulgars (despite the anti-Russian tendencies of the present Yugoslav and Bulgarian governments).

(iii) In the northern confederations the Poles ought to have no difficulty with the other member-peoples (except perhaps with the Czechs). Magyars and Austrians (if the latter were members) could get on together. Difficulties might be expected between Magyars and Slovaks, Magyars and Czechs and to a much lesser degree between Czechs and Slovaks.

(iv) In the Southern Confederation the Bulgars would have difficulties with all the other parties, but much less with Serbs and Rumanians than with Greeks. The most difficult relation would be those of the Albanians with the Greeks and Serbs, and next again those of Serbs with Croats.

Note 2. On the Assumptions

8. In taking the existing plans as a starting point and the intentions of their authors concerning additional members as assumptions, two provisos should be added.

9. Removal of Axis control may result at once in war. This is most likely in the case of Hungary and Rumania but it

may also affect Bulgaria and her neighbours. If there were a general flare-up, the final groupings might reflect the military alliances of the time and be quite different from those now planned.

10. There may also occur, in countries of Eastern Europe, revolutions having the active support or benevolent assistance of the USSR. Exiled or previously established governments may than be overthrown and their prior commitments disowned. Groupings may arise on ideological foundations, especially between Serbs and Bulgars, but elsewhere also. If the new governments were very left-wing, this would tend to increase the influence of the USSR in the area and might isolate States which do not undergo such revolutions.

11. Yet ever if the present plans come to nothing, the breakdown of these embryos should not be allowed to invalidate the idea of federation and might even make possible some improvements in its application.

I. Membership

12. *Note.* Throughout this memorandum, reference will given at the end of each section to the fuller F.R.P.S. material on which much of the memorandum is based.

Hungary and Bulgaria

13. The greatest problems arising from the membership lists given above (para. 4) are those due to the inclusion of Hungary and Bulgaria. These two States have suffered least from Axis control and will accordingly lack the principal immediate motive for membership, namely the determination that such control shall not recur. They also have less anti-German feeling than most of the other member-peoples. Moreover their relations with their neighbours are bad and may even result in war when German control is removed.

14. Yet, despite these obstacles, the Confederations would be mere torsoes from every point of view, military, political and economic, if these States were excluded and liable to be used, as before, as German tools. Accordingly pressure may be

needed to bring and to keep them within the Confederations, and the difficulties of their unpopularity must be faced. There may be concerted attempts by other confederators to benefit territorially at their expense. Such attempts, if they succeeded and especially they succeeded as a result of fighting, would postpone indefinitely the day of willing Magyar and Bulgar co-operation.

15. It should be recognised that the process of compelling States to join and to remain in a Confederation is not an easy one, and that resentful members within the organisations may be an even better field for German infiltration than if they remained outside. It is therefore in the general interests of security that the exiled Allied Governments should not return to their territories with the aim of treating them as ex-enemies, but should be prepared to consider their legitimate territorial interests.

16. It is noted below (para. 102) that the existence of confederations should enable more attention to be paid to ethnic boundaries than in 1919. This will make possible some improvement for Hungary and Bulgaria in their 1919–1939 frontiers. It would also be an advantage if the necessary surrender by Hungary of historic claims were matched by an equal surrender by other States of claims which have only a historic basis.

17. The force of these arguments may seem lessened by the fact that Hungary is assumed to be in one Confederation and two States (Rumania and Yugoslavia) which have claims on her present territory in the other. But the cooperation between the two Confederations which is laid down as essential in the Czech-Polish Agreement[2] would require the maximum reduction of Hungarian grievances here also. It is obvious that a permanently discontented Hungary would be a source of danger to both Confederations.

Rumania

18. The assumption that Rumania will belong to the Southern Confederation is in almost every way regrettable. While their way of life is perhaps more Balkan than Danubian, the Rumanians regard themselves as a Central European people. They have few economic connections with the rest of the

Southern Confederation; and their membership of it makes impossible the most promising solution of the problem of Transylvania, namely that this debated area should belong, as a separate unit, to the same confederation as both Rumania and Hungary. (see below para. 126).

Austria

19. Strategically the case for including Austria in the northern confederation is obvious. If she is in the Reich, or independent and thus liable ultimately to accept an Anschluss,[3] the Czechs would be almost encircled, and their southern frontier, like that of Hungary on the west, would be indefensible. Germany would also be able to strike direct at the Southern Confederation if that suited her strategic plans.

20. Economically and strategically, the inclusion of Austrian industries would strengthen the Northern Confederation and round off its economic structure, though this would require, on the part of the other members, tolerance of Austrian competition, rehabilitation of their old links with Vienna, and the encouragement of further industrialisation in Austria itself. Considerable economic dislocation would also be caused, in the initial stages, in undoing the integration of Austria into the German economic system.

21. The main argument against Austrian membership is the possibility of a fifth column six and a half million strong added to the two or three million Germans who may have to be included in Czechoslovakia anyhow. This danger depends on the degree to which recent pan-Germanism has destroyed the older Austrian tradition, which would make co-operation with Czechs and Magyars more palatable to an Austrian than German domination.

22. Germany would probably resent her severance from Austria in any case, and, if Austria were included in the Confederation against her wishes or without a plebiscite to discover them, the fifth column danger would be increased and supplemented by resentment in Germany both against the Confederation and against the Western Powers for such a violation of heir declared principles. Yet consultation of the Austrian

people will be difficult and may be possible only after a period of time during which she should be included in any schemes for relief and reconstruction and ruled by a puppet government with strong allied support. (*Note*: For further detail on Austria cf. Austria and Eastern Europe (RB IX/11/iii).

Albania

23. Albania is strategically vital to the Southern Confederation. On its landward side it is wholly surrounded by Confederation territory, and it commands the entrance to the Adriatic. It is too weak and backward to be completely indepen-dent, and the only other alternative to this membership, from the point of view of security for the Confederation, would be the unlikely one of occupation (under mandate or otherwise) by a Great Power friendly to the Confederation. Albania has also suf-fered from the hostility of her neighbours, which may tempt them even to consider partitioning her between them. But the tenacious survival of the Albanians suggests that they could not easily be digested either by Yugoslavia or by Greece. Such par-tition would, moreover, clearly violate the principles of the Atlantic Charter,[4] to which both States have adhered.

24. Albanian membership of the Confederation would therefore seem the only sound solution. Albania is so weak and backward that she might need some special assistance from Western experts and advisers (as proposed for Abyssinia) and this assistance might also enable her to maintain her status in the Confederation which might otherwise be an unenviable one in view of her past relations with her neighbours. Her inclusion in a Confederation so loose as that now planned raises general difficulties which are discussed in the next section.

Other Small Units

25. There are many cases where internal difficulties within the States of Europe, as they existed from 1919 to 1939, suggest the possibility of units smaller than those States. Slovakia, Croatia, Slovenia, Sub-Carpathian Ruthenia, Mace-donia—these are areas each with a unity of its own, resisting

submergence in the national unity of the State to which it previously belonged.

26. In a loose Confederation such as that suggested by the published terms of both the Greek-Yugoslav[5] and the Czech-Polish Agreements there would be great difficulties in making any of these areas separate members of the Confederation. (For a possible "tighter" confederation between Poles and Czechs, see below paras. 45, 47). A loose Confederation leaves the ultimate control of all policy to the Governments of the member-States: and these areas are too small and generally too untried and undeveloped to be in effect sovereign States.

27. In a close federation these difficulties would be diminished. The federal organs would exercise genuine control in their own sphere; and the control of the remaining functions (education and other affairs in which local differences count) would not beyond the powers of such smaller units to administer.

28. Federal representation would probably bear some relation to population. While this might seem to admit domination by the larger areas, the greater the unification of policy the less this would be felt, and the greater the benefit to small and backward groups. They would benefit by services which , if they were independent, would be beyond their means, and possibly even by more direct aid, financial, technical and administrative, from the more developed areas of the federation.

29. The conclusion is that none of these small areas can easily be envisaged as members of the Confederations, unless the Polish-Czech Confederation turns out to be closer than our present information gives us conclusive evidence to expect. The special characteristics of these areas will be dealt with separately below (paras. 89-98).

II. Form and Structure

(a) Analysis of the Present Proposals

30. The following analysis is based on the F. O. documents (R 472/43/67 and C 13 370/6/12) given us with our terms of reference. They are called in what follows "The Greek-Yugoslav Agreement" and "The Polish Plan." Reference is also

made to the Czech-Polish Agreement of 23rd January, 1942, the text used being that published in The Times of 24th January.

(i) Spheres of Confederal Control

31. The general subjects over which co-operation is intended are the same in both confederations and comprise foreign policy, defence and security against external attack, and economic affairs of common interest to the member-States.

32. The Polish plan goes into greater detail in setting out the objectives of confederal policy, but most of its detail is no doubt implied in the more general terms of the Greek-Yugoslav Agreement. In regard to foreign policy, the Poles place treaties, negotiations with external powers, and the despatch and reception of ambassadors under the Confederation Government. In defence, the Greek-Yugoslav Agreement specifies "common defence plans, a common type of armament, etc." In economic matters, both plans aim at an ultimate abolition of tariffs as between members and an ultimate imposition of common tariffs in relation to the outside world. Both plans agree to stabilise the currencies of their member-States relatively to each other, but neither suggests a common currency or the interavailability of national currencies. Both prescribe common economic planning and the Poles propose joint distribution of public works and co-ordinated economic development with the aim of absorbing all free labour locally. Both refer to improvements of inter-communications of all kinds, the Poles adding uniform freight rates, internal postal rates and liberty for citizens of any member-State to move freely without visas and to take work anywhere within the territories of the Confederation.

33. What is noticeable about all the above proposals is that they imply everywhere the continuation of effective action by the States concerned in all fields in which co-operation is envisaged. The States retain their own armed forces, coinage, posts, passports, railways, etc. Uniformity, reached by consultation and agreement, is the aim and not centralised control in any sphere. (The only exceptions are the Polish references to a single supreme commander of the joint armies in time of war and to distribution and finance of public works by the

Confederation Government.) This impression is confirmed when we pass to the examination of the finance and organisation by which the confederal policies are to be carried out.

(ii) Finance

34. The Greek-Yugoslav agreement makes no reference to confederal finance. Since, however, no field of executive action is subject to confederal control, the only financial need would be for the salaries and expenses of the two research bureaux. This could be divided among the member-States equally (or proportionately to their national expenditure or population) and met by grants from State budgets, as was League of Nations expenditure.

35. The Polish plan mentions a Confederation budget. No source of income is suggested and the only filed of expenditure named is the financing of public works. Even this expenditure seems limited to capital supply, as the works are to be "distributed", presumably among the member-States. In other matters, the assumption seems to be that the States themselves should carry out improvements of communications etc., though on a joint and uniform plan.

(iii) Organisation and Personnel

36. The essential difference between federations and confederations lies not in the general spheres submitted to central authority but in the nature of the organs established to work in these spheres. It may be summarily stated that, in this respect, the Greek-Yugoslav Agreement foreshadows a very loose confederation. The Polish arrangements look closer, but there is so much vagueness and obscurity in their terms, and the vagueness occurs at such vital points, that it is difficult to say how close they would be in practice. The Greek-Yugoslav plan will therefore be examined first, and it will then be considered what important additions the Polish proposals might make to it.

Greek-Yugoslav Organisation

37. The supreme organ of the Greek-Yugoslav Confederation, on the political side, is composed of the Foreign Ministers of the two States, meeting at regular intervals. No joint bodies for executive action, for diplomatic or consular representation, or for the settlement of political difficulties between members of the Confederation are mentioned. The only permanent political organ of the Confederation is a Bureau to study questions and prepare material for ministerial consideration. In this field, therefore, the Confederation is hardly distinguishable from an alliance.

38. In the field of defence there is an appearance of closer union. There is to be a single general staff. But member-States are to be represented on it by their chiefs of Staff and there is no reference to members other than these. It is clear from the references to "Chiefs of Staff" and to "standardized equipment" that each state retains its own separate armed forces. Accordingly if there are other members of the joint general staff they will also be chosen from the national forces. It would thus seem likely that the general staff (at least in peacetime) would be in fact a two (or three or four) Staff conference to agree on uniform methods and a joint plan. It would differ from the "Staff talks" which any alliance usually involves only in the frequency and regularity of its meetings.

39. In the economic field the political machinery is repeated. The supreme organ is composed of two representatives of the government of each State meeting at regular intervals and supplemented only by a permanent Bureau, studying problems and preparing material.

40. Thus in the political and economic field all control of policy lies with ministers or government representatives, who remain responsible to the governments or parliaments of their own States. Continuity of policy is guaranteed no more and no less than it is in any sovereign State by the tradition that foreign policy should not be reversed by successive governments. Any change of government in the member-States dissolves the central organs of the Confederation. Over any attempt at a genuinely centralized policy hangs the fate of the "Hoare-Laval plan".[6]

Polish-Czech Organisation

41. The published text of the Polish-Czech Agreement says only that " the establishment of common organs will be necessary". In the Polish plan, three organs are mentioned—the Supreme Council, the Confederation Government and the Confederation Assembly. It is on the powers and inter-relations of these three bodies that the nature of the new unit would depend. On one extreme view the result would be little more than the Greek-Yugoslav Confederation, i.e., a close and permanent alliance. On the other the result would be a genuine federation.

42. At all crucial points where a decision between the two interpretations should be discoverable from the terms of the agreement, the language of the Polish plan is so vague as to make a confident decision between them is impossible. The Polish document, however, explains that the vagueness is intentionally maintained in order not to alarm the Czechs. From this it presumably follows that the second interpretation is nearer the truth than the first since the first would hardly alarm anybody.

43. The explicit statements in the text are as follows. Supreme authority is vested in the Councils which appoints the Government. The Government has the executive power. It directs foreign policy, administers the joint budget, and directs the joint defence and common economic affairs of the Confederation. The Assembly passes the Confederation budget, legislates on matters within the competence of the Confederation and controls the Government. There is no further light on how the three bodies are to be elected or appointed, nor on their mutual relations of responsibility. These statements seem open to a weaker and stronger interpretation.

44. On the weaker interpretation the Supreme Council is really supreme. It meets often, makes decisions of principle and appoints and dismisses the Government. ("Appoints" is in the document, "dismisses" is not.) The Government is a permanent Civil Service plus secretariat carrying out in detail the decisions of the Council. The Assembly is like the League Assembly, an organ for debate and publicity. Its "legislation"

would be the formal passing of measures proposed by the Council. Its "control" of the Government would be the French sense of "control"—general supervision and the power to call for reports and to ask questions.

45. On the stronger interpretation the Council would be titular Sovereign and is suggested to avoid the difficulties of a personal sovereign. It would "appoint" the Government as the King appoints British Ministers. (Hence the silence about dismissing them.) It would meet seldom and (except in a crisis) do nothing. The Government would be a real government, like our Cabinet. It would take all decisions of principle, submit bills to the Assembly, negotiate with Foreign States, etc. The Assembly would control the Government as the House of Commons controls the Cabinet. It would have the real power to dismiss governments by defeat on major issues or on votes of confidence, and to appoint them by giving majorities to policies put forward by opposition leaders. It would also control the Government by votes on bills and on the budget.

46. The first of these is said to be the weaker interpretation because it leaves the key powers to the Council which consists of an equal number of representatives of each State in the Confederation. As the Council is supreme, it is presumably neither elected by the Assembly nor responsible to it. Its members must therefore be appointed by the Governments of the member-States and be responsible to those Governments. The result of vesting the Council with active controlling powers would therefore be that anticipated in the Greek-Yugoslav Confederation, namely the subordination of confederal policy to decisions and changes in the governments and parliaments of the member-States.

47. If the Assembly were, as seems the intention, directly elected by the citizens of the Confederation, and if the Assembly and the Government between them exercised the real working sovereignty in the Confederation, in finance, legislation and executive action, the result would be a genuine federation. The policy of the Confederation would be independent of political changes in the member-States (as a Conservative Government can sit firmly at Westminster, while Labour and Conservative majorities alternate on the L. C. C.). Hence this is called

the stronger interpretation.

48. Among the gaps which would have to be filled in the text of the Polish plan to justify this stronger interpretation are the following: direct election of the Assembly; sources of income for the confederal budget; some indication of the independence of the Assembly; and limits on the exercise of "supreme power" by the Council. The silence on the method of election of the Assembly is natural, if direct election with seats allotted according to population is intended. For this would involve a considerable preponderance of Poles in the Assembly.

(b) Difficulties to be anticipated

49. In the following sections the experience of previous unions of States is used to indicate points on which difficulties in these arrangements may arise. The first set are those likely to occur in the execution of the plants at present envisaged; the second are those due to limitations in these plans and requiring other arrangements for their solution.

(i) Difficulties in executing the present plans

50. In foreign and defence policy the central difficulty will be to make the Confederation anything more than an alliance. In foreign policy this seems all that the Agreement allows. Joint defence policy might, however, be assisted if members of the Confederation General Staff, except the two Chiefs of Staff, had this duty as their whole-time work and had the prestige necessary to give the Staff strong service backing and the power to control all large-scale manoeuvres. Language difficulties will arise here, especially when the Confederation is enlarged to include more than two States. Standardized arms, maps and equipment would of course be essential.

51. The other difficulty previous experience foreshadows concerns the tariff proposals. Whenever a tariff union has been tried, there has emerged a clash of interests between the (usually dominant) industrial elements desiring to protect their manufactured goods and the farmers desiring an opposite policy. This clash occurs, of course, within any economically diver-

sified State; but it is usually settled without disruption of the State. In confederal units, however, when the line dividing these interests falls more or less along State boundaries it may threaten disruption. The discontent of agricultural South Carolina had this effect on the United States and similar discontent in Manitoba and Western Australia were among the difficulties which threatened the unity of Canada and Australia.

52. It is unlikely that this difficulty will threaten the unity of the proposed Confederations, though the less industrialised regions in the northern confederation might see dangers in their own association in a Customs Union with Bohemia-Moravia, Austria and Upper Silesia. Most of the States to be confederated have previously protected their industries against goods from outside the area altogether, and their association in Customs Union would therefore make little difference to this policy, while assisting freedom of movement of goods and peoples inside the area. The agriculturalists in the area have not in the past been sufficiently active or effective to resist industrial protection, and there is therefore little reason to expect them to cause serious trouble in the future.

53. Finally finance is likely to create a problem. For the Confederations to be a reality some financial independence seems to be desirable. Complete dependence on State grants would make it difficult for them to pursue any continuous policy and impossible for them to get loans.

(ii) Difficulties suggesting Closer Union

54. It is clear that, in foreign policy, defence and economic action, closer relationships would strengthen the confederations. These, however, could be achieved only by taking the decisive step which separates confederations from federations, that is by rendering the confederal organs independent of control by State Governments and by giving them independent financial resources.

55. Where this step has once been taken, closer federation has grown steadily. It seems natural that the existence of a common tariff policy should suggest the endowment of the confederal budget with the proceeds of customs and excise. Yet

where this has been done, the power of indirect taxation has soon been followed by that of direct taxation. Then the position anticipated in the Greek-Yugoslav confederation has been reversed. Instead of the Confederation subsisting on grants-in-aid from the States, the States have required grants-in-aid from the Federation.

56. A further difficulty in loose confederations is that they cannot afford to include as member-States units which are weak, small and backward. (See above paras. 25–29). Accordingly many Eastern European peoples will have to remain in a position which requires their political allegiance to be given to States in which they are subordinate and often despised minorities.

57. Closely connected with this is the more general point that a Confederation cannot hope to be, for its citizens, a centre of loyalty so powerful as to override the national loyalties on which frontier claims and minority oppressions batten. Member-States may abate their frontier claims on each other and refrain from oppression of some of their minorities for diplomatic reasons, but the Confederation cannot expect to draw out any positive loyalty from the minorities themselves. For example, unless the Czech-Polish Union turns out to be so close as to make Slovakia a possible member of it, there is nothing in its existence which is likely to lead to greater satisfaction of Slovak claims and feelings.

58. There is also a danger that areas in a Confederation may quarrel, if one of them becomes "depressed" and the common economic policy of the Confederation provides it with no relief. In a unitary State, depressed areas can be assisted by subsidies and freedom of movement of men and capital. This therefore is an additional argument for closer union.

Arguments against Pressure for Closer Union

59. The two motives for closer union are security and economic advantage, and these have proved in the past singularly weak stimuli to federation. In other areas, long after the grounds for federation have been obvious, no action has been taken. When it did occur, it took the form of loose confederations

during a trial period before full federation could be achieved. (Cf. Switzerland, the United States, Germany.) But large areas in Eastern Europe have had previous experience of closer union, which might help in future to accelerate it.

60. As to the argument that small units are impossible in loose confederations, it may recoil on its own supporters. For if antagonism between Czechs and Slovaks or Croats and Serbs raises claims which only separate membership could satisfy, these same antagonisms might make the closer union unworkable. Similarly, the more bitter are frontier and minority disputes, the more difficult it is to imagine them laid to rest by the immediate imposition of a single federal loyalty.

61. Since for these reasons it is unlikely that the peoples themselves will wish to form close federations at once, the problem arises whether the Great Powers should attempt to put any pressure on them to make the unions closer than they at present propose.

62. Any such attempt in the political field would seem to be self-defeating. Leaders will make a success only if policies in which they believe, and their peoples will grow loyalty only on an adequate and tested basis of unity. In fields where in the last resort loyal backing from the populations is the only strength, pressure form outside would fail. This would seem to rule out attempts to persuade these Confederations to establish federal constitutions (with directly elected federal assemblies and federal governments independent of governments in the member-States). It would also rule out immediate attempts to get them to place their foreign policy or armed forces at once on a federal basis.

63. In other fields, however, where ultimately efficiency and welfare, and not sentiment or loyalty, confer strength, there might seem to be a case for pressure. In the economic field, in post-war relief and reconstruction, in communications and postal arrangements, in industrialisation and public works, it might seem that confederal authorities could be established which would not have to face the difficulties of unitary diplomacy or unitary defence.

64. But for two quite different reasons pressure with this object is also inadvisable. In the first place the confedera-

tions could not perform these functions unless they were financially independent of the State governments and had their own sources of revenue. This means close federation and raises all the previous difficulties.

65. Secondly, the economic improvements which might be achieved by co-operation within such areas as those covered by the proposed Confederations are very limited as regards immediate benefits, though perhaps more important in relation to long-term developments. But in either case they are much less than those which could be brought about by a reasonable and generous attitude of the outside world to the areas in question.

66. Thus while the running of immediate post-war relief and reconstrucion through the Confederations would give them practice in cooperation between their member-States and some initial prestige in the eyes of their citizens, it seems that these economic activities would be more effective if they were carried through on a wider basis. Some particular problems where this comes out most clearly are noted below. (See paras. 122–142 on Transylvania, Trieste, and the Danube.)

67. It would, therefore, seem better to establish these economic activities on an independent "functional" basis for Eastern Europe as a whole. This might help the Confederations indirectly by deflecting attention from political issues and bringing Eastern European peoples to see that they have interests in common, in regard to which frontiers and minority squabbles are irrelevant. (The view that only such methods as these can solve the problems of Eastern Europe, and that Confederations such as those here examined promise little assistance, is briefly stated, as an individual opinion, in a Note on Eastern Europe, RR IX/10/i).

68. Finally, in relation to the more immediate object of preventing the economic domination of Germany, it would be inadequate merely to urge the Confederations to closer economic union. For both Confederations, Germany will continue to present the nearest and largest single market and the nearest source of supply of manufactured goods. Closer internal economic relations in the Confederations could not altogether remove such dependence (especially in the Southern Confedera-

tion). Only appropriate action by the outside world (see below paras. 155–159) can remove this danger.

Conclusions on Pressure for Closer Union

69. The conclusion would seem to be that pressure on the Confederations to make their union closer is inadvisable in the political field because such pressure would be self-defeating, in the economic field because its aims would be better achieved by action on a wider scale, independent of these political groupings. It is also to be hoped that this action would indirectly diminish political difficulties and thus lead ultimately to closer political relationships in the area as a whole.

III. Territorial Problems

(a) External Western Frontiers of the Confederations

70. These frontiers have been dealt with in a previous F.R.P.S. Memorandum, Frontiers of European Confederation, dated 20th February, 1942. The section which follows summarises that memorandum. For details on particular frontiers references to more detailed F.R.P.S. material are given at the end of each part of this and the following sections.

The Polish-German Frontier

East Prussia and Danzig, under German control, constitute a strategic menace to Poland, creating a second front within a hundred miles of Warsaw. Danzig is also strategically and economically vital to Poland as it controls the mouth of her on great river, the Vistula. Upper Silesia, a highly industrialised area, containing great war potential, would also be a considerable asset to Poland both economically and strategically. Danzig and East Prussia (excluding the Allenstein district) are inhabited by 2 million Germans, whose transfer might be necessary if the full strategic advantages of annexation are to be secured by Poland. Allenstein and the part of Upper Silesia east of the Oder which was under German rule before 1939 contain a mixture of

Germans and Germanised or partly Germanised Poles. Both areas voted for inclusion in Germany after the last war. If transfer were adopted here also, an option to remain might reduce the numbers to be moved from these two areas to something between 500,000 and 1 million in addition to the 2 million mentioned above (and to the 1,250,000 represented by the new settlers and the German minority in pre-war Poland who presumably will flee or evicted in any case). On these proposals there would thus be a minimum figure for transfer of 3,750,000 which would involve an operation unprecedented in history. (Some of its difficulties on the technical side are examined in the previous F.R.P.S. Memorandum, Transfers of German Populations, dated 13th February, 1942.)

72. Even if Poland is given the Oder frontier in Upper Silesia, Czechs and Poles may still urge that German territory comes close to the vital Silesian industries and projects in a deep salient between Poland and Czechoslovakia. This salient could be diminished only by pushing the frontier into purely German areas, and eliminated only by annexing Middle and Lower Silesia. As this would involve moving still more Germans (of whom there are three million in Middle and Lower Silesia) into the still further reduced territory of the Reich, it would seem a most undesirable addition to the difficulties of settlement, and is mentioned here only because it may be raised by extremists.

73. All the annexations mentioned in the preceding paragraphs would be indubitably contrary to the second clause of the Atlantic Charter,[7] and the resentment they would cause in Germany would be exacerbated by transfer. It may, however, be urged that the annexation at least of East Prussia and Danzig is essential for the disarmament of Germany laid down in the eight clause of the Charter.[8] (Cf. East Prussia, RB XI/8/iii; Danzig RB XI/19/ii; Upper Silesia, RB XI/11/iii; Polish Pomerania, RB XI/21/i).

The Czech-German Frontier

74. *Note.* The F.R.P.S. has for some time had no expert on Czechoslovakia on its staff. Accordingly this important prob-

lem has not been worked out by us and the following paragraph must be regarded as tentative and inadequate.)

75. Restoration to Czechoslovakia of the German-inhabited areas in Bohemia and Moravia would give her once again her strong mountain frontier, and, in both areas, but especially in Moravia, industrial regions of great economic and strategic value. The numbers of Germans included might conceivably be lessened by some 700,000 if Czechoslovakia was prepared to give up to Germany the Schluckenau and Friedland salients and the Egerland-Karlsbad triangle. There are likely to be suggestions for evicting the remaining Germans (about 2,600,000 at a minimum figure). The Czechs would find it hard to replace these Germans, especially in the Bohemian industries, and their evictions would be a violent and brutal expedient.

The Austro-Italian Frontier

76. If, as is possible, Austria is a member of the northern confederation, the Austro-Italian frontier will raise the problem of the South Tyrol. Recent population transfers have probably created Italian majorities in all the areas south of the Brenner. Return of the South Tyrol to Austria might be used as a bribe to induce her to join the Confederation. In this case the recent transfer of the Tyrolese Germans, which is still far from complete, would presumably be arrested or even reversed. This would be easy as they have been planted near at hand and placed in unfamiliar occupations.

77. But, even with Austria in the Confederation, the other members may feel that Italy is so little a danger that she might be left the Brenner frontier as a counterweight to the large cessions they will urge on the Eastern and Northern Adriatic shores. In this case the exodus of the Tyrolese Germans would presumably be maintained and even completed.

78. A third possibility which would satisfy Italy's economic interests and give Austria some consideration would be a partition of the South Tyrol leaving to Italy the areas round Bolzano and Merano where Italian penetration has been going on longest and where industries (especially hydro-electric) important to all north Italy are located. (Cf. South Tyrol, RB Xa/14/iii.)

Other Austrian Frontiers

79. The Austro-Czech, Austro-Yugoslav and Austro-Hungarian frontiers have been dealt with below (paras. 85, 99), as if Austria were a member of the northern confederation. This is not meant to prejudge the issue of Austrian membership; and, even if she were independent or left to Germany, the frontiers suggested below could still stand unaltered.

The Yugoslav-Italian Frontier

80. Yugoslavia is certain to claim from Italy, at the very least, the Adriatic islands and the towns of Zara and Fiume along with the Eastern half of Istria to screen the latter's land and sea communications. This half of Istria is solidly Yugoslav in population. But even these minimum concessions would still leave a considerable number of Yugoslavs in Italy. A frontier on the ethnic line would give Yugoslavia in addition the hinterland of Trieste and Pola. She is sure to claim, however, to push her frontier to the Isonzo or even beyond it, and thus to annex Trieste, Pola and Gorizia. (On Trieste see further below Paras. 137–140.) The degree to which such cessions would promote permanent conditions of security in this area depend on the danger to be expected from Italy and advisability of permanently antagonising her, as the loss of Trieste and 300,000 Italians east of the Isonzo would do. If this happened, the 300,000 Italians might have to be transferred to save them from reprisals for Italy's minority policy between 1922 and 1939 and her recent treatment of the Yugoslavs. But on strategic grounds, Italian minorities are generally less of a menace than German minorities. (Cf. The Italo-Yugoslav Frontier, RB IV/16/ii.)

(b) External Eastern Frontiers of the Confederations

81. It was suggested in our terms of reference that it would be unprofitable at present to consider the frontiers between the Confederations and the USSR, though some general points in this connection have been noted elsewhere. (Cf. paras. 6, 147.)

Greek-Turkish Frontier

82. On the European mainland the only problem on the Greek-Turkish frontier is the relatively unimportant question of the Karagatch enclave and the Greek territory which cuts the Oriental railway from Istanbul to Edirne (Adrianople). A more serious difficulty is that of the Dodecanese Islands, presumably to be freed from Italian control. They are Greek-inhabited, but also of strategic interest to Turkey, and many of them have economic contacts with the Turkish mainland. It is possible that the islands vital to Turkey might be held as joint Greco-Turkish bases, or that they should be ceded to Turkey with autonomy or transfer for their Greek inhabitants. Greece might then be awarded the larger and more distant islands, particularly Cos and Rhodes. (Cf. The Greek-Turkish Frontier, RB IV/21/i; Greek Irredentism (Part II), RB Xa/3/ii).

Bulgaro-Turkish Frontier

83. This frontier appears to present no serious difficulties, as the pre-1940 line is approximately ethnic and the old Bulgarian claim to Adrianople has or some time been in abeyance. (Cf. The Frontier between Bulgaria and Turkey, RB IV/29/i.)

(c) Frontiers between the Confederations

84. The Hungaro-Rumanian frontier raises the problem of Transylvania, which is discussed below (Paras. 122-134). The short frontier between Rumania and the Sub-Carpathian Ruthenes is not important enough to require discussion here. In any case, it depends on what happens to Ruthenia. (Cf. Maramures, RB IV/20ii.)

The Austro-Yugoslav Frontier

85. The Austro-Yugoslav frontier falls into two sections, the Carinthian and the Styrian. The pre-1919 frontier in Carinthia included in Austria the south eastern part of the

Klagenfurt basin which had in 1910 a Slovene-speaking majority, but which showed in the 1920 plebiscite a majority for inclusion in Austria. The frontier thus established on the
Karawanken mountains is strategically the strongest possible
and the economic connections of the whole Klagenfurt basin
run northwards into Austria. In Styria the pre-1939 frontier
was generally linguistic and economically favoured Yugoslavia
by giving her Maribor (Marburg) and the Drave valley west of
it. If Austria belongs to the northern confederation this should
improve her connections with Yugoslav territory. It therefore
appears that the pre-1939 frontier is adequate in both sections.
(Cf. The Austro-Yugoslav Frontier, RB IV/16/ii.)

The Hungaro-Yugoslav Frontier

86. In its western half this frontier follows in the main
the Drave river. In the extreme west, Yugoslavia's claim to
recover the Croat-inhabited Medjumurje is exceedingly strong.
The case of Prekomurje, with its Slovene or "Wend" inhabitants
admits of more debate. The 1919 frontier represented a maximum of satisfaction to Yugoslav desires.

87. The greater difficulties arise in the western half
where the 1919 frontier gave to Yugoslavia a corner of the
Baranya, the Backa and part of the Banat, areas containing a
very mixed population, mainly Magyars, Serbs, Germans and
Slav races related to though not identical with the Serbs. While
the mixture is predominantly Magyar in the north and Serb in
the south, the central difficulty of fixing an ethnic line (on the
assumption that the Banat is not given undivided to any of the
competing States) is due to the settlements of Slavs, particularly in Subotica and north of Zenta, cut off from the Serb majority areas by stretches with Magyar majorities. Some exchange of
populations might ease this local difficulty; and, as the country
concerned is of the same character throughout, exchange would
be easier than usual.

88. It may be held that Yugoslavia, as an ally and a victim of aggression here, is at least entitled to her 1919 frontier.
On the other hand the desirability of reducing Magyar hostility
may be urged in favour of meeting her claims. Even without

exchange, some rectification in Hungary's favour would be possible; but a larger one, with exchange, would probably settle the whole business and would still leave Yugoslavia with the larger part of the debated area which she got in 1919. (Cf. The Hungaro-Yugoslav Frontier, RB IV/9/iii.)

(d) Territorial Problems within the Confederations

(i) Special Areas

89. There are several case where a question arises whether an area should be itself a unit in a Confederation or should be part of a larger unit. The general issues are discussed above (paras. 25–29.). The local conditions which give rise to each problem are briefly noted in the following paragraphs. In each case the people concerned feel themselves to be a unit distinct from the surrounding peoples.

Slovakia

90. The Slovaks may demand separate membership for Slovakia or at least such considerable autonomy that few spheres would be left, neither under Slovak control nor under direct confederal administration, but subject to a Czechoslovak Government. The Czech demand for a unitary Czechoslovak State based on Masaryk's[9] policy, on the co-operation of many Slovaks in the Central Government, on a close affinity of language, and on the relative backwardness of Slovakia, was continuously and increasingly attacked by Slovak autonomists from 1919 to 1938. While the Hlinka Party[10] was the only explicitly autonomist party and while it never had a majority in Slovakia until Germany took the Slovak question in charge, there were probably many Slovaks who would have voted for autonomy if it had been the only issue but who disliked the Hlinka Party and supported other parties on other issues. Slovakia was under Hungary when the Czechs were ruled by Austria; and, while hardly any trace now remains of the old pro-Hungarian feeling in Slovakia, the differences of religion, tradition and outlook between Czechs and Slovaks are still considerable. The taste of

"independence"[11] Slovakia has had will also add to the difficulties of re-establishing a unitary Czechoslovakia. While the inclusion of Slovakia as a member-State of the Confederation would have some of the difficulties suggested above (Paras. 25–27.), it should also be noted that if the Polish plan were accepted by the Czechs and the "stronger interpretation" of it (Cf. para. 45) were found to be justified, this inclusion or at least very far-reaching concessions to Slovak autonomists would be possible.

91. The autonomists at present in control are likely to be thrown out and discredited after the war, and the removal of German control may well tend immediately to draw Czechs and Slovaks closer together. Yet there would be dangers in attempting to settle this problem by agreement between Czechs and Slovaks in exile, as this might revive autonomist opposition in Slovakia, unless the agreement included concessions to the autonomist view.

Sub-Carpathian Ruthenia

92. The Ruthenes who live in a compact mass in the mountain valleys of this area are akin to the Ukrainians of the Ukraine and East Galicia by ethnic origin and language, but divided from them by widely differing histories, cultural traditions, and economic interests. They thus have no ethnic links with either Czechoslovakia or Hungary , the two Danubian States chiefly concerned with their fate. They are a primitive and backward people, but are now acquiring a self-consciousness previously lacking among them. They were promised autonomy within Czechoslovakia[12] (to which State they were assigned in 1919) but were in fact ruled authoritarianly but efficiently by Czech officials. They have also been promised, but have also not received, autonomy from Hungary, which re-occupied the area in 1939.[13] The brief time of "independence" which they enjoyed in 1938–39 was in fact subjection to Germany and purely nominal. There is no reliable guide to their present political feelings as between Czechoslovakia and Hungary. Czech rule brought them many improvements and modernisations. On the other hand, their economic connections are all with Hungary.

93. Economically the area is very important to Hungary. It contains timber which Hungary needs. But, more important than this, here are the upper waters of the Tisza, the regulation of which is essential to prevent alternate floods and droughts in the great Hungarian plain. Hungary is now engaged on large-scale works in Ruthenia, in connection with a great national drainage and irrigation scheme. Should Ruthenia not be assigned to Hungary, it is suggested that special arrangements should be made to leave these works, and the control of the waters, in Hungarian hands, or in those of a Confederal or International body on which Hungary is adequately represented.

94. Further, Ruthenia is an area of great strategic importance. Should the USSR claim it on grounds of ethnic affinity, this would give her a frontier across the main Carpathian range and a threatening position commanding the Danube valley. Czechoslovakia valued Ruthenia above all as giving her communications with Rumania and a corridor to the USSR (for when she acquired Ruthenia it was expected in some quarters that East Galicia would ultimately become Soviet territory). Hungary and Poland both wished Ruthenia to go to Hungary so that the two States should have a common frontier (since Poland at the time held East Galicia). If Hungary, Poland and Czechoslovakia were in a single Confederation, this conflict of their strategic interests would presumably disappear.

95. If Ruthenia does not return to Hungary, there will be the problem who should have the southern strip which Ruthenia lost to Hungary in 1938.[14] This strip is a continuation of the debated southern fringe of Slovakia discussed below (paras 107–110) and the arguments stated there are relevant here also. The strip contains a large majority of Magyars over Ruthenes.

Croatia

96. The great differences of tradition, culture, history and religion between Croats and Serbs have created a problem here similar to that between Czechs and Slovaks. Here too the taste of "independence" which Croatia has had (though only under a puppet government) will increase the estrangement.[15]

The problem here is complicated by two further factors not found in Czecho-Slovak relations. One is the difficulty of a frontier delineation between Serbs and Croats in Bosnia-Hercegovina. The other is the Croat conviction of their own superiority to the Serbs in culture and civilisation and the animosity between the two peoples which has always smouldered below political compromises and has flared up frequently in the past and recently again under German and Italian incitement. (Cf. Croatia, RB IV/23/i; Bosnia-Hercegovina, RB IV/28/i.)

Slovenia

97. While religion and culture tended also to estrange Slovenes from Serbs, this relationship is far less difficult for several reasons. During the existence of the Yugoslav State, the ruling Serbs were inclined to leave the Slovenes to manage their own affairs. They were in any case less politically-minded and have therefore advanced fewer claims than the Croats. They have also enjoyed no recent independence even of a Quisling brand. For all these reasons they may turn out to be a valuable unifying factor in the new Yugoslavia.

Macedonia

98. The population of Macedonia is claimed as their kinsmen both by Serbs and by Bulgars. It is split by internal feuds and factions. The Macedonians were probably mainly Bulgarophil in 1919, and members of this race have played a dominant and dangerous role in Bulgarian politics. In a federal State, Macedonia might well be a unit, but in a loose confederation it is certainly too backward and primitive to be a member-State.

(ii) Frontiers raising no serious problem

99. In the remainder of this section, only those frontiers are discussed which may require more than merely local variations of the pre-1938 lines. The Czech-Austrian and Austro-Hungarian frontiers raise no serious problem though if the latter is left unaltered the special arrangements for Sopron should

be maintained. Even if Austria is left in Germany, neither of these frontiers can be strategically strengthened against her by local rectification. The Greek-Yugoslav and Romano-Yugoslav frontiers appear to require no alteration, especially if it can be assumed that the existence of a Confederation will ensure to Roumania free passage on the railway through Yugoslav territory from Temesvar to Bazias on the Danube. The peaceful return of the Southern Dobrudja from Rumania to Bulgaria,[16] along with the population movements which have occurred there, has adequately settled this frontier dispute also.

(iii) Principles of settlement of disputed frontiers

100. It would seem most natural to draw any new frontiers in Eastern Europe on ethnic lines. The two main reasons for departure from the ethnic principle (if we exclude force and history) have always been strategy and economics. Joint membership of a Confederation with a unified defence and economic policy should remove these two reasons. The members no longer require strong frontiers against each other. Even local difficulties of markets and communications should disappear, if tariffs and visas within the confederation are abolished and railway traffic facilitated.

101. It was on economic or strategic grounds that the 1919 settlement included Magyar areas in Rumania, Slovakia, Ruthenia and Yugoslavia, and Bulgarian areas in Yugoslavia and Greece. Acceptance of the above argument would thus involve adjustments of the pre-1938 frontiers in favour of Hungary and Bulgaria.

102. While feeling against these two States will run very high among their neighbours, who may therefore resist any such concessions, it may be urged upon them that some concessions may be wise if they are to live together with their old enemies at all. Approximation to ethnic frontiers will also minimise the minority problem and make transfer less difficult, if it is anywhere desirable, by equalising the minorities on their side of the frontier, and making possible an exchange. Even without exchange, such equality would help to encourage some degree of reciprocity in tolerance of minorities, in contrast with the pre-

1938 position when Magyar and Bulgar minorities in other States greatly outnumbered the minorities in Hungary and Bulgaria.

103. The States on which such surrenders of economic and strategic claims are urged may reply that they dare not risk their security and economic existence on plans so hazardous and tentative as the plans for Confederations are. Frontiers must be fixed before it can be seen whether the Confederations are successful. These States may therefore hold that claims to territory vital to them cannot be surrendered on the chance of this success. On the assumptions of this memorandum, however,—that Confederations with joint strategic and economic policies are established—the argument of Paras. 100–102. appears sound. The frontiers advisable on the assumption that such joint policies cannot be trusted to work might in many cases be different, and would presumably be those appropriate to completely independent sovereign States. Even so, it does not follow that the 1919–1938 frontiers would be those to be accepted. For local strategic advantages have proved to be of little value and are in any case dearly bought at the price of permanent antagonism from the losing State. And, if neither side has a substantial grievance, even a very uneconomic frontier can be made to work reasonably well. (Cf. Upper Silesia and the Austro-Hungarian Frontier.)

104. There are, however, special difficulties about determing the ethnic line which affect most of the disputed frontiers. These are due to changes in the character of the populations which have taken place in these areas at various times in the last eighty years, as first one side and then another ruled each disputed area and used its political power to increase by education or colonisation the numbers of its own relatives or supporters, and to diminish those of alien race or language. Thus each party in a dispute will select, as the definitive time for determining the ethnic constitution of the area the date at which its own population percentage was highest, and will plead that all subsequent changes in the population figures were due to illicit colonisation, or forcible assimilation, or even to straightforward falsification of the census figures. Population changes are still going on in the most of the disputed regions,

and after the war no statistics may be obtainable which will give even a remote approximation to the actual position.

105. All the general considerations   in the foregoing paragraphs (100–104) are relevant to the discussion of the particular frontiers dealt with below, and will not be repeated on each occasion.

(iv) The Czech-Polish Frontier

106. The vital area here is Teschen (the small hill districts of Spiz and Orawa being quite unimportant). Teschen was disputed by Poland and Czechoslovakia from 1918 to 1939. In 1919 two-thirds of the Duchy had Polish majorities and the remainder Czech, with a considerable German population in both sections. The Czechs occupied more than half the total area early in 1919, and were confirmed in their possession of this territory by the Allied Powers, on the ground that the main railway lines through the territory and the coal it contained were both much more needed by them than by the Poles. As the Confederation will have unified economic and transport plans these considerations will be less important. The only serious factor operating against an ethnic frontier, apart from Czech doubts about the value of the Confederation (see Para. 103), is likely to be Czech resentment at Poland's use of the Munich crisis in 193817 to establish that frontier by force. The Germans will probably have to be evicted, at least from any section given to Poland. (Cf. The Teschen Question, RB XI/9/ii.)

(v) The Hungaro-Slovak Frontier

107. The main ethnic line between Magyars and Slovaks —which had remained unmodified for 150 years—ran roughly along the Carpathian foothills. Czechoslovakia obtained in 1919 a frontier which, along most of its extent, ran well to the south of this line, giving her the towns of Bratislava (Pozsony) and Kosice (Kassa) and a strip of plain bounded in its western half by the Danube. The purpose was to give to Czechoslovakia an outlet to the Danube along a wide front, for military and economic purposes, together with lateral communications, admin-

istrative centres and corn-producing land to balance the economy of the Slovak mountains. The result was to include in Slovakia a Magyar-speaking population numbering nearly 900,000 according to the Hungarian census of 1910, or 570,000 according to the Czechoslovak census of 1930. The number of Slovaks left in Hungary near the frontier was negligible; but there were considerable numbers of half-assimilated Slovaks (descendants of 18th century immigrants) in the Hungarian plain.

108. The Vienna Award of 1938[18] reverted to the ethnic principle, but took as basis the Hungarian census of 1910, restoring to Hungary the areas which had then shown Magyar-speaking majorities. Two important exceptions, however, were made, both Bratislava and Nyitra, with their surroundings, being left in Slovakia. These two areas had, in fact, become mainly Slovak between 1910 and 1938. In the area acquired by Hungary under the Vienna Award there are probably, out of a total population of some 860,000,[19] about 125,000 indisputable Slovaks and under 120,000 persons, mainly in the towns, of mixed or dubious ethnic allegiance. In Slovakia there remained 50,000 to 60,000 Magyars. The Slovak-speaking elements of Central Hungary number 100,000 to 150,000.

109. The 1938 frontier is thus not far off ethnic justice, although enquiry on the spot might make possible some local corrections, which would probably be more in favour of the Slovaks than of Hungary. There are, however, still arguments for departing from the ethnic line, though the existence of a Confederation should enable these departures to be less than in 1919. Slovakia's strongest claim is that for Kosice. This town has a mixed population, largely bilingual with a strong Jewish element and many officials. It is likely to show a majority for the party which happens to be in possession of it. It has strong historical associations for Hungary and her recovery of it in 1938 did much to console her for her failure to get back Bratislava. On the other hand, it is of the first importance for Eastern Slovakia as a center of administration and of communications.

110. The rest of the frontier is economically difficult. The ethnic line cuts off the mountains from the plain and leaves in Hungary the easiest transverse communications between the

Slovak valleys. In a comparatively close federation with free transit for goods and persons this need present no difficulty. The Slovaks will presumably claim back all or most of what they lost in 1938. Failing adequate transit arrangements it might be necessary to give back to Slovakia a strip in the west; but this would cause great bitterness in Hungary. The only ideal solution economically remains the complete abolition of any frontier in this area, yet makes the growth of Slovak national feeling the reincorporation of Slovakia as a whole in Hungary inadvisable.

(vi) The Yugoslav-Bulgarian Frontier

111. Two purely Bulgarian districts (Caribrod and Bosiljgrad) were awarded to Yugoslavia on strategic grounds, which, never very strong, should cease to count in a Confederation. The main debated area is Macedonia. As the dispute here concerns the ethnic character of the population it cannot be solved by any frontier line. (See above para. 98.). A plebiscite would be inadvisable in an area so disturbed and unruly. There is therefore a case for giving the pre-1939 frontier the benefit of the doubt. Recovery of Caribrod and Bosiljgrad might help to reconcile Bulgaria to giving up the parts of Yugoslav Macedonia she has recently overrun. (Cf. The Yugoslav-Bulgarian Frontier, RB IV/19/ii.)

The Greek-Bulgarian Frontier

112. By the population transfers following the Treaty of Neuilly[20] (1919) the disputed territories on each side of this frontier were practically cleared of minorities. In 1941 Bulgarian troops overran Greek territory here and have evicted thousands of Greeks and settled Bulgars on their lands. If the pre-1941 frontiers were re-established, Bulgaria would still have a case (as in 1919) for an outlet to the sea at Dedeagatch. The port is economically unnecessary to Greece, and is a strategic asset to her only on the assumption that Bulgaria is an independent and hostile State. If Bulgaria joins the Southern Confederation, the cession of Dedeagatch to her is a possibility. Alternatively she might be given special facilities in Salonica,

Cavalla and Dedeagatch by means of free zones under a mixed regime on which she was represented. (Cf. The Greek-Bulgarian Frontier, RB IX/8/iii.)

The Frontiers of Albania

113. Albania will have disputed frontiers with Greece and Yugoslavia. The pre-1939 Yugoslav-Albanian frontier left in Yugoslavia more than a quarter of the total Albanian population, separated Albanian tribes from their traditional market towns, and left several towns in Yugoslavia vulnerable to raids from Albania. On the other hand, most of the areas thus included in Yugoslavia had their main economic contacts with other Yugoslav territories and were cut off by mountains from the rest of Albania. In 1941 the frontiers of Italian Albania[21] were extended eastward to include all mainly-Albanian-inhabited territory.

114. A compromise line which takes account of economic connections might be found here. It would leave to Albania such of her recent accessions as have economic contacts with pre-1941 Albanian territory, but would return most of the disputed areas to Yugoslavia. The principle suggested above (Paras. 100–102.) of laying down ethnic frontiers and leaving economic contacts to be established across them by the internal arrangements of the Confederation, seems less applicable here for two reasons. Mountain frontiers are desirable in areas so disturbed and primitive. Moreover, toleration by Greece and Yugoslavia of Albania's equal status as a member of the Confederation or even of her continued existence as a State may require Albanian claims to be toned down so as to avoid the permanent resentment of her neighbours. (Cf. The Albano-Yugoslav Frontier, RB IV/18/iii.)

115. The Greek-Albanian frontier is also disputed as Albania has claims in Northern Greece and Greece in Southern Albania. The position is complicated by the Greek successes in their invasion of Albania and the recent extension of Albania to include part of Chamuria. (The report of this awaits confirmation.) Both these events will make the disputants more intransigent.

116. Satisfaction of the Greek claims in full would cut off from Albania her most civilised districts, those with which most Albanian emigrants are connected. It would also diminish Albania's resources so greatly that she would probably be incapable of survival.

117. It is impossible to decide on a reasonable ethnic frontier, because no one can say whether the inhabitants of the disputed areas are Albanianised Greeks or Hellenized Albanians. A plebiscite to discover their wishes would be of doubtful value, because of the primitive character of the people, the passions already aroused, and the uncertainty which would exist, even while the plebiscite were being held, about the survival of Albania.

118. It may perhaps be assumed that the 1939 frontier will not be altered to Greece's detriment. Almost any frontier here would cause problems of markets and communications but it is to be hoped that Confederal arrangements will minimize these. (Cf. The Greek-Albanian Frontier, RB IV/30/i.)

IV. Problems Concerning Relations between the Confederations

(a) Co-operation

119. In their Agreement of 23rd January, 1942, the Governments of Czechoslovakia and Poland say they are "confident that only the co-operation of these two regional organisations can assure security and develop prosperity in the vast region stretching between the Baltic and the Aegean seas." Both Confederation will presumably included in a wider system of international security. But help can reach them only with difficulty from the west and cannot be relied on absolutely from the east. Accordingly, if they are to maintain their security, a common foreign policy, an alliance or pact of mutual assistance, with regular staff talks, consultations and plans for swift joint action would be an added insurance.

120. Similarly, while their resistance to German economic domination will depend much more on the outside world

than on any joint plans they may make, it would add an element of safety if their economic policies were so arranged that Germany was not able to play off one against the other (e.g. Hungary against Rumania, both being sellers of wheat).

121. There are several special problems which involve relations between the two confederations. They include Transylvania, Croatia and Slovenia, Trieste and Fiume, the Danube and the problem of minorities.

(b) Transylvania

122. By far the most difficult problem in the whole area is that of Transylvania. (The name will be used in this section to describe the whole of the territory ceded by Hungary to Rumania in 1919, though such a usage is historically inaccurate.)

123. While the south-eastern corner of Transylvania, where unfortunately the Hungarian Szekels live in compact masses, has economic contacts with Rumania, the whole western half is economically connected with Hungary. The cultural traditions of Transylvania are also Danubian rather than Balkan. On the other hand, Rumanians are in a clear, though not a large majority throughout, except in the Szekel counties and in considerable areas on the western border, where there are Magyar majorities. There is also a large German minority.

124. The western Magyar areas with no Rumanians could have been included in Hungary in 1919 by the adoption of a very irregular frontier following no natural features and cutting across railway communications. They were given to Rumania to complete her communications and also to reward a friend and punish an enemy. But the Szekels were cut off from Hungary by large territories with Rumanian majorities. A corridor to them through central Transylvania would necessarily have included many Rumanians and would have left northern Transylvania in the air, economically and administratively. If northern Transylvania also were restored to Hungary—the solution adopted in 1940[22]—this would mean putting back a very large number of Rumanians under Magyar rule. It would also, however, leave a considerable number of Magyars still in Rumania.

125. Thus the 1919 line left a million and a half Magyars in Rumania and a negligible number of Rumanians in Hungary, while the 1940 revision in order to return two-thirds of these Magyars to Hungary had to take about a million Rumanians with them. The 1940 line is also unsatisfactory economically as it cuts across natural north-south connections in many places.

126. The most hopeful solution of this difficult problem might have been the inclusion of Transylvania as a member-State in a Confederation in which Rumania and Hungary were also members. This solution, unfortunately, is ruled out by our assumptions, but its advantages are so strong as to constitute a major reason for regretting that this assumption must be made.

127. The status of Transylvania is further complicated by the deplorable suggestion (para. 6) that the USSR will wish to compensate Rumania at the expense of Hungary for the loss of Bessarabia and Northern Bukovina. It is difficult to see how Rumania could regard anything less than her pre-1941 frontier with Hungary[23] as "compensation." If, however, this frontier is not to be re-imposed by USSR pressure, two alternative frontiers may be considered. (If the present frontier were maintained, local corrections might ameliorate it, but it is, as noted above, economically bad, and neither party is in the least content with it.)

128. The first alternative would give to Rumania all areas with Rumanian majorities in addition to the Magyar majority areas in the south east. This would involve some concessions to Hungary on Rumania's western frontier and would produce an irregular line, cutting across communications and trade connections. But if the two Confederations had some degree of tariff, transit and visa co-operation, the inconveniences might be somewhat lessened. This solution would satisfy the maximum number of inhabitants of the whole disputed area though it would still leave a very large number dissatisfied. It would, however, be ill-balanced as between the competing States, leaving over a million Magyars in Rumania and few Rumanians in Hungary. In this respect it would resemble the 1919 line and arouse the same undying resentment in Hungary.

129. The second alternative would be a partition of Transylvania by a frontier drawn from north to south with the

Bihor Mountains as its central point, and giving one third of the disputed area to Hungary and two-thirds to Rumania. The Rumanian majority areas thus included in Hungary might be held to balance the Szekel counties included in Rumania. The minorities would be roughly equalised at about three quarters of a million on each side of the line.

130. If local feeling is so acute as to outweigh the hardships of transfer (as might be the case if removal of Axis control is followed by a Rumano-Hungarian war) the minorities might then be exchanged. This, however, would be a very large and difficult operation because the two peoples are very thoroughly mixed up in most areas, because no Hungarian land would resemble that which the Szekels would leave, and because many exchanged Rumanians would be townsmen. It would, however, be far less extensive than the evictions of Germans mentioned above (paras. 71–75).

131. If all or most of Transylvania were returned to Rumania it might be suggested that its connections with the west should be recognised by making it politically a part of the Southern but economically a part of the Northern Confederation. If, however, this meant a customs frontier across Rumania, it would be clearly unworkable. Any special provision for Transylvanian goods and migrants would be likely to limit unduly the economic sovereignty of the Southern Confederation or to cause it to maintain such barriers between its other territories and Transylvania as to drive the latter politically as well as economically into the northern confederation or into independence. The only way in which the special position of Transylvania could be recognised would be by agreements between the two Confederations not to erect trade barriers between them which would disrupt the natural economic connections between Transylvania and Hungary. It should be noted, however, that the economic issues are of much less importance in the Transylvanian problem than questions of history, tradition, strategy, ethnography and local feeling.

132. In view of the difficulties of its partition, the establishment of Transylvania as an independent unit should be considered. Internally it might be proposed that it should be organised on a cantonal basis, as in Switzerland, though the mixture

of populations almost everywhere would require this to be supplemented by a scheme of cultural autonomy, which would be
relatively easy to devise. The new unit could not, according to
our assumptions belong to the same Confederation as both
Hungary and Rumania. Its historic and economic connections
would draw it to the northern, its Rumanian majority to the
southern Confederation. In the former case the Rumanians, in
the latter the Magyars, would need strong safeguards for their
cultural and linguistic rights.

133. In view of these rival attractions and as either solution would cause resentment, a final possibility would be its creation as a buffer state with complete independence. The aim
would be to make it internationally as well as internally like
Switzerland, to which in area and total population it roughly
approximates. Though it has none of the traditions of local government and democracy which have enabled Switzerland to
build a civic loyalty on a diversity of languages and cultures, it
has some traditions surviving from the days of its old special
status in Hungary. Szekels feel themselves a special type of
Magyar, and Transylvanian Rumanians feel a sense of distinct-
ness from (and superiority over) the Rumanians of the old
Kingdom. There is therefore not quite a total absence of basis for
Transylvanian unity.

134. While its independence could rest only on the tolerance of its neighbours (whether or not it was guaranteed by
Treaty) the two Confederations might be at first so evenly balanced and later so linked by common interests as to ensure this
tolerance. Neither Hungary nor Rumania would welcome this
solution but no solution would satisfy them both. Both would be
likely to keep up intrigue and propaganda within the area. An
independent Transylvania might also be faced with economic
difficulties, unless the whole economic life of Eastern Europe
were integrated across political frontiers. (For further details on
this very complex problem—including detail of considerable
importance, omitted here for brevity—see Transylvania, RB
IX/10/iii.)

(c) Croatia and Slovenia

135. These areas because of their history and traditions, and particularly on grounds of culture and religion, have affinities with the Northern rather than the Southern Confederation. These affinities, however, are perhaps not strong enough to link them with Austria and Hungary but only to estrange them from the Serbs. Their economic conditions with the north form another reason for encouraging economic co-operation between the Confederations, but it is difficult to see any other way in which these connections can be specially recognised. (Cf. Para. 131 on the similar problem on Transylvania.)

136. It is difficult to forecast what the feelings of the Croats will be towards their northern neighbour States after the war. But it is quite certain that the Slovenes after their sufferings at the hands of the Germans and Austrians will be a powerful factor in unifying Yugoslavia and drawing it away from connections with the north. The Croats on the other hand are likely to stress their northern affinities and a close federation with the Serbs might harden their grievances, while a looser association might enable them to keep their northern contacts. Many Serbs might even welcome the separation of Croatia and its inclusion in the northern confederation.

(d) Trieste and Fiume

137. Before 1914 Trieste was the main, and almost the only, commercial port of Austria and Fiume served as an outlet to the sea for the trade of Hungary. Since their annexation by Italy, Fiume has been dead and Trieste dying. Such trade as still reached the Northern Adriatic through Yugoslavia was diverted by the Yugoslavs to their new port of Susak (formerly a small suburb of Fiume).

138. Trieste has a predominantly Italian population and a Yugoslav hinterland coming down to the suburbs of the city. If Austria, Czechoslovakia and Hungary belong to the northern confederation their nearest ports in Confederation territory will be Gdynia and (if Poland annexes it) Danzig. Trieste is a natural outlet for all three states. It is not of any value as a port to

Italy or to any State in the Southern Confederation, except for the Slovene area of Yugoslavia.

139. A customs union between the two Confederations might ease this problem and that of Fiume. But there may be a case for going further than this and giving the northern confederation freedom of access to Trieste and special rights in it, or even for the establishment (despite the gloomy example of Danzig) of a free port under an international condominium.

140. The value of Trieste as the only means of access other than Salonica trough which Western armed aid might reach both Confederations may give it (at least during a transition period) international strategic significance. (Its use would presuppose the impotence or friendliness of Italy and the removal of Italian control of the Straits of Otranto.) If it was used as a base from which the United Nations exercised transitional control in Europe the changeover to a condominium for economic purposes would be greatly eased and might also avert the resentments which cession either to Yugoslavia or Italy would arouse.

141. No such far-reaching solution is necessary for the smaller port of Fiume, but failing an inter-Confederation Customs Union, some special rights for Hungary's trade are advisable here.

(e) The Danube

142. The Danube will be one of the main lines of communications within both Confederations and between them. The interest of Germany in its upper waters and of the USSR in its mouth should justify the revival of the International Danube Commission without its old atmosphere of diplomatic intrigue and supplemented perhaps by a Danube Valley Authority to develop irrigation and the use of water power. The former would benefit mainly Hungary and the latter (if the barrage were at the Iron gates) Rumania, Yugoslavia and Bulgaria. It therefore follows that if the international commissions not revived, this is an obviously necessary sphere of inter-Confederation agreement and action.

(f) Minorities

143. Any settlement of frontiers will leave in each Confederation minorities related to member-States of the other Confederation. As everywhere in Eastern Europe minorities can hope for an improvement of their lot only from a diminution of nationalist feeling. Arrangements of a legal or constitutional kind can never ensure fair treatment. Nevertheless it is to be hoped that any such arrangements according protection to any minorities within the Confederations will apply to these special cases also. In their case too the arguments against transfer are slightly weaker than in the case of most other minorities.

V. Relations between the Confederations and the USSR

144. An attempt has been made above (para.7) to summarise the present general attitude of Eastern European peoples to the USSR. This whole problem will depend so much on the strength of the USSR and the position of her armies at the end of the war, on her attitude to a general collective security system, on the nature of the regimes in Eastern European States, and on the demands of the USSR upon them that only certain general comments are possible.

145. It is clear that no pooling of strength can enable Eastern Europe to resist both the USSR and Germany. Moreover, while some peoples may think the USSR the greater danger of the two, it will be impossible for them, immediately after a German defeat, to choose co-operation with Germany as the lesser evil and to carry either Confederation with them.

146. The Confederations cannot be confident of putting up an effective resistance against a revived Germany without direct and immediate aid from some Great Power. The western powers cannot count on the Baltic route as a safe supply line to the northern confederation; and the Southern Confederation can be reached only by the long sea route to Salonica (or possibly Trieste). (See below para. 154.)

147. The Confederations are therefore likely to be secure against German attack only if they can count on USSR support.

Thus it will pay them to conciliate the USSR both over her claims concerning frontiers and bases, and by so conducting their relations with her as to allay the inevitable Soviet suspicion that any Eastern European blocs must necessarily be aimed against the USSR.

148. It must be added, however, that excessive or exclusive reliance by particular States on USSR support may defeat its on aims by destroying altogether the possibility of effective confederations. Thus it is important that in their relations with the USSR the foreign policy of the member-States should be, from the start, a concerted policy.

149. The above argument is not intended to give the slightest support to the view that Eastern Europe should be abandoned to the USSR as her special sphere of influence or that the Confederations should fall under USSR control. It suggests only that they will be well-advised to make an early bid for Soviet goodwill. To ensure that this does not lead to Soviet control, the Western powers must not set up the Confederations and then leave them to sink or swim. All possibilities of supporting them from the West should be worked out and established on an international basis. The priority of the USSR aid need only be that it can be given directly and at once.

150. USSR control would lead to two results fatal to peace in this area. It would make Germany permanently hostile to the Confederations, and it would cause the considerable anti-USSR elements within them to look to Germany for help. Accordingly the peace of Europe (and in the long run the security of the USSR also) are more likely to be preserved by the existence of genuine buffer units between the USSR and Germany than by groups of Soviet satellites in this region. It is also open to question whether British interests would be compatible with Soviet control in Eastern Europe.

151. The whole argument of paras. 146–149 above may also be met by maintaining that an immediate attack on Germany by the Western Powers in the West would give more direct and instant help to the Confederations than any possible alternative. There are many Eastern European peoples who would put more faith in the hope that the Western Powers have learned the necessary lessons from the Munich crisis and the invasion of Poland than in Soviet support.

VI. Relations between the Confederations and Turkey

152. It has been assumed that Turkey will not be a member of the Southern Confederation. Her strategic position and her military strength make it desirable that the Confederation should be on good terms with her, and that neither old memories nor new associations with the USSR should give it the appearance of an anti-Turkish bloc. Fortunately, in view of the recall of the Turkish minorities from the Balkans and Kemal's[24] renunciations of Turkish imperialism, there are hardly any grounds for conflict. Good relations should also be aided by the fact that Turkey took a lead in the most recent attempts to unify the Balkans. A friendly adjustment with Greece over the Dodecanese and the stretch of the Istanbul-Edirne (Adrianople) railway which crosses Greek territory should be easily achieved. Turkey's economic interests should be recognised, especially over goods exported both by her and by States in the Confederation.

153. An application by Turkey for membership of the Confederation would raise a difficult problem. The record of her efforts for Balkan unity and the added strength she would bring to the Confederation might make it difficult to refuse. On the other hand Turkish membership would entangle the Confederation in the affairs of Western Asia and might arouse in the USSR fears of "encirclement."

VII. Relations between the Confederations and the Western Powers

Strategic Problems

154. In relation to defence and security the most serious difficulty is that of access. This may compel the Western Powers to keep control of the Baltic outlets, especially the Kiel Canal. But these outlets would always be very vulnerable if a hostile Germany revived. The Western Powers might be compelled also to keep large forces at a Mediterranean base from which

Salonica or Trieste could be easily reached, or even at one of those ports themselves. Such bases and controls will be easiest to establish immediately after Germany's defeat, when they will least be needed, and it will be difficult to maintain the will to hold them until the period, ten or twenty years later, when if ever the need may be urgent. It is therefore all the more necessary that the USSR should be associated with the Western Powers in the support of the Confederations, especially so far as immediate and direct aid is concerned.

Economic Relations

155. It has been noted above (para. 65) that such economic cooperation as the Confederations may achieve internally, or even with each other, cannot by itself ensure their continued prosperity or enable them to resist German economic domination. As their nearest and largest single market, Germany will be able to re-impose her control as soon as she revives, unless positive steps are taken by the outside world to meet this danger.

156. The Western Powers have an interest in averting this danger and also a wider and more permanent and positive interest in the prosperity of the whole area. The most obvious step they could take would be to accept Eastern European agricultural products. While some help might be given here—e.g. over tobacco—its development on any large scale might involve quotas or preferences in Western States for these products as against those of their own empires or neighbours. This may be too much to expect, and the Western Powers have shown little demand fro these products in the past. (Polish hams are a notable exception.)

157. It may therefore require less alteration of trading arrangements if Western aid were to take the form of assistance (capital and technical) to the Confederations to industrialise their economy and develop their resources (especially in the potentially rich but undeveloped Balkan areas). The work of Italy in Albania shows what can be done.

158. Agricultural production in many Eastern European States, while it has produced surpluses for export, has actually

been inadequate for the needs of these areas themselves, or any reasonable standards of nutrition. Assistance in improving agricultural technique might increase production; and, in view of the more balanced economy which industrialisation would produce, surpluses could go to German markets without giving Germany a stranglehold on the area.

159. The need for the whole area is a co-ordinated programme in which all the above factors—the development of agricultural technique and agricultural markets, industrialisation and transport development—should have a place. As results could not be achieved immediately, an outlet for surplus population is likely to be needed, at least for a time. Emigration should therefore be included in the programme, if possible. It is clear that no such programme can be launched without capital assistance from the West, or carried into effect without Western aid in planning and technical assistance.

VIII. Minorities and Population Transfers

160. There is no mention in the Greek-Yugoslav Agreement or the Polish plan of this difficult issue. It cannot be dealt with fully here but some points may be suggested. The tension between States and their minorities is likely everywhere to be increased by recent events. It is generally agreed that the League system did not give minorities adequate protection. The use made by Germany of German minorities as spies and fifths columnists has further increased the urgency of the problem.

Transfer as a General Solution

161. These difficulties have led otherwise liberal thinkers to believe that no minority protection is possible in Eastern Europe, and that transfer must be adopted wherever possible to remove the problem at a single stroke. Some of them advocate compulsory transfer (forgetting or minimising the difficulties of identifying members of minorities in mixed areas). Others would allow to remain behind only those who are willing to let their children be educated in the majority language. This,

they claim, would remove the problem of selection and would result in the immediate departure of the more violently nationalistic elements and the assimilation of the rest in a couple of generations. Advocates of transfer refer to the "success" of the Greek-Bulgarian and Greek-Turkish exchanges of population, and they add that vast population movements are likely to occur in Eastern Europe anyhow.

General Arguments against Transfer

162. It should hardly be necessary to mention that transfer causes great suffering to innocent people. If large migrations are to occur anyhow, this inevitable suffering will be greatly increased because the limited technical aid and relief available will already be fully stretched, without adding to the calls on it. In the previous "exchanges" whose success is invoked, all migrants except the Turks were really refugees fleeing from violence, in movements belatedly recognised and completed as "exchanges." The measure of success achieved by Greece brought the State into financial difficulties and involved remarkable efforts and sacrifices by the whole population, as well as losses to Western investors who are not likely to support further loans for such purposes. Turkey had large vacant spaces in Anatolia for her newcomers. No such spaces are available in Europe.

163. It is also doubtful whether transfer does solve the problem completely. It would concentrate people in homogeneous groups, thus heightening the nationalism which is the main enemy of cooperation and adding to it a bitterness among the uprooted populations which might make them even more dangerous than they would have been if left undisturbed. Many of the territories they leave would still remain irredentas.

Transfer in Special Cases

164. If transfer is not generally adopted, there may still be special cases where it should be considered. These are briefly noted below, those where the case for transfer is strongest being placed first. (For fuller detail on the following sections, especial-

ly in regard to German minorities, see Memorandum on Transfer of German Populations, dated 13th February, 1942.)

165. (i) Those settled after evictions. There is the strongest case for expelling people who have been settled on a territory as a result of aggression and by the forcible eviction of the previous inhabitants. There are many cases of this all over Eastern Europe, e.g. Hitler's[25] new settlers in Poland and the Bulgars who are being settled in Greek territory. These unfortunate people may, however, take to flight and solve the problem themselves.

166. (ii) German minorities in oppressed territories. Where Heydrich[26] and his like have ruled, no German life is likely to be safe after the war. This would apply to the pre-war German minority in Poland (750,000) and most of that in Yugoslavia (500,000). Here gain flight and massacre may reduce the numbers. (When the Greco-Turkish Exchange Commission set about evacuating the 500,000 Greeks estimated as remaining in Anatolia after the flight from Smyrna, they found only 160,000 were left.) The case of the German minority in Czechoslovakia is peculiar because they form so large and economically important an element in Czechoslovakia.

167. (iii) Germans in Strategic Annexations. The use made by Germany of her minorities has led most States to believe that they would gain little strategic advantage from annexing German territory unless they also evicted the Germans. This argument, however, might well be used for reducing such annexations to a minimum rather than for justifying additional evictions.

168. (iv) Germans minorities elsewhere. Where anti-German feeling does not run so high as in Slovenia and Poland, transfer may still be advocated as a safeguard against fifths columns and espionage. But this fear might be met by measures less drastic than transfer, e.g. by depriving minorities of citizenship and thus bringing them under "alien restrictions," if transfer is the only alternative.

169. (v) Non-German minorities. Here too transfer may have to be considered where feeling runs so high as to make living together impossible. Otherwise, however, the existence of Confederations should weaken everywhere the case for transfer.

Fears for espionage should be diminished, Government oppression mitigated and, especially if ethnic frontiers have been adopted, toleration should be encouraged by reciprocity. (Cf. para. 102).

170. If, however, Eastern European States are determined to make a wide use of transfer, it is all the more important that frontiers should be drawn on ethnic lines so as to reduce minorities to a minimum and to enable them to be exchanged and not unilaterally evicted.

171. Previous peace settlements involving transfers of territory have usually allowed inhabitants to opt for citizenship of the State which loses the territory and to depart to it within a fixed period. It might be possible to extend this system by giving special assistance to such voluntary transfers. Some part of this assistance might reasonably be provided (to a degree depending on circumstances) by the State from which they migrate.

Alternatives to Transfer

172. The existence of Confederations makes possible the extension of certain methods of minority protection. Minority provisions might be included in the initial agreements (though there is no trace of them so far in our texts).

173. Precedents suggests, however, that such provisions would not be likely to be applied in fact, if their implementation was left to the ordinary processes of diplomacy. There would be more hope if the organs of the Confederations included a Minorities Commission in which specialised knowledge and skill could accumulate. But the looseness of the proposed plans (unless the Polish plan is accepted and its "stronger" interpretation verified) does not hold out much hope of this.

174. Such a Commission could function effectively only if it had local branches in the minority areas, able to find facts on the spot and to arbitrate directly between the parties concerned. The great success of the Upper Silesian Commission (1922–1937) gives an excellent precedent for this. It also suggests the value of a neutral chairman for any such local body. He might be a member of a nationality represented in the

Confederation but not in the mixed area concerned.

175. All these arrangements, however, would not, without special care, protect minorities not related to States in the Confederation, such as Magyars in the Southern, Serbs in the northern confederation and Jews and Germans in both. (The Jewish problem is not further dealt with in this Memorandum.) It is also doubtful whether the difficulty of controlling administrative discrimination by any such constitutional devices has not grown so great as to make these devices ineffective.

176. For these reasons, and because the complex organisation suggested above may be too much for the new Confederations, it may be more profitable to conclude with solutions which do not throw responsibility on central organs. In most areas, cantonal or regional autonomy would be inapplicable because the populations are so mixed. (The Szekel counties, if they do not remain in Hungary, are an exception to this rule.) The most suitable method seems that of cultural autonomy, so successful in Estonia. It involves the voluntary registration of individuals on a minority list which then constitutes an electorate with the power of self-taxation for educational and cultural purposes and the control of its own schools. This solution has nothing in particular to do with Confederations; but its acceptance would be made easier by the friendlier relations which Confederation implies and by the reciprocity which the adoption of ethnic frontiers would make possible. (Cf. para. 102.)

177. In the last resort, however, the only sure protection for minorities lies in the disappearance of racialism and nationalism. One trend which might well lead to this desirable result is the increasing emphasis on social and economic problems and the increasing integration, cutting across national boundaries, which their solution will require.

J. D. Mabbott[27]
September 1st, 1942.
Foreign Research and Press Service,
Balliol College, Oxford.

Minutes

1.
Minute

I have not myself yet read every word of this massive document , but it seems to me very much on the right lines even though it is perhaps more an encyclopaedia than an essay. A great deal of material could be used whatever form of confederation in Eastern Europe we may as a Government decide to back, and the whole paper can, I think, be regarded as a sort of quarry from which the stones of our constructive schemes can eventually be drawn. May I, however, say a word regarding policy, notably in reply to Mr. Roberts' minute of 10th August on R 4813 (see also minute on W 8805)?

The F.R.P.S. paper makes a great point of the undesirability of including Roumania in the Southern Confederation. I am not quite sure myself why the assumption was made that Roumania (including Transylvania) must necessarily be in the Southern Confederation. I suppose it was the northern confederation might be thought to be too big if Rumania came in as well and that geographically it looked better if it was lumped with Yugoslavia, Greece and possibly Bulgaria. Yet it is undeniably true that all the natural trade connexions of Rumania (apart from sea exports) are with Central rather than with South Eastern Europe and it is indeed rather difficult to see how the Southern Confederation will get along without any primary or indeed secondary industries.

I know that the basic assumptions were, as Mr. Roberts said, made because we have got at least two "embryos" in the shape of the Polish-Czech and the Greek-Yugoslav declarations. But is it really in our interest to found our own policy of these as yet rather immature efforts? If in fact we build up everything round the Czech-Polish Agreement (which incidentally I believe is not working out very well), are we not foregoing any chance we otherwise might have of pressing for the inclusion of Austria in a northern confederation and would not this, in spite of the arguments to the contrary, really be the one practical step towards impeding the otherwise inevitable Drang nach Osten[28] of the great German Reich. Even therefore if we conceived of a Southern Confederation of Yugoslavia, Greece and possibly of

Bulgaria under the reformed Government, might not Roumania as a whole come into the northern confederation? I know that this would increase the number of "ex-enemies," but I think that this phrase is really rather meaningless so far as post-war politics in the part of the world is concerned. It might even be that the inclusion of Roumania would make the inclusion of Austria more palatable to the Poles, though no doubt it would hardly be welcomed by the Hungarians.

I continue to think in any case that my idea of a "District of Columbia" in Bratislava has a good deal to recommend it and I do not think that it need be dismissed as fanciful.

Gladwyn Jebb[29]
12th August, 1942.

2.
Minute

Comments on F.R.P.S. Paper
"Federations in Eastern Europe"

A. General Comments

(1) The paper as a whole seems to me to suffer from the rigidity of the preliminary assumptions as defined in paragraphs 1–7. It is obviously necessary for a study of this sort to be based on certain hypotheses, but if these hypotheses are too rigid, there is a danger of the paper's practical value in helping us to formulate policy being reduced and of our finding ourselves tied down to unnecessarily limited conceptions.

This seems to apply in particular to paragraph 4. In the first place, should we be so definite as to say that it is not possible to envisage a single large unit may not appear immediately practicable, but I feel that there might be something to be gained by examining the pros and cons. It looks at present as though the Polish-Czech and Greek-Yugoslav Confederations are likely to be very loose, and this being so, it should be less difficult to arrange some sort of union between them than if they were both likely to develop on very close and rigid lines. We should obviously neglect no possibility of avoiding setting up rival confederations which would be a source of weakness rather than of strength in South-Eastern Europe.

More obvious limitations are imposed on the memorandum by the assumption that Roumania must come within the southern confederation. It is pointed out that Roumania's principal trade connexions are with the countries of the northern confederation and with Germany, and it also seems possible that the inclusion of Roumania in the northern confederation may prove the only means of solving the Transylvanian problem and the difficult question of Roumania's relations with Hungary. The pros and cons could be discussed more objectively if no preliminary assumption regarding Roumania's position were laid down.

I feel it might be useful if it were made clear in the preliminary assumptions that merely because we mention certain existing units such as Roumania or Czechoslovakia, we are not at this stage committed to any pre-war frontiers in this area, nor necessarily to the maintenance of the integrity of pre-war units. Thus there is a case to be made for the inclusion of Transylvania as a separate unit, and it also seems possible that the only solution of the Slovak problem and the Czechoslovak-Hungarian difficulties may lie in the granting of a degree of autonomy to Slovakia. There is also a possible case to be made out for the separation of Croatia from Yugoslavia. Such cases might, I think be more satisfactorily examined if the position was made quite clear in the preliminary assumptions.

Paragraph 6, I think, might also be expanded to make it clear at the beginning that the memorandum does not concern itself with the problems of the eastern frontiers of the confederations. I feel, however, that it might be useful if some rather fuller indication were given of what these problems are likely to be. I have in mind particularly the case of Lithuania, which the Soviet Government will clearly wish to incorporate and which the Poles have already expressed the desire to join with Poland in a federation.

(2) I feel that in general the memorandum does not give enough consideration to the political forms of government which

exist at present and may come into being in future inside various member states of the possible confederations. There are already signs that this question may come to have considerable bearing on the formation of the confederations. For instance, the Czechs are already showing signs of wishing to make it a condition of entry into their confederation that member states should roughly have the same liberal democratic form of government which the Czechoslovak Government in London upholds. The article by Dr. Ripka[30] on Hungary in C 8260/8260/21 is of interest in this connexion. It also seems that the time is bound to come when H.M.G. will have to formulate a policy on this question. The time has long passed when we could afford to say that the internal affairs of other countries are not our concern, and, as the war draws nearer to end, there will be strong agitation here for active support by H.M.G. of subversive and revolutionary groups in the countries now under German domination.

This question is touched on in paragraph 10 of the memorandum, but I think this might well be expanded and the definitions of "attitudes" in paragraph 7, which take no account of the possible effects of changes in the internal form of government, may need modification.

(3) The usefulness of the paper also suffers to my mind the fact that little attempt is made to assess the viability of the two confederations from the political, economic and military points of view. What we are chiefly concerned to find out is what unit or units grouped round the existing nuclei of the Polish-Czech and Greek-Yugoslav declarations are likely to form the most stable basis for the future of South-Eastern Europe and to provide the strongest bulwark between Germany and the USSR. It would, for instance, be useful to have some study of the effects, from the point of view of the balance of power, of including Roumania in either the northern or southern confederation. It may be, for instance, that the inclusion of Roumania in the northern confederation would make the northern group so much more powerful than the southern that the balance would be dangerously upset, and the hope of effective collaboration between the two groups dangerously reduced and the effectiveness of the central bulwark correspondingly reduced.

B. Particular Comments.

Paragraph 27.

Is it necessarily a fact that all the members of a loose confederation would have to have equal representation? It seems worth recalling the analogy of the League of Nations, where, once the principle of formal equality had been affirmed, the practical difficulty arising out of the great differences in power and influence between the member states was got over by a limited degree of discrimination in favour of the great powers in the constitution of the Council. It should not be impossible to evolve some such arrangement in a confederation in which say Croatia or Slovenia were members alongside Czechoslovakia or Roumania.

Paragraphs 32–50.

I feel that in these paragraphs too many deductions are made from the so-called "Polish plan" of November, 1941. This plan is admittedly a useful indication of Polish aims, but the measure of what has so far been proved practicable is to be found only in the Polish-Czech declaration of 19th January, 1942.

The texts of the Polish-Czech declaration and of the Greek-Yugoslav declaration of 15th January, 1942 should, I think, be appended to the memorandum as suggested in Mr. Mabbott's covering letter.

Paragraphs 60–70.

The conclusion in paragraph 70 against pressure on the confederations to make their union closer seems disappointingly negative. As regards the political field it is true that as stated in paragraph 63 limits are imposed upon what is possible by the traditional animosities and loyalties of the populations concerned but I do not think it follows that any attempt to modify those traditions must inevitably be self-defeating. They seem bound in any event to undergo considerable development as a result of the common suffering imposed by the war and of the revolutionary developments which seem likely to follow it. Surely we should not rule out in advance all possibility of directing them into new channels. This will mean considerable preparation and there seems no reason why we should not use every opportunity of suggesting discreetly to the governments concerned the advantages of closer union and our ideas of how it might be obtained; and even of preparing the ground for such union by suitable propaganda to the occupied countries.

Nor do I find the economic arguments convincing. It is true that as suggested in paragraph 65 a loose confederation such as seems to be contemplated at present would not have funds to set up inter-state economic undertakings, but surely a start could be made with semi-official corporations in spheres such as transport which could be to some extent self-supporting and independent of national revenues, and if the necessary the foreign capital assistance which is foreseen as necessary in paragraph 158 could be directed into these channels. As regards the arguments that effective action can only be taken on a much wider scale I do not see how this fits in with the argument in paragraph 158 regarding the need of the whole area of South-East Europe for a co-ordinated programme and that in paragraph 120 where the need of avoiding economic rivalry between units of the confederations is emphasised. Obviously the ideal would be to treat the whole of Europe (or why not even the whole world?) as one unit. But there will surely be scope for making a start on the basis of such confederations as do take shape in South East Europe and the admitted need of such confederations for outside economic assistance seems to provide an opportunity.

Paragraph 100.

I think that here the principal of ethnography receives too much emphasis at the expense of strategy and economics. Reference is made in paragraph 103 to the population transfers which have already taken place and I feel that it would be safer to draw frontiers primarily according to the dictates of strategic and economic needs and adjust the ethnographical overlaps as much as can be managed afterwards. I feel that these paragraphs and paragraphs 159 to 175 might examine rather more fully than they do the possibility of allowing in certain cases a degree of option when population transfers are arranged. On the whole it seems to be rather too definitely assumed (particularly in the case of the Sudeten Germans mentioned in paragraph 76 and 165) that the minorities are necessarily coherent groups to be treated as a whole. This may not necessarily always prove true although of course in allowing certain elements of a minority to remain behind the Fifth Column danger has to be borne in mind.

Paragraph 135.

It seems worth considering whether in the discussion of Croatia some examination should not be made of the pros and cons of attaching Croatia to the northern confederation. The arguments in paragraphs 137 to 141 concerning the importance of assuring to the northern confederation some access to the Adriatic seem to have a bearing on this possibility.

Paragraphs 76,
105 and 165.

These are the principal passages dealing with Czechoslovak problems which Mr. Mabbott fears in his covering letter may be unfair to the Czechoslovak case. They are admittedly rather sketchy but I feel that they indicate the main points fairly adequately. The principal problems, particularly concerning the German-Czech frontier, are fully dealt with in the memorandum on frontiers of European confederations in C 2167/241/18 and there seems little point in going too deeply into these questions here. However there might be no harm in the memorandum being shown to Professor Seton-Watson[31] as suggested.

D. Allen[32]
28th August, 1942.

3.
Minute

When I was at Balliol last Saturday I had a long talk with Sir Alfred Zimmern[33] and Mr. Mabbott about the F.R.P.S. paper on Confederations. It seems that Mr. Mabbott is producing a new version now received this encyclopaedia but that he was uneasy about the whole thing seeing that in his view the existing terms of reference made it difficult to put up constructive proposals which would be in any way likely to work in practice. I asked Mr. Mabbott why he objected to the existing terms of reference, and he said that the inclusion of Hungary in the northern confederation and Roumania in the southern would raise insuperable difficulties of an economic and political nature. I replied that the existing instructions were based on the fact that there was at least the nucleus of one confederation in the north and another in the south, but Mr. Mabbott replied (and in this he was vigorously backed up by Professor Zimmern) that the Polish-Czech arrangement was really largely artificial and that the Greek-Yugoslav one would never get beyond the paper stage.

I then said that if this was the view of F.R.P.S. what would they suggest? Would they like to have one huge confederation extending from Danzig to the Piraeus? They replied that this would indeed in their view be preferable to two rather artificial confederations and that it would certainly be easier to work out the economic side of the business if there was one bloc however loosely held together rather than two. (I now observe that the one-bloc theory is being vigorously pushed by Mr. Sumner Welles.)[34]

There followed a long discussion in which I maintained that the one-bloc conception would really be too unwieldy. I suggested, however, on the other hand, that it might be conceivable for Poland to be left out of our calculations and to be treated as a Great Power in itself. This would flatter the Poles and at the same time would not prevent them coming to any sensible arrangement with Czechoslovakia which might seem mutually desirable. I think that the exclusion of Poland would have this advantage: immediately at the conclusion of hostilities there might be a possibility of representatives of Russia, the United States and Great Britain establishing themselves at, say, Bratislava, and declaring that they would, with the existing forces at their disposal, constitute for a given period the central authority of the entire region comprising Czechoslovakia, Austria, Yugoslavia, Roumania, Hungary, Bulgaria, Albania and Greece, and that, whereas during this period the legitimate governments of the countries concerned would either return to or be set up in those countries, certain powers would be reserved during the period indicated by the three Great Allies. Such powers might include the right to redefine frontiers (1939 frontiers would be observed until such redefinitions had been made); a general right to over-rule any State on economic or financial policy; and all decisions relating to the administration of relief.

It seemed to me, I said, that only in this way would you get the initial impetus towards the establishment of any centralised authority, and further, that if such an impetus were not given immediately at the conclusion of hostilities it would never be given at all.

Sir Alfred Zimmern and Mr. Mabbott were much impressed by the possibilities of such a scheme, but I immediately told them that they must not to mention anybody else that such ideas had even been discussed with me, since it would be obviously fatal if any whisper of them got round at this stage to the representatives of the Central European Powers concerned.

On return from Oxford I discussed these possibilities with Sir O. Sargent, who said that he agreed that there was much in the plan, and also agreed that it should be kept entirely dark, at any rate for the time being. I should, however, like to have permission to authorise Sir Alfred Zimmern, in concert with Mr. Mabbott and perhaps Professor Fisher,[35] to prepare a more detailed plan on the lines suggested. When this is received and we have made up our own minds in regard to its practicability, it might be possible to discuss the matter confidentially with Mr. Welles and perhaps with Mr. Maisky[36] as well.

Gladwyn Jebb
8th September, 1942.

4.
Minute

I agree that F.R.P.S. were set a difficult problem owing to the rigidity of the original terms of reference. This point had already been made in the attached minute written by Mr. Allen on the 28th August with which I agree generally. Since arrangements in Eastern Europe are likely to be extremely fluid there is certainly advantage in considering all possible alternatives and I therefore see no objection to F.R.P.S. being allowed to produce another paper with less rigid terms of reference pressing, if they so desire, the advantages of a single confederation.

But I should regard it as rather dangerous for us to frame a policy upon the assumption of a single confederation, even if this should seem the most desirable theoretical solution. The new arrangements in Eastern Europe are going to be difficult enough in any case and it therefore seems to me essential to base them as far as possible upon existing factors. There is, so far as I can see, no solid foundation whatsoever for a single confederation stretching from Lithuania to the Aegean and it will surely crumple at the first jolt. There is, however, a foundation for a union of states between Germany and Russia. The nucleus of such a union is the Polish-Czech federation plus Hungary. I should be prepared to include Roumania within this Federation and to work for a separate Transylvanian component of the federal system. The case of Austria will require very careful weighing up.

Although this is not strictly my affair, the interests of the purely Balkan states and in particular of Greece seem to me quite different from those of the more Northern States. Therefore although the northern confederation would be much bigger and more important than the Southern I should have thought it was wiser to retain the two separate entities restricting the Balkan one to Greece, Yugoslavia, Bulgaria and Albania.

I am not attracted by Mr. Jebb's suggestion of a separate Poland and a federal system covering all the other states under discussion. Our object is not to satisfy Polish vanity, which is already only too dangerous an element in Polish political reasoning, but to create a strong Eastern neighbour to Germany. On her own Poland cannot be such a neighbour for a long time to come. Supported by Czech industry in particular and also by Roumanian oil etc. Poland will be an important factor in European power politics. Moreover the powerful influence of Poland in any confederation should be directed towards our primary aim of keeping Germany down. I am not so sure that a loose Central European structure without Poland, more particularly if such a structure includes Austria, can be relied upon in the long run to follow a sufficiently resolute policy vis-a-vis Germany.

In considering all these problems I think we must also be careful not to loose sight of our obligations towards our Allies. In a theoretical paper it is quite in order to discuss the advantages of e.g. separating Croatia from Yugoslavia, leaving Sub-Carpathian Ruthenia with Hungary etc. but in terms of practical politics it seems to me out of the question for us to impose upon our Allies purely for theoretical reasons really important diminutions in the territories possessed by them before the war, more particularly if this in fact struck at the very roots of their state systems. This argument does not of course apply to Eastern Poland since the arrangements reached there will be purely a matter of power politics and not based upon theoretical speculations.

To turn now to the F.R.P.S. paper the following points occur to me.

I agree with Mr. Allen that more should be made of the question of the social structure of the component states in any confederation. The Czech lectures to their neighbours are rather tiresome but there is considerable force in their arguments that excessive divergences could not exist happily side by side. A connected question which is also not touched upon in the paper is that of political regimes. It seems to me difficult for monarchies and republics to exist side by side in a confederation. The most that could be expected would presumably be something approximating to the pre-war Little Entente[37] which did consist of two monarchies and a republic. We do not of course know what the position will be at the end of the war but as things now stand the Polish-Czech system consists of republics and the Greek-

Yugoslav system of monarchies. If Roumania remains a monarchy and Hungary at least in theory a monarchy they might be difficult to fit into the Polish-Czech structure but it seems very possible that there will be a revolution against the monarchial system in these ex-enemy states after he war.

For reasons which I have already explained I think Mr. Allen goes rather too far in suggesting that these papers should not be influenced by pre-war frontiers etc. Nor do I think that it is possible at present to discuss the Eastern frontiers of the confederation or the problem of Lithuania at all usefully.

I also agree with the writers of the paper rather than with Mr. Allen as regards the pressure which can usefully be brought to bear to make these federal schemes acceptable. At this stage our encouragement should be discreet and we should allow growth to be as organic as possible. The time for pressure will come at a later stage of the war and it will certainly then be necessary to use all our propaganda machinery and to give very definite if unpalatable advice to our allies and ex-enemies. In particular I very much agree with the passages in this paper stressing the need for tolerant and statesmanlike treatment of Hungary and Bulgaria, which are essential members of the new structures and which, unless treated tolerantly, will remain a constant Fifth Column menace. In case of Hungary we shall have to give some very unpalatable advice to the Czechs at the proper moment.

The passages regarding the Sudeten problem rather ignore Dr. Benes[38] intentions of reducing the Sudeten population very drastically not merely by 700,000 but by some two to two and a half million. However it is perhaps not necessary to refer to this in the paper.

Equally the paper does not refer to the Czech-Soviet agreement[39] that Czechoslovakia is to return to her old boundaries including Ruthenia.

I am not very happy about the suggestions at the end of the paper regarding minorities. It will I think be essential to do all we can to escape from the conception of minorities after the war. Irreconcilable minorities should be transferred and, in the case of those who remain, the aim should surely be not give them minority rights and thus perpetuate difficult problems but to insist upon the integration of the minorities within the states to which they will belong.

It seems to me that Austria and Transylvania, if such a state is created, will call for rather special treatment. The object in each case may be to build up something approximating to Switzerland. In the case of Austria in particular the solution might be in an independent Austria neutralized and encouraged to grow into a second Switzerland. Separate papers dealing with these possibilities would I think be useful.

Finally as a minor point F. R.P.S. now have a Czech expert, admittedly on a part-time basis. He has already taken up his duties and it is to him and certainly not to Prof. Seton-Watson that this F.R.P.S. paper should be shown for any comments from the Czech angle.

F. K. Roberts[40]
13th September, 1942

5.
Minute

It occurs to me that we are perhaps allowing ourselves to be unnecessarily disheartened by the F.R.P.S. paper. The difficulties inherent in a confederative solution for Central and South-Eastern Europe which it brings out were always appreciated here. Roumania and Transylvania in particular were always recognised to present a very thorny problem. We knew that the existing Polish-Czech and Greek-Yugoslav agreements were feeble and nebulous instruments, concluded by refugee Governments who might not hold the actual power when the war ended. We also realised that the peoples themselves would have their own point of view in these matters and might readily resort to violence between themselves.

The F.R.P.S. paper brings out and illustrates these and other difficulties, but it does not suggest that they are necessarily insuperable. So far as the Southern Department are concerned there are two main problems.

The first is Roumania. We were aware from the earlier papers that F.R.P.S. hold the view that Roumania is so overwhelmingly linked economically with the Danube Basin that she cannot properly belong to a Balkan Confederation. But all impulses other than economic pull her in the direction of the Balkans. As a former Turkish province her ties are naturally with the other Balkan States, and natural political affinities have grown up between Roumania, Yugoslavia and Greece, to say nothing of Turkey. The strongest argument in favour of Roumania's inclusion in the southern rather than the northern European confederation is that without her the former would be too light a body and would be desperately short of raw materials.

It would be useful to have the considered opinion of F.R.P.S. on the viability of a southern confederation excluding Roumania.

For the second problem, Transylvania, the ideal solution would obviously be found if Roumania and Hungary were included in the same confederation. But I do not think that the Transylvanian problem is in itself an overwhelming argument in favour of including Roumania and Hungary in the same confederation. We ourselves suggested a possible solution in the memorandum in R 3793/43/67—cantonment on the Swiss model —and the F.R.P.S. do not reject this suggestion.

I should deprecate throwing over our confederation scheme in favour of an entirely new scheme such as that suggested by Mr. Jebb until we are quite satisfied that confederation is unworkable. Not only is it our official policy to build on the Graeco-Yugoslav and Polish-Czech agreements as a prelude to the type of arrangement we should welcome in post-war Europe (see the Secretary of State's minute on R 216/G), but I think we should have the greatest difficulty in persuading many of our Allies to agree to anything like Mr. Jebb's scheme, and with Mr. Roberts I feel that it would be quite wrong to leave the feelings of our Allies out of account. The Greeks and the Yugoslavs (at least on the performance of their present Governments) who look to us as a counter-weight to Russia and the Balkans, would certainly regard any such scheme as a surrender to Russia.

An alternative means establishing the control which Mr. Jebb's scheme aims at would be by the establishment of

British or Anglo-Saxon naval and air bases in the Aegean and Adriatic. Although this was not said in the memorandum in R 3793, it has always been at the back of our minds that confederation in Europe would need the sanction of Anglo-Saxon control to have any hope of making it effective. The Greek Government have freely offered us the use of bases in their territory and the Yugoslavs would no doubt agree; there should be no difficulty about establishing them in Albania. The primary object of the control thus set up would be to prevent the outbreak of inter-Balkan quarrels in the immediate post-war period and then gradually to lead the individual States to divest themselves of individual sovereignty to the extent necessary to make collective sovereignty of the confederation effective.

P. Dixon[41]
20th September, 1942.

6.
Minute

I am afraid I must inflict these lengthy minutes on you since they raise an important question of principle.

You will remember that, before going on leave, I mentioned to you a suggestion regarding the Confederations which emanated from my recent talk with the pundits of F.R.P.S. This proposal was recorded in my minute of September 8th and has now given rise to minutes by Mr. Dixon, Mr. Roberts and Mr. Allen, which are attached. I am appeared to be attracted by the idea.

I must say that I do not find myself in agreement with Mr. Dixon and Mr. Roberts and that I continue to believe that in practice the only way to solve the vexed question of unity in Eastern Europe is for ourselves, the Americans and the Russians jointly to agree in advance to administer to a large extent the bulk of the area concerned immediately on the close of hostilities and to do so under the guise of relief. The obvious snag about any proposal of this kind is that the Poles, rightly or wrongly, consider themselves to be a Great Power and consequently will be unlikely to agree to any form of tutelage which might be agreed to be the governments of the other countries concerned, even if we do not feel in a position to impose it on them. It is not, I suggest, a question of "satisfying Polish vanity" or of suggesting any system which would have less chance of standing up to Germany than has been suggested up to now. On the contrary, the system I recommend might conceivably result in some measure of unity both in the north and in the south, whereas the proposal to build up on the existing Polish-Czech and Greek-Yugoslav agreements has always seemed to me to be quite chimerical, partly because the arrangement suggested cuts across natural economic lines of development and partly because, unless some measure of force is applied somewhere, the first thing the nations concerned will do is to quarrel among themselves.

Incidentally, I suggest that there is really not very much point in insisting on Greece forming a part of any southern confederation. Greece is really an island dependent for her support and livelihood on an active seafaring population. She is quite capable of standing alone, provided she maintains good relations with Turkey and generally comes under the aegis of any British power established in the Middle East. She could in fact be an independent State forming part of a large "Middle Eastern" area.

Hence the real problem is how to re-create something on the lines of the old Austrian Empire or, as I should call it, an "Eastern European Federation." This should by no means be an impossible proposition provided that we, the Americans and the Russians work in harmony. Poland after all would remain a pretty large State even if her eastern frontiers approximated to the Curzon line:[42] at any rate she would, I should hope, absorb East Prussia and perhaps Upper Silesia as well.

With regard to Mr. Dixon's suggestion for the establishment of naval and air bases in the Aegean and Adriatic, I have no doubt that it would be useful to attempt to organise them, but we need not delude ourselves into thinking that their mere establishment would result in unity in Eastern Europe; and here again the establishment of such bases without Russian agreement would merely convince the Russians that we were pursuing an anti-Russian policy.

I must say, therefore, that I should like your authority to tell F.R.P.S. to work out another scheme on the assumption that Poland should be a separate State and an Inter-Allied Commission of Control would establish itself at some central point immediately on the conclusion of hostilities and declare that it reserved to itself for an indeterminate period certain powers in the whole area now included in Czechoslovakia, Austria, Hungary, Roumania, Yugoslavia, Albania and Bulgaria.

The exact function which might be reserved for such an allied commission and those which should be left to the local governments would be one of the things to be decided in the F.R.P.S. paper.

I suggest that, even if you are not convinced of the desirability of such a scheme, it would be at least useful to get F.R.P.S. to elaborate it.

Gladwyn Jebb
25th Sept., 1942.

7.
Minute

I remember your mentioning to me the fact that the F.R.P.S. were not satisfied with the bases on which they were compelled to construct their report, and I agreed that there was no reason why they should not be encouraged to work out further schemes on other bases. I do not, however, remember your explaining to me the actual basis which you refer to in your minute of the 8th September.

Anyhow I am still of the opinion that we need not be tied to any one scheme, and that the F.R.P.S. is there to be used for working out alternative schemes on the bases which we may suggest to them.

It would, however, I think be a mistake to give the F.R.P.S. a completely free hand, and unless they are going to waste their time and paper they must work within the framework laid down by the Foreign Office. As, therefore, there is a general feeling that other alternatives should be explored, I would suggest that a meeting should be held at the Foreign Office to draw up further bases on which the F.R.P.S. should be invited to construct other edifices. At such a meeting it would be possible to discuss all the various suggestions that have been put forward in these minutes and decide which to work on and which to discard.

Incidentally, I do not agree with the view that two Confederations based upon the existing Czech-Polish Agreement and the Greek-Yugoslav Agreement are necessarily chimerical. At any rate I cannot agree that they would be any more chimerical than the idea of a vast Confederation extending from the Baltic to the Mediterranean, which seems to be the alternative you contemplate.* Moreover, I do not understand why a union between Poland and Czechoslovakia or one between Greece and Yugoslavia should be held to cut across natural economic lines of development. On the other hand, I quite agree that any scheme in Central Europe or the Balkans will have to be more or less imposed upon the various States, and that the Great Powers will therefore have to be ready jointly to use a certain amount of coercion. But naturally it would be everybody's desire that this coercion should be reduced to a minimum and therefore the scheme to be imposed should coincide as far as possible with the wishes and tendencies of the nations concerned.

O. G. Sargent
Sept. 26th, 1942.

8.
Minute

"Confederations in Eastern Europe"

At a meeting held in Sir Orme Sargent's room on 2nd October the following conclusions were reached:
1. Foreign Research and Press Service Paper "Confederation in Eastern Europe" subject to final revision by Foreign

---

* Taken here to comprise Poland, Czechoslovakia, Austria, Hungary, Roumania, Yugoslavia, Bulgaria, Albania and Greece as constituted in 1937.

Research and Press Service, should go forward.

2. Foreign Research and Press Service should be asked to undertake further studies on the post-war settlement of Eastern Europe with the following terms of reference:

Assuming that the object of any scheme is to provide durable safeguards against German penetration and to promote the security and prosperity of the area, and accepting the necessity of giving satisfaction to the strategic and political interests of the Union of Soviet Socialist Republics, Foreign Research and Press Service are asked to consider:

(1) Assuming the existence of two confederations (as described in the existing Foreign Research and Press Service Paper), what unity of the whole area could be achieved in the economic field; and if a sufficient degree of unity could be achieved, would this ease the problem of the retention of Roumania in the Southern confederation.

(2) The future status of Austria, including the circumstances in which she might form part of any confederation.

(3) The possibility of solving the Transylvanian problem either by partition, by transfer as a whole either to Roumania or Hungary, or by the creation of a separate Transylvanian state, and in the latter case whether it should form part of any confederation or exist as a buffer state between the two confederations contemplated in the existing Foreign Research and Press Service paper.

(4) The possible ways of dealing with the Yugoslav problem if the present state disintegrates and we have to deal with at least Croatia and Serbia as separate states.

(5) The desirability and practicability of a Danubian Confederation; what Danubian states should be included in such a confederation; how far it could be extended to include non-riparian states and what would be the position of the states remaining outside the confederation?

(6) How best in any combination to meet what we may expect the Soviet Government to demand in order to guarantee their strategic security and their economic and political interests vis-a-vis any confederation or confederations?

N. B. Ronald[43]
6th October, 1942

[U 723/58/72]

DOCUMENT 2

Economic Possibilities in Eastern Europe with Reference to Political Structure

[*Note*. This paper is intended to throw light on the nature of the economic development which is most desirable (and, in favourable conditions, most probable) in Eastern Europe, and on the extent to which various forms of political organisation would probably tend to favour or to inhibit this desirable development. Development has been going on for some time at a considerable and increasing rate; sometimes on sound lines, sometimes in directions which are not consistent with the best development of the area as a whole. The existing development is not considered in this paper, except in so far as it is necessary to mention it as affecting future possibilities; the main attention is fixed on what is known of the permanent resources of the area and the lines of development which they suggest.]

Summary

1. The main economic problem of Eastern Europe (agricultural over-population and growing population-pressure) can be solved in the absence of emigration facilities on a scale surpassing all reasonable expectations, only by means similar to those used to solve the not dissimilar problem in Japan—rapid industrialisation. The most advantageous lines of development can be followed only if foreign markets are available for new Eastern European exports of various kinds, but a mere improvement in the terms on which it can sell abroad exports of the kind it has specialised on hitherto can make only a minor contribution to the solution of its problem.

2. The distribution of resources in the area is such that

the best use of them demands a considerable division of economic function between its parts. The regions which have far the greater part of the power resources, and should therefore contain most of the heavier industries, are Silesia, Bohemia-Moravia, and Eastern Austria. The natural endowments of these three areas are such that their functions, again, should be encouraged to develop largely along complementary rather than competitive lines. The most suitable secondary centres of heavy industry, based on water-power and aluminium as well as (or instead of) on coal and iron, are the regions around the Iron Gate and perhaps part of the Dalmatian coast.

3. Light industries, perhaps led by textiles based on artificial fibres of cellulose, should be capable of developing in the Carpathians, Transylvania and the Balkans. Agriculture, and the food industries depending on it, would benefit by more specialisation on milk and fresh vegetables near the industrial areas, on animal products in Poland, on pastoral production in the mountain areas, on fruits, tobacco, etc., in the Balkans and Greece, and by irrigation, making possible higher grain yields, vegetable-growing, and more cattle in the Danube Valley. Many of the specialised products could then be canned or otherwise packed for export.

4. The chief developments of communications required are the improvement of the Danube as a waterway, the completion of the Danube-Elbe and Danube-Oder Canals (with a connexion to the Vistula), the canalisation of the Vistula, and the building of a Belgrade-Salonica Canal, together with extensive road-building some railway improvements.

5. A prior condition of the optimum division of function between any two or more parts of the area is the establishment of complete political confidence between them. In spite of the fact that the development adumbrated would lead to a greater diversity of industries than hitherto in most countries, and would have manifest economic advantages (especially if co-operation were made the condition of assistance from outside), the political difficulties will obviously be great. It might be possible to demonstrate the advantages of economic co-operation and to start development in the right directions under international supervision in the post-war relief period.

6. Since there is only one region in the area which is likely to become of the first industrial importance and to achieve high income-levels in the near and middle future, it follows that, if there is more than one confederation in Eastern Europe, either (a) part of the area will be cut off from the most direct access to first-class industrial resources and from the advantages which political connexion with wealthier areas can give, or (b) the main industrial area will have to be split, which would tend to reduce its effectiveness. The dilemma might be partly avoided through economic agreements between the two confederations, but this would not make possible the transfer of income from the richer to the poorer areas, which happens only where there is a common system of public finance. This creates a presumption in favour of one confederation covering the whole area.

7. If there are two confederations based respectively on Poland-Czechoslovakia-Hungary and Yugoslavia-Greece (associations which would be quite advantageous economically), Roumania and perhaps even Bulgaria would have stronger economic interests in entering the northern than the southern. The same is probably true of Austria, but her interest in both, and her position astride the communications, is an additional argument for one confederation of the whole area.

General Considerations on the Whole Ares

1. Considered as a whole, the area between Germany and Russia, between the Mediterranean and the Baltic,* in which about 117 million people lived before the war, is a poor, mainly agricultural region, over-populated (at least in the limited sense that if its economic structure remained anything like at present it would provide better standards of living with fewer people) with a rapid, though diminishing, rate of natural population growth and poor prospects of finding an adequate outlet in emigration; it is not rich in those combinations of resources which provide the basis for the great industrial agglomerations of Western Europe or the United States; and in its external

---

* Taken here to comprise Poland, Czechoslovakia, Austria, Hungary, Roumania, Yugoslavia, Bulgaria, Albania and Greece as constituted in 1937.

trade relations, it is for the most part, a weaker competitor of much larger and more fortunately-endowed producers overseas.

2. This position is not a promising one, but it must be remembered that other regions, whose prospects have, in the past, been little less gloomy, have achieved striking changes in their economic structure and striking improvements in their standards of life. In some respects, Japan provides perhaps the most instructive example. Sixty years ago, the standard of living there was much lower than in Eastern Europe to-day, power and metal resources little better, population two or three times as dense in relation to arable land, and the rate of natural increase high, yet, in spite of these handicaps, the Japanese economic structure has been completely transformed, the numbers on the land have not increased, and the average levels of output and consumption per head have trebled or quadrupled. It is plain, therefore, that even a great scarcity of natural resources can be overcome by the determined application of capital in the appropriate forms, accompanied by the corresponding transformation of occupational structure.

3. In Eastern Europe, as in Japan, the extent to which the problem can be solved by applying capital to agricultural production, which now occupies some 60 or 70 per cent. of the population, is limited. It is true that the small yields per acre of most Eastern European agricultural products are due largely to the facts that fertilisers cannot be afforded by the peasants, that livestock is scarce, and that the areas with the best soil are too dry, so that investment on fertilisers, irrigation, drainage, livestock and technical education would bear fruit. For these applications of capital to agriculture which would displace labour, however, there is little scope in an area where already probably a quarter or a third of the farm population could be removed without reducing output, and where large areas of soil now under the plough are so poor that, in less poverty-stricken countries, they would be less intensively rather than more intensively used.

4. The absorption of the 1.5 million persons (or the 3/4 million men) who are added to the population of productive age each year in Eastern Europe, in such a way as to prevent their overcrowding the land still further (not to mention the gradual

removal of some of the 8 or 10 million men now on the land whose labour there is superfluous), is clearly an enormous task. The absorption of the annual natural increase in active male population alone into handicrafts, factory industry, and wholesale and retail trade of the kinds established in Palestine between 1930 and 1937 (probably quite a suitable parallel), would require a capital investment of about (300 million per year (at pre-war prices). If the present surplus population on the land is to be reduced, this investment will, of course, have to be correspondingly increased, and it must also be noted that the above figure does not include either the cost of agricultural improvements or expenditure on public utilities, dwelling-houses, etc., the need for which would increase greatly as a result of rapid industrialisation. It seems safe to say that an annual investment equivalent to (500 million before the war would be necessary to bring about a really satisfactory rate of improvement in the economic life of Eastern Europe—a rate, that is, which would enable the surplus agricultural population to be transferred to other occupations, and agriculture itself made reasonably productive within not much more than a generation. Any substantial emigration from the area would, of course, reduce these requirements.

5. Such an investment is equivalent to about 15–20 per cent. of the area's aggregate national income in a moderately prosperous pre-war year. Similar rates of investment, in relation to national income, have been achieved by Japan and the U.S.S.R., with average income-levels, probably not far different from those occurring in Eastern Europe, while Britain, in the middle of last century, when incomes were no higher than they were before 1939 in the more prosperous parts of the area, also attained a proportionate rate of saving as high as this. It is obvious, however, that the political, social and economic organisations of the countries named were so far different from those prevailing in Eastern Europe as to make the parallel of little immediate relevance and that the great quantities of investment goods and technical advice required for the transformation under discussion would make it necessary for Eastern Europe to import largely—and hence to borrow considerably—from abroad, especially in the earlier stages.

6. The economic troubles of Eastern Europe can obviously be attacked, not only by the measures to increase production inside the area which are referred to above, but also by measures aimed at improving its terms of trade with the outside world. These measures would probably, in the first instance, tend to reduce the physical volume of the area's exports to some extent, since even a smaller physical export would then serve to buy more imports than have hitherto been available, and any improvement in the standard of life would result in a increased consumption of (among other things) the food-stuffs which have been among the area's chief exports. Such an attack on the problem can be made, however, only either through the payment of specially favourable prices for Eastern European products by some outside country or countries, or through a change in the terms of trade between primary and manufactured products in the world market as a whole, and in any case the contribution which such an attack would be likely to make in practice to the raising of the standard of life would probably be of only the second order of importance. This must not, of course, obscure the fact that the optimum internal development of the area will probably depend on its finding markets for new export products.

7. The regeneration of the region's economy therefore demands (failing a truly enormous increase in the facilities for emigration, which is hardly likely), a very large programme of industrialisation, accompanied by measures to increase the productivity of its agriculture. What forms the industrialisation and agricultural improvement could most suitably take, and what local division of function within Eastern Europe they would (in their most desirable forms) involve, must now be considered.

The Distribution of Resources

(a) Power and Fuel

8. It is stated above that Eastern Europe is not rich in those combinations of resources which have formed the basis for industrial agglomerations in the West. The coal and lignite (the latter expressed as an equivalent amount of coal) which are

thought to exist in workable seams in the area amount to only some 113,000 million tons, or less than 1,000 tons per head of the area's present population, as compared with 292,000 million tons (4,180 tons per head) in Germany and 175,000 million tons (3,700 tons per head) in Britain. The iron-ore reserves, though less reliably estimated, appear also to be small as compared with those of the West—almost certainly less (probably very much less) than a quarter of those of Lorraine alone. Water-power, the potential total of which at normal low-water levels has been estimated at about 11.5 million horse-power, is also much less abundant, in relation to population, than in Western Europe. Nevertheless, the amounts of these resources per head of the population are greater (with the possible exception of water-power) than those of Japan, their absolute magnitude is very considerable, and they are supplemented by mineral resources of other kinds. The agricultural resources, again, though at present very meagre in relation to the population which tries to live on them, are, absolutely, of impressive magnitude and diversity, and should be capable of considerable improvement. The proper development of the resources available, both agricultural and industrial, is essential to the economic improvement of the area, and it is not hard to see, in rough outline at least, what territorial division of economic functions is conducive to this proper development.

9. The industrial resources of Eastern Europe are (like similar resources in most parts of the world) very unevenly distributed. More than 80 per cent. of the solid mineral fuels of the area are packed into the small space of Polish Upper Silesia; a further 12 per cent. are in the neighbouring districts of Czechoslovakia and in the lesser coal-fields and the high-quality lignite beds elsewhere in Bohemia and Moravia (the lignite is mainly in the Erzgebirge and the coal-fields are scattered).

10. The coal and lignite resources of the rest of Eastern Europe are small indeed: Austria, Roumania, Hungary, Bulgaria, Albania, Greece, Yugoslavia, Slovakia and Central, Northern and Eastern Poland together have scarcely 90 tons per head, against more than 5,000 tons per head of the 20 million or so inhabitants of Bohemia, Moravia and South-West Poland. These smaller coal and lignite resources of the area are

distributed as follows (reserves expressed in millions of tons, and lignite as its coal equivalent):

Yugoslavia (total 2,149).
   Lignite: 2,110, in Slovenia, Eastern Serbia and at vari--
   ous places in, and south of, the Middle Save Valley
   Coal: 39.
Poland (excluding Silesia).
   Lignite: 1,400, mostly in the neighbourhoods of Lwow
   and Bydgoszcz.
Austria (total 1,419).
   Lignite: 1,400, largely in the Mur Valley.
   Coal: 19 in the Lower Danube Province.
Hungary (total 710).
   Lignite: 500, mostly around Miskolc in the north.
   Coal: 210, near Pecs.
Roumania (total 1,950).
   Coal: 1,620 mostly in the Banat.
   Lignite: 330, in the Banat, Transylvanian Alps, and
   small deposits in Transylvania
Bulgaria.
   Lignite: 330, along western frontier and in north-east.
Greece..
   Lignite: 15, mostly in Boeotia and Euboea.

11. The other power resources of the area are consider-able but not great by comparison with the coal and lignite resources of Bohemia, Moravia, and Silesia. The potential water-power of the whole of Eastern Europe (at normal low-water levels) is equivalent to only half the power which could be obtained from the pre-war Polish and Czech output of coal and lignite, if this were used with the efficiency normal in power-stations, while the petroleum output of Galicia, Roumania, Hungary and Albania and Austria—which could probably not be increased much without rapidly exhausting the relatively small reserves known to exist—is equivalent to only about a sixth of this coal and lignite output. The water-power available might pos-sibly be raised above the amount obtainable at low water by the construction of storage dams, but against this must be set the

impossibility of harnessing all the sources comprised in the cal-
culation, while the coal and lignite output could certainly be
raised far above the pre-war level and maintained there for centuries without exhausting the reserves.

12. Statistics of petroleum reserves are so misleading as
to be hardly worth quoting, but it is a concrete fact that the
wells of Galicia have given a decreasing yield, now about 1/2
million tons per year, that the Roumanian yields have also been
decreasing since 1936 and are about 5.5 million tons annually,
and that the new wells of Hungary now produce about 1/4 million tons annually, those of the Vienna basin field about 3/4 million tons, and the Albanian wells about 100,000 tons. The
Roumanian yield is the only one of more than local importance,
and it would be prudent to expect a decline rather than an
increase in it in the future. The natural gas of Transylvania,
also, has an uncertain future, and it would be unwise to enter-
tain any positive expectations of an increase in its importance.

13. The distribution of water-power in Eastern Europe
is fortunate in that it is often found where other power
resources are scarce. The distribution between countries (and
the capacities of hydro-electric plants existing before the war)
are as follows:

	Potential h. p. at Ordinary Minimum Flow	Capacity of Installed Plant, 1936
Austria	1,550	1,000
Bulgaria	400	54
Czechoslovakia	700	310
Greece	350	10
Hungary	160	5
Poland	1,350	90
Roumania*	3,000	127
Yugoslavia*	4,000	250
Total:	11,510	1,846

* It is not clear how the great power available from the Danube at the Iron
Gate is divided between Roumania and Yugoslavia in this estimate.

It is plain from this that Roumania and Yugoslavia may obtain power from hydro-electric sources in sufficient quantities to make up largely for their lack of coal—7 million h. p., continuously generated day and night in fairly efficient steam power-stations would require something like 20 million tons of coal per year. Austria and Poland, also, have large power resources still untapped (Austria's actual output of hydro-electric energy in 1936 was only about a fifth of that which could be obtained at normal minimum flow according to the above estimate), while Czechoslovakia's smaller resources are important because they lie largely in Slovakia and Ruthenia, away from the main coal-fields, and because the energy from them could be conveniently transmitted to Hungary if that were desirable. Bulgaria's poverty of hydro-electric power might be made up from the great resources of Yugoslavia and Roumania, but Greece lies further from the main sources of power, which, in view of her lack of mineral fuels, is a serious matter.

(b) Iron Ore

14. To assess the iron ore resources of Eastern Europe is more difficult. These ores occur widely, but the deposits, according to present knowledge, are small. The biggest reserves in the area are probably those of the Erzberg region of Styria, with a total iron content which has been variously estimated at 100–200 million tons (the content being put, apparently, at about 36 per cent. of the ore). These deposits were yielding about 1 million tons of iron a year on the eve of the war. The Greek reserves, notably those of Kopais and Euboea, have been estimated to contain some 45 million tons of iron. The Yugoslavian deposits are numerous and their size somewhat uncertain, but the chief ones appear to be those of Bosnia, which may be provisionally regarded as containing 20–50 million tons of iron. They are probably surpassed by the reserves both of Bohemia and of Slovakia. The former probably contain over 100 million tons of metal, though of varying degrees of accessibility; the latter (in the ore mountains of Central Slovakia) probably contain 30–35 million tons of iron. The deposits of South-Eastern Poland have been variously estimated from 12 million to 100 million tons of

iron, but the useful iron content seems to be much nearer the lower than the higher of these figures. Minor deposits occur elsewhere in Eastern Europe; in the Banat and the adjoining part of Transylvania there is perhaps 10–20 million tons of iron, and smaller amounts occur further east in Transylvania. Others occur in Albania.

(c) Non-Ferrous Metals

15. In the non-ferrous metals, Eastern Europe is relatively much richer. Poland and Yugoslavia have large zinc and lead resources, Yugoslavia has the second large copper deposits in Europe at Bor, not far from the Iron Gate, and Greece, Albania, Yugoslavia and Roumania have considerable reserves of chromite; Roumania, Bulgaria and Hungary (especially the first named) have manganese ore deposits, Czechoslovakia and Yugoslavia have large resources of antimony, and Roumania has some molybdenum. Considerable deposits of pyrites occur in Albania, Roumania and Greece, and smaller ones elsewhere in the area. It is in the ores of the light metals—bauxite and magnesite—however, that the area is really outstanding among the regions of Europe. The largest bauxite deposits in Europe—perhaps as much as 500 million tons—are in the Bakony Hills in Hungary, but Yugoslavia has about 80 million tons (chiefly along the Adriatic coast), Greece has some 5 million tons, and Roumania has about 20 million tons in the region of the Bihor Mountains. The biggest reserves of magnesite are in Greece (Euboea) and Austria, while Yugoslavia has smaller deposits.

(d) Agricultural Resources

16. As regards soil and climate, Eastern Europe presents the greatest variety, but the combination of the two factors is frequently not a fortunate one for the prospects of agriculture. The chief regions may be distinguished as follows:
(a) Bohemia-Moravia, the lowlands of eastern Austria, Hungary west of the Danube, Silesia and Galicia—good (or at least adequate) soil and climate for mixed farming, including root-crops.

(b) The Hungarian Plain east of the Danube, the Old Kingdom of Roumania and Northern Bulgaria—excellent "black earth," but danger of drought, which is responsible for many crop failures, and which prevents the growing of root-crops.

(c) The Carpathians, most of Transylvania and the highlands of Yugoslavia—poor soil, mostly wet climate, not very well suited for cereals of any kind.

(d) Northern and Central Poland—poor soil, not containing enough humus for high yields of cereals (unless cultivated at uneconomically high costs as in East Prussia).

(e) Polesia and Volhynia—very poor soil, largely unfitted for arable cultivation of any kind, though some of it could be improved by draining.

(f) Inland valleys of Yugoslavia and Bulgaria—hot, dry climate, suitable for intensive growing of fruit, roses, tobacco, etc.,

(g) Coastal areas of Yugoslavia. Albania and Greece true "Mediterranean" climate.

17. It is their relation to the populations living on them, however, that determines how these resources are, in fact, used. Throughout Eastern Europe population is dense and capital scarce (by most Western standards) in relation to agricultural lands, so that the varieties of agriculture practised are more labour-intensive (e.g., tend towards cultivation of land which in happier circumstances would be though fit only for pasture) and less capital-intensive (i.e., less reliant on expensive live-stock, irrigation and machinery, and less directed towards conserving the fertility of the soil), than they would be if there were less farm population and more capital. The areas where these effects of overcrowding on the way in which land is used are most marked are Southern and Eastern Poland, much of the foothill country of the Carpathians, some of the highland regions and the Old Kingdom of Roumania. In these areas especially there is either more cultivation altogether, a more exhausting mode of cultivation without adequate rotations, or too few live-stock in relation to the use for which the land would be best fitted if population and farm capital were better distributed.

Appropriate Directions of Local Specialisation

18. The above brief survey of the distribution of resources opens the way for a consideration of the directions in which the various parts of Eastern Europe can best specialise in the course of their development. It is convenient to start with those specialised activities which demand bulky raw materials and large quantities of power and capital, namely, metallurgy, heavy engineering, electrochemistry, etc., It is obvious from what was said in paras. 8–13 above about the distribution of power-sources within the area that such industry can best develop in the neighbourhood of the Silesian coalfield; indeed, it has already done so, for Silesia, Bohemia-Moravia and Eastern Austria are the chief centres of such industries. It would be most advantageous if these industrial areas continued their development with a fairly marked degree of specialisation; what would happen to them if they were all included in the same free-trade area is suggested by the not unilluminating parallel of the somewhat similarly endowed German areas of the Ruhr (a great coalfield corresponding to Silesia), Saxony (which has developed similarly to the adjacent areas of Bohemia), and Berlin (which present some points of analogy with Vienna). Silesia, probably, ought to continue as the chief centre of ferrous metallurgy, heavy engineering and the preparation of heavy semi-manufactured iron and steel products; Bohemia-Moravia (so far as its metal industries are concerned) should specialise more on engineering as a whole (as Saxony does), with the emphasis rather on the branches which need less power and fuel; Austria should concentrate in general on the lighter branches of engineering (perhaps electrical engineering and motor vehicles), since its main fuel supply would have to be brought through the Moravian Gate from Upper Silesia. Budapest has recently developed some of the light engineering and ancillary industries, and these also should be encouraged to fit in with the division of functions outlined above.

19. This pattern of development would necessitate a continuation and expansion of the importation of Swedish iron-ore by Upper Silesia. Local ores would, of course, play their part; Austrian ores and pig-iron would travel over the Moravian

Gate to Bohemia and Silesia, providing return freights to balance the coal coming the other way; Bohemian ores would probably continue to be used locally (they supplied before the war only about half the needs of the local industries), and Slovakian ores would also be brought to Silesian coal.

20. The more distant Eastern European iron ores might not be worth bringing to the western industrial area, however, in view of the high cost of upstream transport on the Danube; it might be worth smelting and working some of them (e.g., those of the Banat and Bosnia), with the assistance of local water-power, at some convenient point (probably on the Danube) to which both they and Silesian coking coal could conveniently be brought. The Greek ores, however, and many of those from the smaller and more outlying deposits, would probably not be worth smelting in the area if free trade prevailed within it, and might be exported, when communications with the middle Danube region were much improved.

21. The area has, however, as was mentioned above, a number of very important sources of non-ferrous metals—notably aluminium, magnesium and copper, and it is likely that this fact will affect its future development. To reduce bauxite and magnesite, all that is required is plenty of very cheap electric power, and it is likely that the development of some of the area's hydro-electric potentialities would supply this need adequately. An annual aluminium output equal to that of all Europe, except Russia, in 1936–38 (about 300,000 tons) would require a power consumption of about 1.2 million h.p., which is less than a fifth of the estimated potential hydro-electric capacity (at low water) of Yugoslavia and Roumania alone. At some point or points near to the major sources of power in this are (near the Iron Gate, for instance), the Hungarian and Roumanian bauxite might conveniently be reduced. Abundant power at the Iron Gate would also suggest the possibility of electrolytic refining there of copper from the near-by mines at Bor. The Greek and Yugoslavian bauxite, however, since it occurs much further away and on the other side of the mountains, could not with such convenience be brought to this main centre. The Dalmatian water-power might make the creation of a subsidiary aluminium industry on the spot practicable, but the

Greek lack of abundant water power would probably prevent the setting up of an equally efficient industry there. The Greek bauxite and magnesite might conveniently be transported to Dalmatia for reduction. Austrian magnesite could be dealt with near it source. It must be borne in mind, however, that the rapid progress of the light metal industries in Eastern Europe after the war would probably meet with strong competition from the Western countries, who will wish to preserve their own, at first over-developed, light metal industries on a large scale for military reasons.

22. As the other metals of the area, though important, are not likely to exercise a major influence on its economic structure, they need not be considered here. It may be mentioned, however, that Roumanian and Polish rock-salt, and Greek, Albanian, Polish and Roumanian pyrites, together with the area's coal, might form the basis for heavy chemical industries in various parts, while, near the main sources either of coal or of water-power, the production of synthetic nitrates to supply the area's agricultural demand may be undertaken.

23. The general nature of Eastern Europe's resources—abundant and cheap labour, but shortage of capital and no great abundance, in general, of power-resources—suggests that it should be excellently adapted for a large range of light industries, of which the textile and clothing industries are probably the most important. These are industries which Czechoslovakia (a country which in many ways exemplifies the desirable direction of advance for the area as a whole) has already developed to a high degree. The Bohemian, Moravian and to some extent the Polish textile industries will probably, like the British, find themselves forced to concentrate gradually on goods of medium and higher quality, leaving the production of cheaper goods eventually to new centres of manufacture further east where unskilled and semi-skilled labour is cheaper.

24. The most suitable location of light industry is not physically determined by proximity to the sources of bulky raw materials and of power as is that of the heavy industries considered above, but its tendency is to seek cheap labour and wide markets for its products. The cheapest labour in Eastern Europe is to be found where agriculture is least prosperous and has

least prospect of becoming so. Fortunately, it happens that the districts where this is the case are frequently the hilly districts with fair potential supplies of hydro-electric power. Indeed, it was in such districts that textile industries developed in the past in Britain and Germany, through a combination of sheep-pastures, water-power, and a mode of farming which did not fully employ all those engaged in it—it was probably only the absence of political stability and other conditions necessary to the growth of wide markets which prevented similar developments in Eastern Europe. In some cases, even a local natural raw material is not lacking—Polish flax, Yugoslavian wool, Greek and Bulgarian cotton and silk—but a great expansion of the textile industries such as seems possible and desirable for Eastern Europe would call for far more materials than the area can supply from such sources. No doubt natural fibres (especially cotton) would be imported on a large scale in connexion with any great development of the textile industries of the area, but there is one class of raw materials which it should be particularly easy to produce on the spot—namely, cellulose fibres. The presence of extensive forests in the same hill districts which possess over-abundant labour and considerable hydro-electric possibilities point to the development of a very low-cost textile industry based largely on these materials—an industry which should be capable of developing an export trade of world importance, but especially to the Middle East. This industry would not, in all probability, be geographically concentrated, but would be dispersed through the foothills of the Carpathians the Transylvanian Alps and the Dinaric Alps in those small technical units which—especially in spinning and weaving—are well adapted to the conditions of textile production.

It is these textile industries which as mentioned in para. 23, are likely in time to displace the Bohemian products from the cheaper markets of the area. The growth of larger and wealthier urban populations in Silesia, Bohemia-Moravia and Austria, however, would give scope for the expansion of the Czech industry, especially in the field of medium- and high-quality goods, while the great agricultural populations further east, both in Eastern Europe and in the neighbouring parts of Asia, would provide the chief markets for the products of the new small-scale industry.

25. After textiles and clothing (with which must be included cheap footwear of the Bata variety), the food-manufacturing industries seem to be those most likely to develop on a large scale in the area. As their nature and location must largely depend on the distribution of agricultural production, however, it will be convenient to discuss them in connexion with it.

26. The short remarks made in para. 16 above about the natural capabilities of the main agricultural regions within Eastern Europe, together with the subsequent suggestions or prognostications about the development of the main manufacturing industries, give some basis for estimating the most desirable developments in agriculture. In the neighbourhoods of the new or growing urban districts, agriculture is likely to take on the characteristic which it always possesses in such localities— namely, an increasing concentration of the production of fresh milk and vegetables for town consumption. In Austria, Southern Bohemia, Western Hungary, and South-Western Poland, where the climatic conditions are favourable to mixed farming, with a considerable emphasis on such products, this development is clearly indicated. Further down the Danube Valley, on the black soil, the absence of sufficient rain makes an emphasis on dairying much harder, but the irrigation which is necessary to increase the yield of the local grain crops would make possible an increase in the productive livestock also, and these could be fed on the lucerne and similar crops, and increase in which, in proper rotation, is necessary to conserve fertility. The products which these areas would sell would, however, as now, be mostly wheat or maize or maize-fed pigs and poultry, these, perhaps, in the form of canned goods, while, with irrigation, the production of tomatoes and other vegetables for canning should become easy. The growth of urban and other factory-employed populations would greatly increase the local food consumption, and the size of the surplus available for export from these very fertile areas would gradually diminish. Industrial crops such as sunflowers and soya beans may have some future in, e.g., Bessarabia but it is doubtful whether there would be a good external market for them in normal conditions.

27. In Poland, as in so many other parts of the area, the

improvement of agriculture, and the development of profitable lines of specialisation are largely dependent on the removal of population from the overcrowded land into industry. In the drier north, grain is probably the most suitable main product of the soil, but the yields which can be obtained without subsidisation in some form are not nearly as high as those which are obtained with the aid of protection in Germany or which could probably be obtained with the aid of irrigation on the Danubian black soil. In the north, a more "extensive" system of farming than the present one—though probably on the same general lines—seems likely to be the only way of increasing agricultural incomes without subsidies, and the natural outcome of easier escape into industry; in the more fertile south, again, the type of production—mixed, with more cattle than in the north—is likely to persist in less overcrowded conditions. A shift of population which would gradually end the attempts to cultivate most of Polesia would probably result from any great improvement in Polish conditions. Poland's agricultural exports—potato-fed pigs and bacon, rye, eggs and poultry—seem likely to remain much as at present under any development, though industrialisation would probably leave smaller surpluses of them for export, and would also probably change their relative importance—animal products gaining.

28. In the Carpathian highlands better opportunities for entering occupations alternative to farming would probably result in the wide abandonment of arable farming in favour of a predominantly live-stock farming system of a less intensive character, while arable farming would decrease also in the highlands south of the Save. In the inland valleys of Yugoslavia and Central Bulgaria the specialisation on fruit, tobacco, roses, etc., would probably be pushed further than at present and subsidiary fruit-canning industries could find considerable scope. In Greece agricultural specialisation has been pushed further than in most parts of Eastern Europe, and the essential character of it would not be much changed, in all probability, as a result of industrial development; but in certain areas (notably the refugee settlements of Central Macedonia) the present very unremunerative subsistence farming would give place to more specialised cultivation of Mediterranean products.

Communications

29. These developments will depend on, and will involve, the extension of communications throughout the area. The Danube is, of course, the main highway of Eastern Europe, and the improvement of its navigable channel, especially at the Iron Gate to take barges of at least 1,000 tons deadweight capacity, is certainly desirable. So is the construction of the projected Danube-Constanza Canal to save the troublesome journey through the delta.

30. The construction of various canals connected with the Danube has long been under discussion, or, in some cases, in progress. The Rhine-Main-Danube Canal (planned for completion in 1945) should greatly increase the ease of communication between South-Eastern Europe and the main heavy industrial area of Germany, bringing about stronger German competition with the coal and heavy industry of Poland and Czechoslovakia, but providing better export outlets for the grain and oil of the Danube Valley.

31. The Oder-Danube Canal, on the other hand, which is also under construction, is of the first importance as part of the internal communications of Eastern Europe itself. It is to run from Kosel on the Oder, up the valley of that river through (or near) Moravska Ostrava, over the watershed of the Moravian Gate into the Morava Valley, and so to the Danube near Bratislava. It would presumably be possible to construct a branch from the neighbourhood of Moravska Ostrava to the Polish industrial area around Katowice, so as not to cross pre-war German territory. A canal joining the Danube-Oder Canal (at Prerov) to the Elbe (at Pardubice) has been mooted, and would greatly improve the internal communications of this important industrial part of Eastern Europe—indeed, the two canals together would provide the connexions necessary for the desirable complex division of function between Silesia, Bohemia-Moravia and Austria.

32. Further east the main suggestion which has been made for improving access to the Danube Valley by water is the canalisation of the Serbian Morava and the Vardar, and the construction of a canal connecting them, so as to make a direct way

from the Danube just east of Belgrade to Salonica. This would
be specially useful for giving the Hungarian plain and the surrounding regions a shorter route for exports to Greece and to the
Mediterranean and Western Europe; it would also make it easier for Greek ores to reach the neighbourhood of the Iron Gate
and for Silesian coal to reach Greece and the Mediterranean.

33. Apart from the Danube Basin, the most important
inland waterway which Eastern Europe seems to require is one
from Silesia to the Baltic, running through Polish territory, e.g.,
a canal from (say) Katowice to Krakow and the canalisation of
the Vistula from there to the sea. This canal could link up with
that leading over the Moravian Gate to the Danube, but its main
function would be to take Silesian coal to the Baltic and to bring
Swedish ore back. It would heavily supplement the facilities
given by the famous Katowice-Gdynia railway. The improvement of the Pripet-Bug waterway would facilitate trade between
the agricultural parts of Poland and the industrial areas of the
Ukraine.

34. There is little to be said about railways and roads
except that any large economic development would call for the
improvement and increase of both. The quantitative importance
of roads in any programme of development would necessarily be
great, but their economic significance would be mainly local, and
they are not, therefore, of great relevance to this paper. The
existing rail routes, which radiate from the western industrial
area, will need to be supplemented (especially, perhaps, in
Poland), but they form a fairly good skeleton for whatever may
eventually have to be built up.

Implications of Development

35. The lines of development sketched above as being
the most advantageous for Eastern Europe would necessitate
considerable movements of population and capital over a fairly
long period of time, and would result in a great development of
the area's internal trade. It may be useful to summarise the
main movements of goods, capital and men involved, in order to
get a clearer view of the political implications (and prerequisites) of the development concerned.

(a) Trade

36. If the economic structure sketched above is to develop, there must be a considerable measure of free trade within the area. In particular, the textile and other light industries at present established in the more advanced western parts of it must not be in a position to secure protection against the new cheap products from further east, the areas (especially Austria and Czechoslovakia) which should concentrate more on milk and vegetable-growing as industrialisation proceeds, must not protect their cereal growers against competition from lower down the Danube, nor must similar protection be allowed to become the policy of the other mountain areas which ought to change over in the direction of dairying and light industry. It is highly desirable, too, that the industrial areas of Silesia, Bohemia-Moravia, Austria, and preferably the Budapest area also, should be allowed to develop as a closely co-ordinated system, not seeking to build up separate complete steel and engineering industries for military or other reasons.

37. The trade in electric power should also be allowed to develop on the widest scale. Hungary, Greece and Bulgaria are relatively poor in power-sources, and will need to purchase power; the hydro-electric power of the area may be expected to show great seasonal fluctuation owing both to variations of rainfall and to freezing; it would be advantageous if areas whose fluctuations were complementary could be linked together, and the net fluctuations of both together adapted to the pattern of seasonal demand through links with steam generating stations suitably sited on the coalfields.

38. The trade between the constituent countries of the area, however, should not be emphasised at the expense of its external trade, on the freedom of which many regions must primarily depend. Poland's agriculture will continue to be largely competitive with that of the Danube Basin, and must continue to sell a considerable part of its products to Western and Northern Europe; the specialised agricultural products of Greece and (increasingly) of Bulgaria, Yugoslavia and Hungary can be disposed of in adequate quantities only in the world market. The cheap textile industry which should grow up should

also eventually become a large exporter. Moreover, it is desirable that the area should be able to export easily in order to
repay, and to pay interest on, the development loans which it
obtains from abroad; and there are many imports which it will
need (and many more which it could advantageously take) and
will have to pay for. The extent to which the area's external
trade is restricted (either by itself or by other countries) will
therefore for a long time be at least as important as the extent
to which trade within it is restricted.

(b) Capital Movements

39. In the early stages of development, it is to be expected that the whole area will be a net capital importer (provided
that external capital is available to it), and the savings of most
parts of the area, which should be encouraged by the development of institutional machinery to harness them, will be largely, if not entirely, needed locally. Later on, however, the industrial areas of Poland, Bohemia-Moravia, and Austria especially,
should be in a position to lend to the poorer east on a substantial scale, and it is highly desirable that no restrictions should
be placed on this lending other than those which may be thought
necessary to ensure that the objects of it are sound.

(c) Population Movements

40. Industrialisation would bring about major aggrega-
tions of population in Eastern Austria, Bohemia-Moravia and
Upper Silesia, with a smaller aggregation in the region of the
Iron Gate and (perhaps) still smaller ones in the bauxite-bear-
ing region of Dalmatia. A few major textile centres might develop in the foothills of the Carpathians and the Dinaric Alps, but,
in general, the development of textile industries would involve
only local population-movements, and the same is true of other
light industries. Where are the populations of these areas to be
drawn from? Probably the areas from which it is most important
that population should be drawn are Galicia, Transylvania,
Ruthenia and Eastern Slovakia, the Carpathian foothills in
Roumania, Polesia and Volhynia and Yugoslavia south of the

Save. With the exception of Galicia, population from which would almost certainly flow into a developing Silesia, these especially over-populated areas (which are also areas of rapid natural increase) are far from the main industrial centres of the west, but population often moves by short stages, each successive zone providing emigrants to fill up the gaps left by departure from the one next to it, so that there might well be a general westward movement such that the chief areas of net emigration were, in fact, the distant and over-populated ones. Long distance migration, inspired by the great contrast in real incomes between the most over-populated areas (which have a tradition of overseas emigration dating from before 1914) and the industrialising ones is not, moreover, likely to be negligible in the absence of political obstacles. The subsidiary industrial centres near the Iron Gate and in Dalmatia would, in any case, be in close proximity to some of the most over-populated districts.

41. It is clear that a great deal of population movement, which will probably be opposed by powerful vested interests, especially those of labour in the areas of immigration, will have to take place if Eastern Europe is to be developed in anything like the most advantageous way. It is important to prevent political sovereignty and national feeling from being enlisted in the cause of these vested interests.

Political Implications and Pre-requisites of Development

42. The political conditions implied in these requirements as to trade policy, capital-movement and migration, would clearly be satisfied if Eastern Europe became either a unitary State and the federal authority were in the same ratio as in, say, the United States. It is more useful, however, to consider what arrangements, short of such total union or general federation, would fulfil a substantial proportion of the conditions, and which would make it difficult to fulfil vital parts of them.

43. In the first place, it is clear that the most important requisite mobilities of goods and factors of production and

adjustments of economic structure between certain parts of the area could hardly be secured by agreements between nominally fully sovereign States, unless, at least, the political relations between those States were as friendly, as completely uninfluenced by the possibility of war between them, as are the relations between say, Australia and New Zealand—perhaps, indeed, not even them. It is highly desirable, therefore, that each country which ought, for its own and the general economic good, to develop on fairly specialised lines (e.g., as a specialist on agriculture and light industry, or on heavy industry and an agriculture incapable of providing the population with the necessary cereals), should have some strong political link with countries whose appropriate structure is largely complementary; otherwise, the separate countries will almost certainly be unwilling to specialise enough in some important respect. Moreover, it is desirable that the areas most in need of outlets for their populations should be linked, if possible, sufficiently closely with areas capable of absorbing population to push political bans on the movement of population from one to the other outside the realm of practical possibility. The same may be said of areas likely to require capital imports and those capable of exporting capital. It is also desirable that poor areas should, if possible, be sufficiently closely linked to richer ones to make it politically possible for them to receive subsidies from them through public channels.

44. How these objects could be secured may, perhaps, best be seen by first considering what is necessary to secure reasonable location of the main kinds of economic activity, and then passing on to the effects of those arrangements on labour and capital mobility and on the prospects of beneficial income-transfers from richer to poorer areas.

45. The desirability of having a fairly extensive division of labour between Silesia, Bohemia-Moravia, and Austria has been touched on in para. 18 above. This suggests that they should all three be closely linked together. If this is impossible, however, Austria is the component which could best be spared, since its industrial function, vis-a-vis Eastern Europe, can relatively easily be taken over by Bohemia-Moravia and perhaps by new industrial areas further east, while desirability of the rest

of the heavy industrial area relying largely on its cheap coal; Bohemia-Moravia could be ill-spared if only because of its geographical position between the Silesian coalfield and the Danube. Austria would, however, herself suffer most, in all likelihood, from anything which diminished her possibilities of trade either down the Danube or over the Moravian Gate.

46. As regards the metal industries of the rest of Eastern Europe, the most important thing is that the low-grade and outlying iron resources should not, in most cases, be developed under protection from the competition of the main heavy industrial area just referred to. Yugoslavia and Roumania have both developed iron industries of fantastic inefficiency which illustrate the point of this; if the ferrous resources of these countries should really be exploited at all (which is doubtful), it should probably be done (as mentioned in paragraph 20 above) at a single centre on the Danube. An economical distribution of the iron and steel industry of Eastern Europe can hardly be assured, however, without including all the countries which would otherwise be tempted to develop high-cost production (i.e., principally Yugoslavia and Roumania, but possibly Greece and Bulgaria also) in a customs union, or, preferably, an even closer economic arrangement which precludes a battle of subsidies, with the western industrial area. In short, the fact that there is only one first-class potential area of heavy industry in Eastern Europe—an area which ought not to be split up—is clearly an argument for including all Eastern Europe in a single political unit for the purpose of formulating economic policy. If the western industrial area were included in a northern federation (or confederation), excluding Yugoslavia, Bulgaria and Greece, at least, the development of the secondary centre of the iron industry based on Yugoslav ores would be made more likely; it would, as mentioned above, probably be a somewhat more efficient centre if Roumania grouped in some way with Yugoslavia, preferably with the participation of Greece and/or Bulgaria.

47. The development of the light metal industries as sketched above requires, ideally, that Hungary and Greece should not endeavour to build up smelting industries based on their own ore but that Greek ore should be smelted in Dalmatia

(which would be relatively easy if there was a close link between Greece and Yugoslavia), and Hungarian ore nearer the Iron Gate, in either Yugoslavian or Roumanian territory, which would be easier if Hungary were closely associated with either of those countries. Failing this, it seems that Hungary would benefit by the use of Slovakian water-power to smelt her bauxite, and reliance on this might be more willingly accepted if the two countries were included in the same grouping.

48. The development of the textile industries of Eastern Europe is much less dependent on the absence of internal barriers than that of the metal industries; nevertheless, it would be facilitated if the established industries of Bohemia-Moravia and Poland were restrained from obtaining protection against, or subsidies to compete with, the cheaper and coarser manufactures from further east—which, again, ideally requires a single direction of economic policy for the whole area.

49. Agriculture and the food industries require especially, for their proper development, absence of agrarian protection (especially of protection for cereals, dairy produce, poultry and canned foods) in the countries which develop the larger industrial centres or specialised types of agriculture, i.e., principally in Austria, Czechoslovakia, and Greece. Czechoslovakia and Austrian agrarian protection have, indeed, had serious adverse influences on the economy of the area in the past. It is also desirable, of course, that economic policy throughout the area should be so co-ordinated as to prevent any subsidisation of agricultural (as, for that matter, of industrial) products which is not generally acquiesced in; but, short of this, the association of each major industrial area with a more or less complementary agricultural area, and of highly specialised agricultural areas also with more or less complementary ones is the best arrangement. The association of Czechoslovakia and Austria, either separately or together, with Poland, Hungary, Roumania, Bulgaria, and Yugoslavia (or some of these States), and of the association of Greece with one or more of them, would help towards this end. It is desirable, however, that the main industrial areas should have connexions not with Poland alone, but with some country or countries of the Danube Basin also, so as not to promote wheat-growing in Poland (or in the other industrial countries),

which is better done in the Danube Valley.

50. The courses of the main lines of communication also give rise to certain presumptions as to what political arrangements would be good and which bad from an economic point of view. The Danube is, of course an international river, in any case; even if Eastern Europe were politically unified, Germany would still have a direct interest, and other countries less direct ones in the conditions of navigation on it which would necessitate regulation by something like the Commission Internationale Danubienne, or (preferably) some similar body backed by a real international authority. The same would apply in some degree to the proposed Belgrade-Salonica waterway. Nevertheless, there are many cases where a direct political tie of some kind between two or more areas may ease what would otherwise be a potentially difficult question of transit facilities, or an incentive to the development of inherently silly routes. The working of the great international waterways themselves would probably be made easier if most of the countries through which they ran were associated together politically. It is clear that the Danube-Oder (or Danube-Vistula) Canal and the parallel rail and road communications would have a better chance of working smoothly if Austria, Czechoslovakia and Poland had some political link stronger than common membership of an international transit commission, and that the important communications of Slovakia and Ruthenia with Bohemia-Moravia could be more easily and rationally developed if political conditions made it matter little that they should cross Hungarian territory. The access of Bulgaria to the Mediterranean, also, would obviously be easier if that country had some political tie with Greece.

51. It is clear that the importance of Vienna as a centre of communications in the western part of Eastern Europe, and as the gateway between Eastern and Western Europe is very great. If Austria were excluded from a political aggregation comprising Hungary and Czechoslovakia (and still more if it comprised Yugoslavia also), the internal communications of that aggregation would be somewhat difficult, since the main railways from Budapest to Prague and from Croatia and Slovenia to both Prague and Silesia pass through Vienna.

52. As regards the effects on migration and the possibility of beneficial internal capital movements and transfers of income, it is desirable that all the naturally poorest and most over-populated areas should be associated with naturally richer ones—that none of them should be "left out in the cold." Within the pre-war State boundaries, the association of eastern and central Poland with Silesia and Western Poland was good, so was the association of Ruthenia and Slovakia with Bohemia-Moravia and of Yugoslavia south of the Save with the richer areas north of that river. The relief provided by these associations was, however, quite insufficient because of the relatively low rate of development prevailing and level of material wealth reached in even the richer areas in the inter-war period and the insufficiency of population movement—due partly to industrial depression. Furthermore, many depressed areas in Roumania, Bulgaria, and Greece lacked even the advantages which association with such richer areas could give. In general, the conditions desirable on the ground that they facilitate useful population movements, income transfers, and capital movements, are the same as those already noted as desirable as promoting a fruitful division of labour, and merely emphasise arguments which have already been used. It is important to note, however, that the fear of being inundated by immigrants from poorer areas (whether well founded or not) is likely to be strong in Austria, Bohemia-Moravia and Hungary; for Austria it might well be thought to offset all the economic advantages of association with Eastern Europe, especially if association with Germany were a practicable alternative. Some agreed regulation of population movements to guard against such an inundation might be a prerequisite of any arrangement designed to allow the desirable movements to take place at all.

Some Further Political Considerations

53. It remains to turn the above considerations to a more concrete use by discussing briefly what kind of political connexion or agreement is required between whatever countries are associated together for the promotion of development such as that outlined above, how that connexion or agreement might be

brought about, and finally, how certain suggestions made or discussed in other Foreign Research and Press Service papers on Eastern Europe appear in the light of the economic considerations advanced here.

54. The point is made in para. 43 above that the degree of interdependence between certain countries of the area which is suggested here to be desirable will not be brought about so long as the fear of war between these countries (or, for that matter, of war in which one of them may have to fight without the active co-operation of the others) continues to exist, even in a small degree. Unless this source of insecurity is removed, the customs unions (or low tariff arrangements), agreements to prevent subsidy wars and to maintain freedom of population and capital movement, which are necessary for the achievement of the most fruitful division of function, will probably not be concluded and certainly not kept; still less will the combined resources of the Governments concerned be used in concert to promote an agreed plan of common development. A very reliable military alliance or a reliable system of external guarantees not only against military aggression but also against hostile economic action by one of the parties to the agreements appears to be a prerequisite for the conclusion of these agreements, unless especially cordial political relations already exist. If a sufficient degree of cordiality can be fostered, however, the common advantages of co-operation may be so large and evident as to overcome any lingering desire to promote national autarky for reasons of military and economic security.

55. Fortunately, it seems that, while the kind of economic co-ordination envisaged would make most countries of Eastern Europe put their eggs into rather fewer baskets than they would use if they were masters of their own development, and could push ahead with it as fast as they liked, it would distribute the eggs of all the countries except, perhaps, Czechoslovakia and Austria, among more baskets than they have been contained in hitherto. Moreover, it is a means of increasing the total number of eggs, and, if aid from the outside world were made conditional on the acceptance of a reasonable international division of function, this aspect of the matter would become still more obvious and important, since the rate at which most

parts of the area could develop without external assistance is bound to be very small for some time. The extent of the control which outside countries will possess over Eastern Europe by virtue of their power to give or withhold assistance will, of course, decline as the area becomes less poor, and the aim must be so to exercise it—and so, eventually, to remove it—that its removal is not followed by a revulsion of opinion against the economic system which it has been used to foster. This is as unhelpful as any other counsel of perfection, but it is hard to make it more practical save in relation to circumstances which cannot yet be predicted. At all events, since development means greater diversification in most of the countries concerned, and a higher degree of specialisation than at present only in, perhaps, two of them, and since development would in all cases be very much slower for some time in the absence of internal co-ordination and the external help which could be made conditional on it, apprehensions about what would happen if internal co-ordination broke down at a later stage should be capable of being relieved.

56. If these difficulties can be overcome, the chief remaining obstacles to the conclusion of the necessary economic agreements would probably be those set up by the private interests, in the countries concerned, which believe they would be hit by the removal of barriers. Where genuine hardship is likely to be caused by economic reorganisation, there is a very strong case for giving compensation in some form—preferably in a form specifically designed to assist adaptation to the new conditions. This assistance may placate many groups which would otherwise be hostile—or more hostile—to the economic agreements necessary for proper development.

57. In spite of the power which outside countries should have at the outset to set co-ordination going, however, it is plain from what has been said above that where political suspicion exists (as it does in so many cases) it will be extremely difficult to achieve a proper division of functions between sovereign States in Eastern Europe. The same political suspicion would also tend to make any form of federation or confederation difficult, though it increases the desirability of such unions. Hence, one is led to ask whether it is practicable to demonstrate the

advantages of closer union and to get the countries concerned "nicely mixed up together," under the shelter of an external authority introduced to administer relief, provide assistance, and effect some of the desirable economic developments. The case for such an authority in part of Eastern Europe is discussed in the Foreign Research and Press Service paper *Dyarchy in Danubia* (17th December, 1942). It is not appropriate here to comment on the political feasibility of such a system, but it seems that, if an international authority could be given charge of the developments financed by external loan, with some power to administer international routes of communication and to veto national economic measures (e.g., restrictions on trade, migration and capital movements) when they transgress certain clearly-stated and initially-accepted limits, the chance of creating common economic interests to cement an eventually political union (or two unions) of Eastern European States would be greatly increased.

58. A final word may be added on the bearing which all the above discussion has on a specific form of political organisation for Eastern Europe discussed elsewhere (Foreign Research and Press Service paper *Confederations in Eastern Europe*, the 1st September, 1942), namely, two confederations based respectively on Poland, Czechoslovakia and Hungary in the north and Yugoslavia and Greece in the south. It is clear that the States named here as forming the kernels of the two confederations would gain considerably from union; the complementary development of Polish and Czech heavy industry, the mitigation of Czech agricultural protectionism, the easier development of the Vistula-Danube and Belgrade-Salonica waterways, the bringing together of Greek ores and Yugoslavian water-power, are the most obvious of the advantages to be hoped for.

59. The disadvantages of having two confederations instead of one are equally obvious; such an arrangement leaves the northern group with agricultural and industrial resources fairly well balanced, but denies the southern group (which is naturally poorer) an equal participation in the development of the main industrial districts of Eastern Europe. Some treaty provision for low tariff arrangements and migration facilities

might be made to mitigate this, but would still leave some of the poorest parts of the area outside the scope of direct help from the richest.

60. The way in which the two confederations might best be extended to include other Eastern European States deserves longer discussion than it can receive here. It is obvious, however, that Roumania would gain most by inclusion in the northern group, which is bound to be the wealthier and to offer the greater industrial demand for her agricultural products, and that the contribution which her water-power and minerals could make to the industrial potentialities of the Southern Confederation is not of the first order of magnitude. Hitherto, she has been the main source of Greek wheat imports, but Yugoslavia would probably take over that function if she were federated with Greece and if the Belgrade-Salonica waterway were built.

61. Austria also would probably benefit more from inclusion in the northern than in the southern group, but her natural economic connexions, and her position astride the main lines of communication, are among the substantial arguments for the closest possible economic co-ordination between the two confederations. Bulgaria's interest also lies in the Northern Confederation on the general ground that it is the wealthier and is likely to be far the greater absorber of agricultural produce, but her agriculture, like that of Greece, is likely to develop its chief external connexions outside Eastern Europe altogether, and the same may be true of her industry if (as is likely) she develops the production of cheap textiles suitable for export to the Middle East.

Foreign Research and Press Service,
Balliol College, Oxford,
February 14, 1943.

DOCUMENT 3

The Future of Austria

I. The Present Administrative System in Austria

1. Immediately after the occupation of the country by German troops in March 1938, Austria was declared to be a "Land" of the German Reich under an Austrian Federal Government in Vienna, with Seyss-Inquart[44] at its head. At the same time the first steps were taken to transform this status into one of complete absorption into the administrative system of the Reich. On the 15th March the German Law of the 30th January, 1934, for the Reconstruction of the Reich was declared valid in Austria. This meant the abolition of representative government in the Länder, as well as those of the former Austrian State, to the Reich. The "Austrian Federal Government" became the "Austrian Provincial Government," and Seyss-Inquart received the title of "Reichsstatthalter in Austria." Bürckel,[45] Gauleiter of Saarpfalz, was appointed Reich Commissioner for the Reunion of Austria with the Reich, and, in May 1938, he divided the country into seven Party Gaue. These corresponded in the main, with some modifications, to the former Austrian Länder, except that the Burgenland was split up and ceased to exist as a unit for this purpose.

2. The next step was taken by the Ostmark[46] Law of the 14th April, 1939. This set out a plan of administration which was put into operation on the 1st April, 1940. Under it the seven Party Gaue—of Vienna, Carinthia, Lower Danube, Upper Danube, Salzburg, Styria and Tirol-Vorarlberg—became Reichsgaue on the model of the Sudetenland. Each was placed under a Reichsstatthalter, who was also the Gauleiter of the

141

party. There is nothing in a Reichsgau corresponding to the Government of a Land in the Old Reich. It is merely an administrative region of the Reich, and its offices are "immediate" offices of Reich administration. The Reichsstatthalter is thus, not merely the representative of the Reich in the Reichsgau (as he is in the German Länder), but the agent of the Reich for the administration of the Reichsgau. He controls all administrative offices, including those which exercise specialised functions on behalf of the various Reich Ministries, with the exception, in the Ostmark, of the offices of Reich Finance, Justice, Posts and Railways. The administration of the Reichsgau is thus highly centralised and closely linked, in the person of the Reichsstatthalter-Gauleiter, with the leadership of the party. The effect of this measure was to destroy Austria as a territorial unit of administration, and the office of "Reichsstatthalter in Austria" was abolished. Some time later even the term "Ostmark," the last symbol of Austrian unity, was dropped, and all laws relating to former Austria used the phrase "Alpen und Donau Reichsgaue."

II. The Probable Situation in Austria Immediately after the War

3. After the war Austria, like Poland and Czechoslovakia, will have to be re-created, but, unlike Poland and Czechoslovakia, it has no Government in exile representing the unity that has been destroyed and ready to return and take control during the period of re-creation. This task of internal reconstruction will have to be undertaken and completed before Austria can even become a candidate for membership of a Danubian or South-East European Confederation.

4. The machinery that links the Austrian Reichsgaue with the Central government of Germany is of recent creation, it is the work of the Nazis, it is closely associated with the party, and it is manned largely by Nazi personnel. Consequently, it would probably be shattered by a revolution which drove the Nazis out of Austria. Austria would not have to make a special effort to detach herself from Germany; she would, so to speak,

fall out of it. Further, if the United Nations occupied Germany and took over control of the Central government, it would rest with them to decide whether to administer Austria as a part of Germany or not. And they would be able to help Austria to complete her disentanglement, especially in the field of finance, while, perhaps, retaining the unity of control over transport and communications.

5. If the links binding Austria to Germany were to snap in this way, it is improbable that the Austrian people would wish to forge them anew even if they were permitted to, at least for some time to come. Austria has always occupied a middle position between the German States of Central Europe and the non-German States of the South-East. She has gravitated first to one side and then to the other, hoping to be able to enjoy the best of both worlds. In 1918 German Austria was ejected from the Eastern Empire in which she had enjoyed a dominant position and naturally looked to some kind of fusion with Germany as a means of escaping from her isolation. Germany was then under the direction of the Social-Democrats and the Catholic Centre party, which corresponded to the two strongest parties in Austria. Germany and Austria were in the same boat. Both had suffered the consequences of defeat, which had struck German Austria more heavily than they had struck Germany. Union with Germany might be expected to lift Austria up, rather than to drag her down. But it was a union on a federal basis that most Austrians hoped for. If an independent Austria emerges after this war, it will do so by emancipating itself from a tyrannical German rule which, so far from giving Austria a federal status, destroyed its unity even as an administrative region. Also, whereas Germany will suffer the consequences of defeat more heavily than after the last war, Austria, in view of the official statements of the British Government, may well hope to escape them altogether by repudiating Nazidom. And the repudiation of Nazidom means, for the time being at least, the repudiation of Germany.

6. It must always be remembered that Austria's history and geographical position do not clearly define her future destiny. She has been at different times the leading State in a German Confederation, the head of a largely non-German

empire in South-Eastern Europe, an independent State, and an integral part of a unitary German State. Any one of these situations might recur in the future, though the last would be the least acceptable both to the Austrians and to the Powers interested in European security. Germany might welcome union with Austria on a federal basis, many Austrian might hope that inclusion in a Danubian Federation would in time give Austria a position comparable with that she occupied in imperial days, and an independent Austria is an obvious possibility. In this respect Austria differs from Switzerland, with which it is often compared on grounds of economic similarity, for Switzerland has no such embarras de choix. She has no alternative but to be an independent State, and she has put her whole heart into making a success of that position. But if Austria is offered a solution which will work, provided there is a real determination to make it work, the Austrians will always be tempted to think that another solution might have been easier. Consequently, the margin of advantage in the solution chosen must be great enough to smother these doubts and to secure the effort needed to overcome the difficulties which are bound to be presented by any solution.

III. Strategic Considerations

7. Considerations of security, which are bound to bulk large at the end of the war, point to the separation of Austria from Germany as desirable. The possession of Austria by Germany would make the southern frontier of Bohemia-Moravia and the western frontier of Hungary practically indefensible, if Germany were allowed to rearm. But, if Austria is to be a bulwark against German aggression, it must be strong enough to prevent Germany from recovering her lost strategic advantages by a "Blitzkrieg,"[47] which she might undertake after a limited rearmament as part of an attempt to remove one by one the obstacles to the recovery of her full military strength. Austria would have to be a bulwark rather than a glacis.

8. It would seem that effective measures for the defence of Austria could best be taken if they were regarded as an integral part of the measures for the defence of South-Eastern

Europe as a whole, and this is an argument for including Austria, for some purposes at least, in a Danubian or South-East European Confederation. On the other hand, it must be considered whether it would be wise to allow a leading part in this general defence system to be played by a country whose population might contain a large number of fifth columnists or German sympathisers. The States of South-Eastern Europe might feel more secure if the integrity and defence of Austria were guaranteed directly by the United Nations, than if Austria were an equal partner in a South-East European Military Alliance or Confederation. The answer to this question involves technical military considerations which lie outside the scope of this paper.

IV. Political Considerations

9. The great majority of Austrians can hardly be said to have been nationally conscious before 1918, and the Austrian Republic started life with no foundations in history or in public sentiment. The Austrians combined a strong provincial loyalty with an international outlook. Furthermore, they were not schooled in the arts of democracy. The political parties, which alone could take the lead after the fall of the dynasty, had been accustomed to the organisation of opposition and to wrangling over State patronage, not to the assumption of responsibility for policy, and they were disciplined with a rigidity which placed loyalty to party above loyalty to State. It cannot be claimed that Austria, during the years of her independence, solved the problem of democratic government. In 1933 and 1934 parliamentary government was replaced by dictatorship[48] and was not again restored. But undoubtedly the growing threat from Germany helped to precipitate this change. On the other hand the growth of national sentiment was strong enough, even before the access to power of the Nazis in Germany, do deprive the idea of an Anschluss of most of its popularity.

10. Similar obstacles to the creation of an Austrian national State under responsible Government will reappear after this war. The first stage in the revolution to expel the Nazis will probably take the form of seizing the operative

machinery of Government, which is now provincial and not national. The blending of revolutionary provincial Government into a national Constitution may present some difficulty, especially if local particularist sentiments are reinforced by political antagonisms, as, for instance, between a Conservative south-west and a predominantly Socialist north-east. Whether there will be a major clash between Republicans and Habsburg Legitimists it is impossible to say, but the latter showed distinct signs of increasing strength between 1930 and 1938.

11. But these questions, though important, do not materially affect the choice for Austria between independence and membership of a confederation. Their solution is a precondition for the success of either scheme. In 1918, when Austria was kicked out of Eastern Europe, amalgamation with Germany appeared to be a way of evading the internal political problems which would arise if she remained independent. But if, after this war, she escaped from Germany and sought refuge in the arms of South-Eastern Europe, these problems would not thereby be evaded. National unity and internal political stability would be as necessary for Austria as a member of a confederation as they would be for Austria as an independent State.

12. Although membership of a confederation would not solve Austria's internal problems, she might regard it as a way of escape from isolation in the international sphere. But independence need not necessarily mean isolation Austria would be a small Power, and her status would depend on the position accorded to small Powers in the Europe of the future. This is a question that does not affect her alone; a solution will have to be found, and there is no reason to suppose that it would not apply as well to her as to the other small Powers. Here, too, the comparison with Switzerland is misleading, for Switzerland, though an independent small Power, was, as the home of the League of Nations and other kindred bodies, a focal point of international activity. She was very far from being isolated. Similar advantages could not be offered to Austria, but steps would have to be taken to make her feel that she was really a member of the European family of nations.

13. If independence did not imply isolation, either strategic or political Austria would not need to seek membership

of a confederation in order to improve her international status. Doubts as to the strength and stability of the confederation and as to the possibility of maintaining harmonious relations between its members, together with the fear of being involved in international issues, such as that of the relations of the confederation with the USSR, from which she could otherwise remain detached, might lead Austria to prefer independence, at least for some time to come. Her choice would probably depend on economic, rather than on political, considerations (see below, paras. 16–21).

14. From the point of view of the confederation as a whole, Austria would be able to contribute certain things which the other States lack or possess only to a smaller degree, such as her high level of culture, her international outlook, and the fruits of her experience as a Great Power. But these are all attributes of leadership, and it is precisely the leadership of the confederation by Austria that the other States are likely to fear. For this reason they would certainly refuse to admit Austria if the Habsburgs were restored to power.

15. There is nothing to show that any South-East European State regards the inclusion of Austria, on political grounds, as essential to the success of the confederation. There are some, however, which would probably agree to her admission (e.g., Czechoslovakia) either for the sake of the economic advantages which would accrue, or for fear that an independent Austria which failed to make good might become a centre of disturbance in the Danubian area. But there is also the fear that Austria would become a centre of disturbance within the confederation, by serving as a stepping-stone for German penetration and as a camouflage for activities pursued in the interests of Germany. Also a rapprochement at a later date between Austria and a revived and reformed Germany would have to be reckoned with. For these reasons Czechoslovakia would certainly regard a satisfactory liquidation of the problem of the Sudeten Germans, accompanied by a large transfer of population, as a necessary precondition for the inclusion of Austria. Otherwise the German element in the confederation would be too strong. Opinion in Hungary is probably divided, but, in so far as there is an influential section of the Hungarian population in favour of the inclusion of Austria, this might well cause

other States to oppose it, since a revival of Austro-Hungarian Dualism would imperil the stability of the confederation.

V. Economic Considerations

16. A careful examination of the Austrian national income and of movements in the volume of employment and the standard of living makes it clear that Austria, as an independent State, did not solve her economic problems. The situation in 1937 was worse than it had been in 1925. This was due partly to the failure of the various Governments to pursue an active policy of finding employment for the labour and capital resources of the country, and partly to the various forms of trade barriers which impeded economic relations with the outside world. The two causes were inter-related, since, owing to the restrictions on foreign trade, the pursuit of an active internal policy would inevitably have increased the adverse foreign balance.

17. It is true, nevertheless, that, theoretically, a sound internal economic policy would have made it possible to maintain, and even slightly to increase, the national income, even in spite of the conditions prevailing in world trade, and that international loans to Austria might have been used as a lever to encourage the adoption of such a policy. but this would have required a Government strong enough to assert itself against vested interests and to demand and secure a great and concerted effort on the part of all classes. Political conditions at the time made this practically impossible, and the prospects, even if it could be done, were no rosy enough to overcome the general pessimism about the future of Austria as an independent State. If the conditions of the period 1918 to 1938 were to be reproduced after this war, the same conclusions would follow: Austria could exist, and, under wise Government, could prevent a deterioration of her economic position, but she would have little hope of securing substantial improvement. And the task set to her Government would be an exceedingly severe one.

18. If, without any change in external economic relations, a confederation were established in South-Eastern

Europe, then Austria would benefit by being included in it and the confederation would benefit by including Austria, provided that the confederation had the power and the will to pursue an active policy within its frontiers. The countries in the area from Poland to the Balkan States are largely complementary as regards economic resources, Poland being, from the point of view of Austria, the most valuable associate. Consequently the scope for active economic development within the area treated as a whole is greater than in its parts treated separately, and the balance of payments of each member could be, to a large extent, adjusted within the area. If Austria were excluded and the confederation pursued a highly protectionist policy against her, she would be driven to seek trade outlets elsewhere and would probably gravitate back towards Germany. The economic difficulties of an independent Austria would be increased by the formation of a confederation that excluded her, unless it pursued an exceedingly active and enlightened policy. On the other hand, if it did not pursue such a policy, she would gain nothing by being included in it.

19. If one postulates a change in external economic relations, the picture is completely altered. The change contemplated is the creation by the Great Powers of an international authority to which the individual States in the area would surrender some of their sovereign rights in such matters as note issue, exchange adjustment, and the direction of capital investment. The first aim of such an international authority would be to see that each State or federated group of States kept its balance of payments in equilibrium, preferably by an appropriate adjustment of rates of exchange. It would also have power to insist that the adjustment of foreign balances should be secured by the lowering of trade barriers.

20. Under these conditions the economic prospects of an independent Austria would be greatly improved, and could be regarded as satisfactory. The creation of a confederation from which she was excluded would cease to be a menace, since the international authority could prevent the wasteful development of competitive industries, the erection of crippling trade barriers, and any interference with Austria's outlet via the Danube or to the Adriatic. It could thus ensure that the advantages of

specialisation were enjoyed to some extent by all countries, whether included in the confederation or not. This implies, of course, that it should show equal interest in all the countries of the area, and not devote itself to the development of the States of the confederation, leaving Austria to fend for herself. In such circumstances it would still be better, both for Austria and for the confederation, if Austria were included, since the larger the economic regions with which the international authority has to deal the better. But the advantages of inclusion would be less decisive. It should be remembered that, if one of the objects of the confederation is to secure free mobility of labour and to equalise the standard of living as between rich and poor regions, Austria, as the country with the highest standard of living in the group, would stand to lose.

21. The general conclusion is that a confederation cannot of itself solve the economic problems either of Austria or of South-Eastern Europe, and it might even make matters worse. Far more important is the establishment of international economic direction and control. If economic control of this kind could work perfectly and without friction it would not matter very much whether a confederation were established, and it would not matter very much to Austria whether she were included in it. But, since perfection cannot be expected in an imperfect world, the substitution of a confederation for a collection of independent sovereign States would be of value as a means of eliminating friction which the international authority could not otherwise overcome, and Austria would benefit from inclusion in it.

VI. Conclusions

22. It can be assumed that the whole East European area will, after the war, be in need of assistance for relief and reconstruction and the maintenance of order, and that the United Nations will take steps to meet that need. In the process of doing this they will necessarily set up some kind of military and economic control over the area. If, as is also to be expected, Austria is detached from Germany, then assistance and control will have to be extended to Austria as well.

23. In these circumstances there would be a single concerted plan covering Austria and the other States, whether Austria were included in a confederation or not. Within such a plan Austria could exist as an independent State, and it should be possible to direct her internal effort for reconstruction in such a way that subsequent inclusion in a confederation, if circumstances made it desirable, would represent a fulfilment of the policy she had pursued in the interim, not a reversal of it. Provided this were done, so that Austria's effort were not paralysed by doubts as to her future status, which might drive her back into the arms of Germany, the United Nations would be free to decide as and when they pleased on the attitude they should adopt towards the inclusion of Austria in a confederation. The ultimate decision would depend largely on the effect of the inclusion of Austria on the balance of forces within the confederation. Would it inflame or allay latent antagonisms between the member-States? Would it lead to the formation of opposed blocs within the area? On the whole the Austrians might be expected to bring with them a spirit of co-operation, not of jealous nationalism, but any judgment on the question as a whole would, at present, be too speculative to have much value.

Foreign Research and Press Service,
Balliol College, Oxford,
February 26, 1943.

DOCUMENT 4

The Problem of Transylvania

Note on Use of Terms

While the term Transylvania is often used for the whole area under dispute between Roumania and Hungary, and can, indeed, conveniently be so used where no ambiguity results, it must be remembered that in 1919 Roumania acquired from Hungary not only Transylvania proper, but also considerable areas west thereof: the districts thereafter know officially as Maramures, Crisana and the Banat. Where in this memorandum it has been necessary to refer to the sum of these western areas, the old title of the "Partium" has been used—a name applied in Hungarian history to parts of Hungary (approximately the same as those mentioned above) which at certain periods were attached politically to Transylvania, although never incorporated within its historic frontiers.

Note on the attitude of the United Nations in regard to the Hungaro-Roumanian dispute.

In this paper, the following political and ethical assumptions are made:

(i) That the United Nations are now quit of all political obligations (implicit or explicit) towards Roumania as well as towards Hungary—the present political situation (resulting from the fact that Roumania as well as Hungary is an enemy State in the present war) having superseded the inter-war political situation (which had resulted from the fact that, in the war of 1914–18, Roumania had been an ally while Hungary had been an enemy).

(ii) That the paramount political interest of the United Nations, in their handling of the present territorial dispute between Hungary and Roumania, is to find terms of settlement which will not leave in the hearts of either party so deep and lasting a grievance as to make this party (whichever it may be) unwilling to enter into some kind of union with the other party, or short of that, unwilling to live on terms of reasonable amity with it.

(iii) That the moral obligation, resting upon any judge in any dispute, to do justice between the disputants as even-handedly as possible remains incumbent on the United Nations in their handling of the present Hungaro-Roumanian dispute.

N.B. The fulfilment of this moral obligation to do justice will be facilitated by the present freedom of the United Nations from any political obligations to either Hungary or Roumania (point (i) above). And, in trying to fulfil this moral obligation to do justice, the United Nations will be adopting the most promising means of securing their own political interest in bringing about a reconciliation between the disputants (point (ii) above).

The Background (Sentimental, Historical, Ethnic, Economic and Strategic)

1. The Transylvanian controversy is notable, not only for the extreme passion with which the two protagonists—Roumania and Hungary—press their respective claims, but also for the very real strength of the case of each of them. Neither of them is putting up, for bargaining purposes, a claim in which it does not believe, or on which it does not feel deeply, and neither case can be dismissed as unreasonable. The two claims are, however, mutually irreconcilable.

2. The sentimental and historical claims, which in this case are particularly strong on both sides, are for the most part in absolute conflict. Roumanians hold Transylvania to have been (as Roman Dacia) the cradle of the Roumanian race. Hungarians, who deny with passion, and perhaps with reason, the justice of Roumania's claim to historic continuity since Trajan's day, look back on some 900 years of practically unbroken Hungarian sovereignty over Transylvania, during 200 years of which Transylvania was almost the sole representative of Hungarian independence and Hungarian national culture. It is

true that Roumanians as a whole feel much less strongly about the Partium; but this does not help much when Hungary feels so strongly about Transylvania proper. Only with regard to the Banat, with its largely German population and former tradition of Austrian imperial administration, are the feelings of both parties distinctly cooler; it would be easier if this comparative indifference were felt by only one of them.

3. Ethnically, Roumanians are in a clear, although not a large absolute majority over all the other nationalities combined, in both Transylvania proper, taken alone, and in the Partium; and in a majority of about two to one over the Magyars (if, that is, the other nationalities, of whom the Germans are the most important, are deducted). Nevertheless, the Magyar population is so large—at least 1.5 million, perhaps nearer 2 million souls out of a total of 5.5 million—as to make it psychologically impossible for Hungary ever to accept with resignation a decision which placed it all under Roumanian rule; Roumania could, of course, no more easily reconcile herself to seeing 3–3.25 million Roumanians revert to Hungarian rule, with all the political and social retrogression that this would almost inevitably entail.

4. An important factor in Hungarian popular sentiment is the rather special position held by the Szekels (i.e., the compact Magyar-speaking population—with a historic local community tradition of its own—inhabiting the extreme south-east corner of Transylvania, in the angle of the Carpathians). The Szekels themselves may not be of Magyar origin; owing, probably, to a mistake made by a 12th century chronicler, they believe themselves to be descended from Attila's Huns—in fact, they probably derive from some other, but kindred, Turkish tribe. But they are certainly not Roumanians, and while they feel themselves rather different from the other Magyars, this feeling takes the form of despising the others as degenerate, if not bastard, cousins. Correspondingly they enjoy a snob value in Hungary comparable to that formerly enjoyed in England by families of Norman descent; and as they have an abnormally high rate of natural increase, and send their surplus population out into the world, the number of Magyars in Budapest and elsewhere who cherish their Szekel descent is very large. A sim-

ilar, although slightly less pronounced, snob value attaches to the other Transylvanian Magyars.

5. Feelings of this sort are mentioned not because they are necessarily reasonable, but because they exist and, reasonable or no, form important factors in the situation.

6. Hungarian feeling regarding the Szekels has been much intensified by an unfortunate and scientifically entirely unjustified attempt on the part of the Roumanians during the last ten or fifteen years to regard the Szekels as proto-Roumanians and to re-Roumanise them. It was this, and also the failure of Roumania to grant the Szekels the autonomy provided in the Roumanian Minorities Treaty,[49] which, in the end— shortly before the war—largely decided official Hungarian circles to give up their more moderate claim for local revision in the west plus autonomy for the Szekels in favour of absolute insistence on the territorial attachment of the Szekel districts to Hungary.

7. A partition of the area proportionate to the relative numbers of the nationalities involved is made difficult by the local conditions—although, as will be seen, it is a solution which might have to be adopted. Unhappily, however, the population everywhere is extremely mixed. In the Crisana and parts of Western Transylvania there is, it is true, a large Magyar population—although even this is considerably outnumbered, except in some comparatively small areas quite near the frontier, by the Roumanian. The Maramures, which is economically most dependent of all on Hungary, is mainly Roumanian in population. Through Central Transylvania runs a corridor where the population is extremely mixed, a substantial Magyar minority being interspersed with a Roumanian majority. The group whose presence constitutes the crux of the ethnic situation, the compact mass of at least 500,000 Magyar Szekels, live at the eastern end of this corridor, and thus in the extreme east of Transylvania, remote from Hungary, near the Roumanian plains, and flanked north and south by Roumanians. North of the corridor some 600,000 Roumanians, with comparatively few Magyars and still fewer Germans among them, inhabit homes which are, indeed, contiguous on the map with those of the Roumanians of Moldavia, but are in reality cut off from them by

the main chain of the Carpathians. The Roumanians south of the corridor, who again constitute a large national majority in that area, are rather less severely isolated from Wallachia; but their economic connexions are still rather northward than southward. The 550,000 Germans live chiefly in Southern Transylvania or in the Banat; only about 50,000 of them are in the corridor, and the same number in Northern Transylvania.

8. Even this description fails to bring out the full complexity of the ethnic conditions. For the historic development of Transylvania had by 1918 brought about the position that except in the Saxon districts (which stood apart, leading their own lives and forming their own compact communities of prosperous peasants and respectable bourgeoisie) the great majority of the upper and middle classes were Magyar or Magyarised; and this was true even in those districts where the bulk of the peasantry was Roumanian. The landlord and urban classes constituted a relatively high proportion of the Magyar population, although there was also a considerable number of Magyar peasants, especially in the Szekel districts and in the Crisana. The Roumanians had, on the other hand, practically no landlord class and only a small and weak bourgeoisie; the great majority of them were peasants, and their economic and cultural standards were considerably below those of the Magyar, not to speak of the German, peasants.

9. After 1918 Roumania made great efforts to alter this position. The land reform largely expropriated[50] the landowners (both individuals and institutions) belonging to the minorities and gave their land to poor or altogether landless peasants, chiefly Roumanian, although the Magyar landless class was in this respect treated by no means ungenerously. There matters rested for some years; but after the onset of the great depression and with the emergence from the high schools of the new generation of young Roumanian "intellectuals," and increasingly vigorous drive began for replacing members of the minorities by Roumanians, first in the official posts, then in business life. Finally there came a series of measures directed especially against the Jews. These various measures were not carried through either efficiently or consistently, and often amounted rather to spoliation of the non-Roumanians than to anything

constructive. Yet, one way and another, Roumania did undeni-
ably create for herself something more nearly resembling a
Roumanian bourgeoisie than had previously existed in
Transylvania.

10. Transylvania proper consists of a hilly table-land
encircled on all sides by mountains, the slopes of which are covered with forests of fir and beech. In the table-land some cereals
are grown, especially maize; but in spite of its low nutritional
standards, the country has to import food-stuffs. There is considerable live-stock farming. There is not, at present, much
important industry, but there are deposits of iron and coal in the
mountainous Western Banat, and gold, salt and methane gas
are found in various parts of the country. The eastern fringe of
the Partium (including the whole Maramures) is composed of
the western slopes of the Transylvanian mountains. They are
forested, and in their lower slopes produce an admirable wine.
The western portion of the Partium is simply the eastern end of
the flat Central Hungarian plain—an agricultural area suitable
for the raising of wheat, and other cereals.

11. Economically, the timber, minerals, salt, methane
and other resources of the area as a whole might be regarded as
equally valuable to the open, grain-growing plains of the
Hungarian Middle Danube or of the Roumanian Lower Danube.
apart from this, however, there is a certain division of natural
economic connexions, which tends, unfortunately, to run precisely contrary to ethnic considerations. The economic life of the
Partium, especially the northern part thereof, quite clearly
gravitates towards Hungary, and these areas undoubtedly suf-
fered economically by their separation from Hungary after 1919.
But the suffering was most severe of all in the case of the
Maramures, whose population, although small, is overwhelmingly Roumanian. The south and east of Transylvania lies much
nearer to Bucharest than to Budapest, and gained economically
from the change of frontiers in 1919. These areas, however,
include those inhabited by the Szekels. The economic connexions of Northern and Central Transylvania are mainly local. It
does not, probably, matter greatly to their economic life whether
they are in Hungary or Roumania; but it does matter to them
that Transylvania itself should not be cut up by frontiers and

tariff barriers.

12. Both parties also advance strong strategic considerations in support of their claims. The Roumanian claim is not only directed against Hungary, but also based on the argument that the population and resources of Transylvania are essential to Roumania. Further, much of the Roumanian armaments industry is located in Southern Transylvania, especially round Brasov.

13. Hungary, were she to desire strategic security against Roumania only, could get this in ample measure by obtaining roughly the western frontier of historic Transylvania. This involves, however, the spiritual renunciation by Hungary of Transylvania proper. Regarding herself as entitled to that area on other grounds, she regards its historic frontiers on the east and south—the main crest of the Carpathians—as alone affording security from the east to the Hungary of her wishes— i. e., a Hungary which should include at least part of Transylvania. In particular, she pressed on Germany at the time of the Vienna award of September 1940[51] the importance of her receiving the frontier of the Carpathian crest, in order to provide a bulwark for Europe against bolshevism. This argument probably induced the Germans to agree to something like the line for which Hungary was asking and to include the Szekel districts in the part of Transylvania awarded to Hungary.

Should the Whole Disputed Area Be Assigned either to Roumania or to Hungary?

14. These data show that there is no easy solution of the Transylvanian problem. the conflict of feelings, claims and interests is so strong that to award the whole area in dispute to either party, undivided and in absolute sovereignty, would certainly arouse in the other party a lasting resentment which would, moreover, be fully justified. These solutions are therefore mentioned not to advocate them, but to point out the objections to them and the safeguards which could, and should, be taken if circumstances made the adoption of either of them inevitable.

15. To give the whole to Hungary would mean that some 3.5 million Roumanians would again find themselves under Hungarian rule—a situation which would arouse in Roumania

a passionate and enduring resentment.

N. B. This solution could only be seriously considered in the case of a complete destruction of the Roumanian State, which would presumably be caused, or followed, or both, by the Soviet Union's advancing its frontiers up to the crest of the Carpathians, swallowing up both Moldavia and Wallachia. In such a case Transylvania and the Roumanian Banat (if not also swallowed up by the Soviet Union) would almost inevitably revert to Hungary, and in that case should be formed into an autonomous province of Hungary, with rights for the non-Magyars—far more extensive than those laid down in the 1919 minorities treaties—specially guaranteed.

16. Neither ought the frontiers of 1919 to be restored and the whole area—Transylvania proper and the Partium alike —be returned undiminished to Roumania; for this would mean restoring a situation of great inequality, for which no justification could be found to-day, and replacing under Roumanian rule a million Magyars who were reunited with Hungary under the Vienna award of 1940, besides the 1/2–3/4 million whom that award still left in Roumania.

N. B. Hungary ought, in any case, to be given a degree of rectification in the Partium. A minor rectification in the north-west would, indeed, probably be accepted in Roumania without extreme revolt; but it would not be regarded in Hungary as anything like a compromise, but only as the removal of a crying injustice. The following suggestions therefore envisage something more than such a minor change.

17. If, on the grounds suggested above, an award of the whole disputed territory either to Hungary or to Roumania is to be ruled out of consideration, there remain the two possibilities of partitioning the area between the two disputants (on one or other of the alternative lines set our below) or keeping together the whole, or the greater part, of it as a unity constituting a Transylvanian State separate from both Roumania and Hungary.

Alternative Schemes of Partition

18. The following would appear to be the principal alternative schemes of partition which might be worth consideration:

19. (i) The scheme of partition which, from the map, would look as if it were the most sensible would be to enlarge the rectification in Hungary's favour in the Partium (suggested in para. 16 above), extending it southward towards (though not necessarily as far as) the Danube. It would not be necessary to follow the exact boundary of historic Transylvania, for the eastern half of the Banat, which is almost purely Roumanian, belongs geographically to Transylvania or Wallachia. Other adjustments could be made further north also. A line could be drawn which would be geographically, economically and strategically reasonable, and would restore to Hungary (as compared with the frontier of 1919–40) a substantial number—some half-million—of Magyars. With these it would place under Hungarian rule an even larger number of Roumanians and Germans—perhaps at the maximum 700, 000 of the former and 300,000 of the latter—but these could be set off against the Magyars remaining in Transylvania whose numbers would be quite as great.

20. These Hungarian and Roumanian minorities which, under this scheme of partition, would find themselves on the wrong side of the frontier, and likewise the German minorities on both sides of the frontier, might be dealt with in one or other of two ways: Either they might all be left in situ with specially guaranteed rights (of the kind suggested in para. 15 above), or the Hungarian and the Roumanian minority might be exchanged against one another (the numbers would be approximately equal if the territorial revision given to Hungary on the western borders of the disputed territory were substantial).

N. B. While the history of the inter-war years sufficiently illustrates the difficulty of protecting minorities in situ by treaty guarantees, it would at the same time be a mistake to think of this exchange as an easy and certain panacea. The argument (whether cogent or not) in favour of transfer would be that, in the long run, Hungarian irredentist feeling in regard to Transylvania would be unlikely to survive on the strength of

historical sentiment alone, unsupported by the continuing presence of an appreciable Magyar element in the population of the
Transylvanian territories attached to Roumania. But not only
would the numbers involved be large, making the operation a
difficult and expensive one. There is the additional complication
that the land and other conditions in the two areas differ considerably, so that the persons transferred would find it difficult
to settle down in their new homes. But, above all, it must be
remembered that the claims of the two parties, but especially
those of Hungary, are not based on ethnography alone, but on
historical and sentimental factors which are very strong, and
which a transfer of population would leave untouched. Hungary
would not much the more easily reconcile herself to the loss of
Transylvania because her Szekels had also lost their homes
there.

21. It is, however, hard to imagine Hungary's joining in
a union with Roumania at any early date on the basis of a partition of the disputed territory on the lines sketched in paras.
19–20 above, assigning approximately the Partium to Hungary
and Transylvania to Roumania. A partition on these lines would
not be so radically different from the Trianon award of 1919
(assigning the whole disputed area to Roumania) as to escape
the odium attaching to the Trianon award in Hungarian minds.
At least for some time to come, Hungary would be likely to
remain hostile to Roumania; and, as it is also hard to imagine
Czechs and Slovaks joining with Hungary against Roumania,
the adoption of this first scheme of partition would probably
mean at least postponing, and perhaps abandoning, the idea of
a Danubian Union.

22. (ii) These objections on Hungary's part would, however, be somewhat diminished if, simultaneously with the grant
of revision in the Partium, territorial autonomy were granted
not to Transylvania as a whole, but to the compact enclave
inhabited by the Szekels in the south-east corner of Transylvania, the frontier between the Partium and Transylvania proper being adjusted as far as possible to leave an approximately
equal number of Roumanians in Hungary and Magyars in
Roumania outside the Szekel enclave. It has been noted in para.
6 above that for some years after 1919 official Hungarian circles

were prepared to agree to a settlement with Roumania on some such lines; but this was, of course, under the entirely different conditions prevailing at that time, when Roumania was a victorious ally of those in power and Hungary a defeated enemy. If the two countries were not in any kind of union, the Szekel enclave would presumably have to be under Roumanian sovereignty, whereas, if there was a union, it might be placed under Hungarian sovereignty. This would be an argument which might induce Hungary to enter the union even if its terms were in other respects unsatisfactory to her. For Roumania the plan would give a considerable proportion of her main points; and, if worse than the treaties of 1919, it would be a big improvement on the Vienna Award.

23. (iii) A third conceivable scheme of partition would be to assign to Hungary not only revision in the Partium and restoration of the Szekel districts, but also a corridor linking the Szekel districts with the main body of Hungary.

24. The advantages of such a scheme would be (a) that it would get rid of the territorial anomaly of a detached enclave of Hungarian territory, and (b) that such a corridor could be drawn on lines that would give back to Hungary the majority of the Magyar population in the whole disputed area, with only about half as many Roumanians, while leaving in Roumania three-quarters of the Roumanian population of the disputed area. Further, as against (ii) above, it would avoid the renewed hardships and sufferings to which the population of the corridor would again be exposed by being subjected for the third time in twenty-five years, and the second in five, to a change of sovereignty.

25. The major disadvantage of Scheme (iii) is that, even if the corridor were whittled down to the slimmest possible proportions, the result would approximate to the present partition, which was imposed upon Roumania by Germany and Italy in the Vienna Award of September 1940[52] (though with this substantial difference: that, by restoring to Roumania the preponderantly Romanian districts north of the corridor, it would, reduce the number of Roumanians in Hungary be some 600,000 and remove the ethnic inequality of the present position under the Vienna Award). All the same, this would be not less griev-

ous to Roumania than Scheme (i) would be to Hungary; and this Roumanian grievance would be just as formidable an obstacle to union between Roumania and Hungary as the Hungarian grievance that would be generated under Scheme (i) by the assignment of the Partium alone to Hungary and of Transylvania to Roumania.

26. Another great weakness of this Scheme (iii) is the absurd geographical and economic situation which would result from it. The ancient economic unity of Transylvania would be cut in two; Northern Transylvania would be left hanging in the air, as, although it would still be contiguous with Moldavia on the map, the Carpathians would form in practice a formidable dividing barrier; and the Szekel districts themselves must suffer severely in their economic life from being placed at this furthest end of so long and sinuous a tail.

27. The Vienna award had taken as its basis the Hungarian proposals, which made the return of the Szekel districts to Hungary an absolute condition and which also stipulated for a territorial connexion between those districts and the rest of Hungary. It conceded the Hungarian claim, however, by drawing the southern frontier along its whole length rather farther north than the line which the Hungarians would have liked. In doing so it cut through some indispensable local connexions, and in this respect the line probably would need minor rectification in favour of Hungary. On the other hand, the award gave to Hungary all Northern Transylvania, including the almost purely Roumanian areas north of the mixed districts of the corridor. These could, on the conditions laid down below, be returned to Roumania. The award was, as a matter of fact, not so inequitable as it was represented; Hungary's share both of the whole disputed territory and of Transylvania proper was not, as commonly stated, two-thirds, but just over two-fifths, and a correction as indicated above would produce something like equality in the degree of the disappointment of the ethnic claims of the two nations (about 500,000 of each nationality left on the wrong side of the frontier). Thus, although it would content neither party, neither could justifiably say that the other had been unduly favoured.

28. Owing, however, to the economic absurdities created

by this line, the populations affected would be bound to suffer heavily unless at the same time Roumania and Hungary were to be included in a federation with an adequate measure of freedom for the movement of men and of goods. This, however, would almost certainly be rendered impracticable by the sense of grievance which a partition on these lines would undoubtedly leave in Roumanian hearts; while conversely, if a union between Roumania and Hungary were psychologically practicable, there would be no economic or strategic necessity that an enclave of territory under Hungarian sovereignty in the Szekel districts should be linked by any corridor with the main body of Hungary.

29. It has already been pointed out (in para. 22 above) that Scheme (ii), involving, as it does, the grant of territorial autonomy to the Szekel districts, would hardly be practicable except within the framework of a union between Hungary and Roumania; and, if the autonomous Szekel enclave was to be placed under Hungarian sovereignty, such union would evidently be a condition sine qua non (see para. 22 above). In thus depending for its practicability on the establishment of a union, Scheme (ii) also constitutes a strong positive argument for establishing a union. This last consideration also applies to the possibility—alternative to all these partition schemes—of creating a separate Transylvanian State.

The Creation of a Separate Transylvanian State

30. There remains this possibility of keeping Transylvania geographically intact and forming it into an autonomous member of a Danubian union. In this case some territory in the Partium ought probably still to be assigned to Hungary outright; the remainder of the Partium would, in these circumstances, probably best be joined to Transylvania.

31. Ideally, this would be the best solution, and conditions exist, even to-day, which suggest that it might be a practical possibility. Apart from its historic and geographical unity, Transylvania still possesses old traditions, the memory of which has not been altogether effaced by modern conditions, of active and fruitful co-operation between different elements of its pop-

ulation. For centuries it possessed not only a real constitutional life, at a time when nearly every other European State was almost or quite an absolutism; but that life was specially adapted to the multi-national character of the population. There were three "nations," each of which enjoyed wide self-government and co-operated with the other two, and with the monarch, in the conduct of affairs of common concern; and they evolved a corporate life some aspects of which aroused the admiration of contemporary Europe.

32. Obviously these old institutions could not be revived without alteration. Thus the three Transylvanian peoples, who in the 19th century formed the famous "Union of the Three Nations," were the Hungarian "nobles," who were not, indeed, exclusively Magyars but in practice mainly Magyar, those among them who came of German or Roumanian stock usually assimilating to the Magyar majority; the Saxons; and the Szekels. All those Roumanians who did not enjoy Hungarian nobility, i.e., the great majority of them, were in practice a national proletariat. The three "nations" of to-day would have to be (1) the Roumanians, (2) the Magyars, including the Szekels, and (3) the Germans, both Saxons and Swabians. Further, the old class-distinction, which excluded not only Roumanians but Magyar non-nobles from the enjoyment of political rights, could, of course, not be revived. Each of the new "nations" would have to represent all its members. Similarly, the equality formerly reigning between the four "received religions"—Catholics, Lutherans, Calvinists, Unitarians — would have to be extended to the Orthodox and Jewish Churches.

33. But the tradition might be able to survive this modernisation, and there are also old institutions which do survive and which could be utilised as the foundation for a separate life. In considering the prospects of that life, the mind naturally leaps to Switzerland, where also there are three peoples, with at least one local minority, living together in that amity which it would be desired to bring about between the peoples of Transylvania. The traditions and circumstances of Switzerland are, however, very different from those of Transylvania, and the institution required in Transylvania would have to be very different, in most respects, from those of Switzerland.

34. The Swiss model could be approached in one respect: the language provisions. In the central organs, legislative or administrative, the three current languages—Roumanian, Magyar, German-would have to enjoy complete equality. Further, there would have to be as much decentralisation as possible, the smaller units being determined as far as possible on national lines (the boundaries of the present counties and departments are by no means sacrosanct, nor even very ancient). In each, such unit all languages current locally would have to be on an equal footing, and provision would have to be made also for the language of any considerable local minority (e.g., Serbs in Timis or Ruthenes (i.e., Cis-Carpathian Ukrainian-speaking Slavs) in Maramures, if included in Transylvania). All public employees would have to be conversant with all languages in official use in their offices, i.e., all three languages in the central services, and one, two or three, as the case might be, in the local administration. This condition would not be a severe one, in view of the prevailing polyglotism.

35. Transylvania has not, however, achieved the comparative indifference to national origin which reigns in Switzerland. There are obviously many matters, both general and local, which interest all citizens of the country, whatever their language or ethnic origin, and these would have to be discussed jointly, whether by the central or by the local organs. But it would be necessary to adopt the institution of "national curiae" such as operated, to the great common benefit, in a couple of Crownlands (Moravia and the Bukovina) of the old Austrian Monarchy. Each "nation" would thus elect its own representatives, in numbers proportionate to the population, (c. It might be possible to dispense with this in some cases, e.g., functional bodies such as chambers of commerce and industry. It would also be necessary to allot to each nation a proportion of the posts in the public services, at any rate in all except the highest grades.

36. In all national-cultural affairs, however, each nation would have to enjoy complete self-government and absolute freedom from interference on the part of the others. The organisation of the bodies through which this national self-government was exercised would be particularly easy. The elements already exist in the different Church organisations; for in

Transylvania religious classifications coincide almost exactly with national. The Saxons, in particular, are Lutherans to a man, and there are practically no Lutherans who are not Saxons. The whole exceedingly extensive national life of the Saxons has for centuries been built up on their Church organisation. The Roumanians are Greek Orthodox or Uniate; the Magyars, Roman Catholic, Calvinist or Unitarian. The Serbs already have their own Orthodox bishopric, and the Armenians and Jews their own organisations. The only important cross-section is in the case of the Swabians, who are Roman Catholics.

37. It would not be difficult for each nation to develop its own "national" organisation for the conduct of its own private affairs. The proper sphere of these bodies would consist only of national-cultural matters, but the Germans, and to some extent the other nationalities also, already have their own economic and social organisations (building societies, co-operatives, friendly societies, (c.), and these should be left in being.

38. It does not seem altogether foolhardy to hope that if arrangements on the lines sketched out above were wisely and carefully drafter, a workable political unit could be created which might in some respects even set an example to the rest of Europe, as the Transylvania of three centuries ago, although always vitiated by the unhealthy position of the Roumanian element, set an example in declaring and maintaining, first of all European States, the principle of religious toleration. In some respects the events of the past twenty-five years, painful as they have been, may be regarded as an essential and even a healthy historic process, since they have enabled the Roumanian element to rise to a position of social equality with the other nationalities.

39. This Transylvania would have a population of a full 4 millions. It would thus be larger in population, and even in area, than several European States whose rights to existence are seldom questioned. It would have considerable economic resources; its standards of living should be fully up to the local average, and surpass those of some of its neighbours.

40. Its economic prosperity would, however, require a degree of freedom of trade, communications and migration between Transylvania and both her neighbours; arrangements

to this effect would be equally important to the neighbouring States, especially to Roumania.

41. While, however, this solution is put forward as the ideal, the considerable opposition which it would encounter must be admitted. It is nearly eighty years since Transylvania ceased to constitute a separate political unit. In the intervening period first the Magyars, then the Roumanians, have had experience of life within a larger national State belonging to their own kinsmen. In each case they have regarded the said kinsmen with some degree of contempt and dislike, but the experience has gradually sapped their particularist spirit, and this has been particularly true of the Roumanians during the past twenty years. In any case, they have preferred their kinsmen to their neighbours and would rather dominate their co-Transylvanians in a Roumanian national State than combine with them outside it. The sincerest "Transylvanians" of to-day are the Saxons, who do not enjoy the alternative possibility.

42. Both Hungary and Roumania, too, would prefer to possess all Transylvania than to see it form a separate unit. There would be a strong pull from each nation on its co-nationals; and the pull from Roumania, in particular, would be much stronger than before 1918 (when union with Transylvania was only an aspiration, not, as to-day, an experience), while in the old days of Transylvanian independence this pull hardly existed.

43. One is forced, therefore, the conclude that the solution of an autonomous Transylvania might not be practicable, and that it certainly would not be so unless both Roumania and Hungary were members of the union of which Transylvania also was a member. It is not easy to be optimistic about the prospects of a Transylvania forming a buffer State between two federations (or confederations). It would probably prove rather a bone of contention than a buffer. It is hard to imagine that either Roumania or Hungary would leave Transylvania even approximately at peace unless. Transylvania were included in a union of which Roumania or Hungary respectively was itself also a member; nor could the respective members of the two nationalities easily acquiesce in such a situation. Obviously, given a sufficiently strong control on the part of the United Nations, any

position desired could be maintained, and it might be that in due time both the inhabitants and the neighbours of Transyl-vania would come to accept this solution; but the time would probably be long in coming, and the efforts during the interval severe.

44. Given, however, the condition laid down above, i.e., that Roumania, Hungary and Transylvania were all three members of the same union, then although outside control would also be required, that control would not need to be so severe, and there seems a reasonable prospect that the experiment might make good and end by gaining acceptance both in Transylvania itself, and among its neighbours.

Conclusions

45. The conclusions reached in this paper may be summed up as follows:

46. (a) To assign, either to Roumania or to Hungary, the whole area in dispute between them (i.e., the whole area transferred from Hungarian to Roumanian sovereignty after the war of 1914–18 under the Treaty of Trianon) would neither do justice nor produce stability.

47. (b) Of the three main possible alternative schemes of partition, two would almost certainly be impracticable because each of these two would favour one of the two parties to an extent that would make it inevitably unacceptable to the other party.

48. Hungary would presumably never voluntarily accept Partition Scheme (i) assigning approximately the Partium to Hungary and Transylvania to Roumania, either with or without an exchange of the Roumanian and Hungarian minorities which would be left respectively on the wrong side of the line.

49. Roumania would presumably never voluntarily accept Partition Scheme (iii), assigning to Hungary not only the Partium but also the Szekel districts in the extreme south-eastern corner of Transylvania together with a corridor linking this Szekel country with the main body of Hungary.

50. (c) If Hungary and Roumania could be induced to accept Partition Scheme (ii) assigning the Partium to Hungary and at the same time granting territorial autonomy to the Szekel districts of Transylvania, while leaving the rest of

Transylvania under direct Roumanian rule, then the autonomous Szekel territory would have to be under Roumanian sovereignty if Roumania and Hungary were to remain wholly separate from one another. If, on the other hand, they were to enter into some kind of union with one another, the Szekel enclave might be placed under Hungarian sovereignty with decided advantage to the Szekels themselves and to Hungary and without serious detriment to Roumania.

51. It is by no means certain that Scheme (ii), in either of its two variant forms, would be acceptable to either Roumania or Hungary. As against Schemes (i) and (iii), Scheme (ii) has, however, at least the negative psychological advantage of not being reminiscent either of the Trianon award of 1919, which is odious to the Hungarians, or of the Vienna award of 1940, which is odious to the Roumanians.

52. (d) The ideally best solution would be to assign a portion of the Partium to Hungary and to combine the rest of the Partium with Transylvania to form a separate multi-national Transylvanian State, with the several nationalities enjoying equal status in the spirit of historic Transylvanian constitutional traditions.

53. (e) Under present conditions, such a revival of the historic principality of Transylvania would only be feasible if the new Transylvanian State were incorporated in a union of States also including both Hungary and Roumania.

54. (f) The break in the historic Transylvanian constitutional tradition and the modern accentuation of both Hungarian and Roumanian national feeling inside as well as outside Transylvania impracticable. If so, it might be necessary to fall back upon Partition Scheme (ii)—preferably with Hungary and Roumania in some kind of union and with the Szekel enclave under Hungarian sovereignty—as a resolution which, though perhaps not ideal, might at any rate prove acceptable to both parties.

Foreign Research and Press Service,
Balliol College, Oxford,
December 21, 1942.

DOCUMENT 5

The Problem of Yugoslavia

A. Introduction

1. The terms of reference lay down the contingency that there will be at least separate Croat and Serb States.

2. Should that situation arise, the Slovenes would be territorially separated from the rest of Yugoslavia by the Croat State. Accordingly, and in addition to all questions of a wider association with non-Yugoslav States, for the Slovenes there would arise the alternatives of inclusion in Croatia, or some form of association with Croatia, or independence. (This problem existed in a limited and somewhat academic form in Yugoslavia. From 1939 to 1941 Croatia had a measure of autonomy. The competence of the Central Government, however, was so wide, and that of the autonomous Croat Government so narrow, as to render the geographical "isolation" of Slovenia of no importance. What is to be remarked is that the Slovene demand both before and during that time was never for a centralised Yugoslavia nor for inclusion in an autonomous Croatia, but for an autonomous Slovenia.)

3. It is here assumed that Italy will be obliged to surrender not only her acquisitions made in 1941 at the expense of Yugoslavia,[53] but also Fiume, her annexation of which was no part of the European settlement effected at Paris in 1919–20.

4. In this memorandum the expression "Serbians" is used to distinguish the Serbs of Serbia from those of other parts of Yugoslavia; and that of "Bosnia" to cover the whole of Bosnia-Herzegovina.

B. Croatia and Slovenia

5. The leaders of the Croat Peasant party,[54] who may still be taken as the authentic representatives of the Croat people, have in the past declared that their ideal was such an association of Croatia with neighbouring countries, as would assure Croatian self-government and promote the interests of peasants. The Croats have long been accustomed to federal relations. A federal Yugoslav State was their desire in 1918. They may reasonably be expected to consider favourably proposals for the inclusion of Croatia in an Inter-State Union. They are hardly likely to favour a Balkan Union, in which they would be outnumbered by the Serbs and associated with other peoples of "Eastern" Culture. They would probably greatly prefer autonomy within a Danubian Union (including Hungary, Austria and Czechoslovakia, with or without Poland, Serbia or Roumania). Even if the Danubian Union did not include Austria, their preference would probably be the same. In that case a fortiori the Slovenes would similarly prefer a Danubian to a Balkan Union. Even more than the Croats, they have long shared the Danubian rather than the Balkan culture and social system. And if Croatia were included in a Danubian Union, Slovenia would have no territorial contact with the Balkans.

6. Strong economic bonds would draw Croatia and Slovenia to Hungary, Austria and Czechoslovakia. For Croatia and Slovenia will desire the northern market for their products as well as the prosperity to be derived from transit trade; while the other States will want their trade to cross Slovenia or Croatia to the nearest seaport with the minimum of formality and payment.

7. The mutual relations of the Croats and Slovenes are affected by such factors as the following: the bonds of sympathy between the two peoples are not strong; the Slovenes are on a higher level of efficiency and literacy than the Croats; the Catholic Church has played a much greater part in the social life and economic organisation of the Slovenes than in those of the Croats; the Slovene language differs considerably from the Croat and is understood by few Croats. If, therefore, a single State of Croats and Slovenes were formed, the Croats might use

their numerical superiority to establish a dominant position in that State; whereupon the Serbo-Croat struggles of the past twenty years would probably be reproduced in the form of Croato-Slovene struggles.

8. The Slovenes desire absolutely assured access to the Adriatic. Were they to obtain Trieste, or, alternatively, were Trieste placed under a form of international control assuring to the Slovenes complete freedom of residence and trade in the city and port, then there is good ground for believing that they would prefer formal independence or at any rate no closer bond with Croatia than that of common membership of a Danubian Union. Failing any such settlement of Trieste, the Slovenes would presumably prefer to share with the Croats the control of Fiume. This might be achieved within the framework of one State, which we will call "South Slavia." But, in such a State, for the reasons given in para. 7, the Slovenes would demand a very large measure of autonomy, perhaps amounting to dualism; and, without a reconciling factor such as is sometimes provided by an established dynasty, the resultant constitutional difficulties might be great. Much simpler would be the creation of two separate States, within the Danubian Union, sharing or dividing the port and railway termini of Fiume between them. (To give the Slovenes adequate access to Fiume, it would be necessary to withdraw the Italian frontier to the west of the Ljubljana—Fiume railway line; as was urged by President Wilson[55] at the Peace Conference of Paris in 1919. The railway line runs entirely through Slav-inhabited territory. Italy's insistence, in the Treaty of London (1915)[56], on carrying her frontier to the east of it was based on strategic grounds.)

9. The boundary between Croatia and Slovenia should present little difficulty. Should a State of Slovenia have such a position in Trieste as would cause it not to desire any control of Fiume, the boundary could follow the traditional and clear line of division between the two peoples (see map*). In the alternative case, that of sharing or dividing Fiume, the Slovene frontier might be advanced along the railway from Ljubljana for the few miles necessary to bring it to Fiume, so as to leave the railway westwards from Fiume in Slovene hands. (This expedient would bring only a very small Croat population under Slovene rule.

---

* Not reproduced.

The situation would be more complicated were the Croat-inhabited portion of Istria taken from Italy and attributed to Croatia.
The Slovenes would then, for a few miles, have the narrow corridor of their railway running through Croat territory. That
complication, however, might be expected to be soluble as
between fellow-members of the same union.)

10. The welfare of such extremely small and weak
States as Croatia and Slovenia or "South Slavia" within a
Danubian Union would depend on the creation of adequate military security and on the adoption of arrangements for securing
an adequate measure of freedom for the movement of men as
well as of goods within the union. Without the latter provision
such a State as Croatia, with chronic over-population in its
southern portions, would suffer considerably.

C. Serbia

11. On the given assumption of the separation of Serbia
and Croatia, there would appear to be four alternative futures
for Serbia: (i) membership of a Danubian Union, along with
Croatia and Slovenia or "South Slavia"; (ii) independence; (iii)
membership of a Balkan Union; (iv) inclusion in the USSR, if
Roumania and Bulgaria were so included.

12. (i) The adoption of the first alternative would create
opportunities for considerable economic advancement. It would
enable Serbia to profit by any economic plans for the Danubian
area with a minimum of difficulty. Whatever régime were adopted for the Danube, it would greatly facilitate plans for the
improved common use of the river. Also it would ease the problems of Serbia's relations with Croatia or "South Slavia." On the
other hand, the culture of the Serbs, at any rate in Serbia and
Bosnia, is not Danubian but Balkan, and the Serbian tradition
of independence is very strong. Opposition to any close association with the more developed peoples of the Danubian area
might be expected from Serbs of the older generation and the
very influential Serbian army and Church.

13. (ii) Independence would correspond with the apparently prevailing opinion amongst the Serbs. It would not be economically advantageous; unless, despite her independence,

Serbia enjoyed very close economic co-operation with the Danubian Union.

14. (iii) A Balkan Union would associate the Serbs with peoples (the Greeks, the Turks, the Albanians) with whom they have little sympathy or traditions of co-operation. It would have the economic advantage of basing the security of Serbian trade through Salonica on the union rather than on a treaty between independent States. But it would not have the advantage of bringing together complementary economies, since the countries concerned are chiefly producers of primary commodities. Past proposals for a Balkan Union, in so far as they professed to aim at the benefit of all the Balkan States, appear to have been chiefly actuated by the desire to provide security against aggression from non-Balkan Powers. For a period after the present war it is to be expected that the danger of such aggression will not exist; and it is to be hoped that the world will be so organised as permanently to exclude the danger. Nevertheless, should a return to power politics between sovereign States occur, the successful establishment of a Danubian Union in the years of peace would sensibly diminish the danger of aggression by non-Balkan Powers, i.e., as far as can be seen, by one or more of the following: Germany, Italy, the Danubian Union and the USSR For, in that case, aggression by Germany could only occur after Germany had either disrupted or conquered the Danubian Union. Aggression by Italy would be likely to encounter the opposition of the Danubian Union on Italy's flank. The probability of aggression by the Danubian Union itself ought to be small, in view of the decentralised and heterogeneous character of any such union. There remains the hypothesis of aggression by the USSR, defence against which may more profitably be sought in the mutual relations of the United Nations than in a Balkan Union.

15. It is possible that a smaller Balkan Union might be formed. Serbia and Bulgaria might be drawn together by the underlying mutual goodwill of their peoples and unite in an Orthodox South Slav State on a federal basis. So long, at least, as Macedonia was in Yugoslav hands there was a considerable current of opinion in Bulgaria in favour of this solution, it being supposed that Macedonia would become a third member of the

federation. It is true that Croatia and Slovenia were commonly envisaged as also belonging to the federation, the Bulgarians believing that those units would prevent the Serbs from dominating the federation. On the other hand, a Serbia unable to command the resources of Yugoslavia might not be so alarming to Bulgarians.

16. Such an Orthodox South Slav State might have any of the four alternative futures suggested as possible for Serbia. The advantages and disadvantages would be much the same as for Serbia. Membership of a Balkan Union, however, is the least likely of the four, since Greece would probably be unwilling to enter into a union with so large a Slav State, even though the alternative might be that she would find herself in an isolated and precarious position.

17. (iv) Serbia's inclusion in the USSR would presumably only take place in the event of Communist revolutions in at least Bulgaria and Serbia. The extension of the Soviet power into the Balkans would have effects, not easy to estimate, beyond that area. It might so draw together the Danubian States, including Slovenia and Croatia, as to unite them in a closer union; or it might result in the Russian absorption of the whole Danubian area.

18. On all these alternatives, except for the second possibility envisaged in para. 17, a frontier would have to be drawn between Serbia and Croatia. Croatia could lay no justified ethnic claim to territory north of the Danube nor to Srem. Between Croatian Slavonia and Serbian Srem a frontier could be drawn with comparative ease and substantial justice. In the extreme south the dividing line is fairly clear between the Croats of the coast as far as the mouth of the Gulf of Kotor (Cattaro) and the Serbs of the immediate hinterland and the coast further south. A difficulty there would be to give Serbia adequate access to the sea without excessive violation of national sentiment. But in Bosnia the mingling of Serbs, Croats and Moslems baffles the desire to draw an agreed frontier. History has here produced an awkward situation. As the Turkish armies advanced northwestwards through Bosnia in the 15th and 16th centuries, there came many Orthodox Serbs, Vlachs and others from the southeast, partly as auxiliary troops serving the Sultan, partly in

search of land and loot, partly in flight from the Turks. The descendants of these immigrants are settled in Central and Western Bosnia and further west up to the limit of the Turkish advance, i.e., the River Kulpa in Croatia. When the Habsburg Monarchy reconquered Southern Croatia from the Turks, this Orthodox population was confirmed in its possession of the land and given liberty to retain its Orthodox faith, on condition of military service along the frontier. These Orthodox, whatever their ethnic origin, came by the end of the 19th century to consider themselves Serbs. Meanwhile, in Bosnia the Catholic Croat population only survived in considerable numbers in the hills west of Sarajevo and in the plain of the north-east, along the south bank of the Save. In most parts of Bosnia, especially the centre, the population is largely Moslem, the descendants of the Slavs who accepted Islam. [The Moslems would probably prefer Croatia to Serbia, but they are so scattered that it would be difficult to give effect to their wishes.] The result is that the Serb strongholds are the districts along the eastern border of Bosnia and the extreme west and north-west. When an autonomous Croatia was created within Yugoslavia in 1939, she received a broad wedge of territory running up from Dalmatia to a point north-west of Sarajevo and the Croat belt of plain in the north-east (see map*). Between these two arms of Croat territory was left a fairly broad corridor of Yugoslav (Serb) territory, widening out to include all Western Bosnia. Tolerable as this arrangement was within Yugoslavia, it would produce a most inconvenient situation as between two separate States. The best method of settlement would be the imposition by the United Nations of a frontier based on geography, economics and, as far as possible, on national sentiment. In view of the difficulties of road and railway construction in most of Bosnia, such a settlement should aim at giving to each State an equitable share of the roads and railways, taking into account existing and possible connexions with each State's system of communications. If, as is probable, many Germans emigrate from the Banat, Backa and Srem, there should be much fertile land available in Serbia. This should enable such Serbs and Croats as wished to do so to migrate, across the new frontier running through Bosnia and Slavonia, to their respective national States; while incidentally

* Not reproduced.

providing land for those of the excess population whose needs
are not met by measures of industrialisation.

D. Federal Yugoslavia

19. It is possible that the terms of reference were not
intended to exclude the possibility of the re-integration of
Yugoslavia in a new form. For the separate Governments of
Croatia and Serbia (and of Slovenia) might wish to form a
Yugoslav Federation. South Slav sentiment is a reality, born of
common speech and other similarities of daily life; although it is
of variable and not easily calculable content.

20. A Yugoslav nationality, which should obliterate the
Serb, Croat and Slovene nationalities, has very few devotees.

21. To most Serbians the idea of Yugoslavia has never
been distinguishable from an enlarged Serbia, in which, at any
rate, the Croats were to submit to Serbian leadership and to
accept the Serbian national and political ideals. Pre-occupation
with the Croats caused the Serbians not to bother about the
remoter, less numerous and economically useful Slovenes.

22. To some Croats the whole idea of Yugoslavia has
been intolerable, but the desire of the great majority, before
1941, was a Yugoslavia in the form of a not too close union of
three (or more) self-governing States, which would support each
other against any possible opponent.

23. To the Slovenes Yugoslavia has presented itself as
the only available protection against the Germans and Italians,
and as a community in which their energy and efficiency would
bring them to prominent positions. They, too, have consistently
demanded autonomy.

24. To the Bosnian Moslems, whose loyalty has been
directed primarily to Bosnia and to Islam, Yugoslavia ceased to
appeal as soon as it became clear that there was little or no
prospect of a self-governing Bosnia.

25. If remains to consider one other element amongst
the Yugoslavs, the Serbs of former Austria and Hungary, the so-
called Precani Serbs, who combine Serb sentiment and orthodox
professions with long assimilation to Danubian civilisation.
After 1918 they were the champions of extreme centralism and

a common Yugoslav national programme, but assumed that leadership should come from Serbs, though not exclusively from Serbians. It was their Yugoslavist programme which prevented their political party (the Independent Democratic party), inaugurated in 1926, from gaining any success in Serbia or any noticeable success in Bosnia. In 1927 they passed over into alliance with the Croat federalist opposition.

26. When in 1939 Croatia received her limited autonomy, Dr. Macek[57], his colleagues of the Croat Peasant party, and their political allies of the Independent Democratic party, became genuine and zealous supporters of Yugoslavia, which they hoped yet further to reform in a federalist sense; whereas nearly all Serbians looked with distaste upon the new arrangement and wished to modify in a centralist sense the autonomy granted to Croatia. In 1940 there were many in Croatia whose Yugoslav sentiments had survived the disillusionments of the period 1919–39 and who believed that a new and better era had begun in Yugoslavia (though few Croats were prepared to fight, against desperate odds, for Yugoslavia). The events of the past eighteen months may have awoken Yugoslav sentiment in yet others or restored it to some of those who had lost it. The future existence of Yugoslavia seems primarily to depend on the willingness of the Serbians to meet the wishes of the Croats and Slovenes. It would be rash to assume that Croat and Serb States could not come together in a new Yugoslavia.

27. But, apart from the present bitterness between Serbs and Croats, there are formidable obstacles in the way of such a reintegration. Serbians and Croats, by themselves, would find it difficult to reach an agreed settlement of the Bosnian question. The Serbians of Serbia would be reluctant to agree to an equal partnership with the Croats and Slovenes; and the Croats and Slovenes could hardly agree to anything less than that. In the given circumstances of separate Croat and Serb States it appears that the concession by the Serbians of an equal partnership in a federation would be an absolute condition of a renewed Yugoslavia. Further, as has been suggested above, the attitude of the Croats and Slovenes to proposals for their inclusion in a Danubian Union would probably be favourable and that of the Serbians unfavourable. Yugoslav sentiment might be

strong enough to overcome these obstacles; and, if so, a federal Yugoslavia could be included in the Danubian Union. Alternatively, were it once decided that the Danubian Union should include the Croats and Slovenes, and were the Croat-Serb frontier imposed, the Serbians might be prepared to enter a federal Yugoslavia within the Danubian Union. It would be most unfortunate for the Danubian Union were Yugoslav sentiment to cause the creation of a Yugoslavia which rejected membership of that Union and separated it from the Adriatic Sea. Such a contingency is not to be excluded, in view of the international bitterness and distrust generated by the war. But its adverse effects on the economic life and stability of the Danubian area might be off-set were the United Nations able and willing to apply economic plans, over-riding State boundaries, to the Danubian and Balkan areas as a whole. What does not appear at all probable is that the Croats and Slovenes should willingly enter a purely Balkan Union.

Foreign Research and Press Service,
Balliol College, Oxford,
November 5, 1942

DOCUMENT 6

Danubian Confederation

[*Note (1)*]. Some subjects briefly dealt with in this paper have been more fully treated in a previous memorandum Confederations in Eastern Europe dated the 1st September, 1942 (Document No. 1). This memorandum is referred to below as C. E. E.

Note (2). The facts and considerations set out in this memorandum are believed to be equally relevant whether or not the relations between the States in the area lying between the USSR and Germany are set in the wider framework of the Anglo-Soviet Treaty.[58] The memorandum, however, deals only with the area taken by itself. It does not consider the possible effect of the treaty upon the problem of organising the security of the area.]

I. Introduction

1. The desirability of closer association between the small countries lying between Germany and Russia arises out of considerations of security in the widest sense of the word—security military, political, social and economic. Each of them taken alone is much weaker than either of its great neighbours; and it is only in combination that they can hope to deter an aggressor or to contribute effectively to a general system of security. For this purpose a simple alliance, on a basis of completely sovereign States, is not sufficient; for, apart from the proved weakness of alliances between small States when one of them imagines itself immune from a threat directed against its partners, the particular conditions of the area are such that its division into sovereign States entails special difficulties. For such a divi-

sion necessarily perpetuates, aggravates, or creates antagonism between the different peoples, which would be reduced by any form of collaboration and greatly reduced if the collaboration developed into a close form of union (cf. para. 26). It also allows and even fosters weaknesses in the economic field, which, again, union might eventually eliminate.

2. The populations are in many places so mixed that no frontiers can eliminate minorities. If completely sovereign States are re-established, a considerable proportion of the population of each will necessarily consist of national minorities, which will be left entirely at the mercy of the national majorities, and thus in a worse position than the smaller nationalities were, for example, in the multi-national State of Austria. The hope entertained in 1919 that the League Minority Treaties would provide a real protection for the minorities proved misplaced. Only a close association limiting the absolute dominance of national majorities can provide real protection.

3. Further, although there must be some minorities, however, frontiers are drawn, yet completely sovereign States demand economic and strategic frontiers against each other, and this greatly increases the numbers of the minorities, many of whom were found, after 1919, in the frontier areas allotted to certain States on economic and strategic grounds. A closer association, so far as it eliminated the need for defensive lines, military or economic, between its members, would at a stroke very largely reduce the number of minorities.

4. There is considerable economic diversity in Eastern Europe, and the products of many parts, placed in 1919 within different States, are to some extent mutually complementary. Thus, within a closer union there might be much trade. In the régime of sovereign States, each State has in the inter-war period tended to be exclusive in its economic policy, and thoroughly uneconomic consequences have resulted. The standard of living has been kept lower than, with rational large-scale organisation, it need be. Difficulties in marketing surpluses were serious, and in the end several States succumbed, after 1934, to German economic domination leading on to political domination.

5. There are also other factors to be considered. Many of

the peoples of Eastern Europe have had long experience of living together (in the Austro-Hungarian Monarchy). Their social standards and habits have a degree of similarity none the less strong because overshadowed by national rivalries and hatreds. There are even institutions, both spiritual and economic (among the latter many man-made communications), which are the fruits of past cohabitation and which should form a basis for future collaboration, if once the disturbing factors can be removed. It would, of course, be useless simply to order the peoples to collaborate without providing a suitable framework; but if this can be created the prospects for the future are brighter than would appear at first sight.

II. Membership

6. The countries which appear to be probable candidates for membership must next be discussed; after which it will be possible to consider in more detail the merits and the organisation of the association. Broadly speaking, members must obviously be selected on the principle of combining those peoples, and only those peoples, whose combination would increase their security, in the side sense defined above. This makes it necessary to consider the exclusion from the union (where such exclusion is compatible with the security of the union) of any areas whose inhabitants would prefer to belong to States outside it. It would also add to the security of the union if it excluded areas whose inclusion would provoke the lasting hostility of the union's neighbours. If these principles are maintained, the USSR and Germany may regard the union as conformable to their own ultimate interests and may come to look on it with reasonable benevolence. If the members of the union are too greedy, they will invite their own destruction.

7. Czechoslovakia.— At present there exists the nucleus of a larger formation in the shape of the projected Polish-Czechoslovak Confederation. It is, however, uncertain whether it will develop into a permanent association, and, if it does, whether it will possess enough vital strength to survive if it remains exclusive. The Governments concerned have themselves stated that their grouping is to be opened to further

adherents, and His Majesty's Government has endorsed their hopes in this respect. The territories included in the projected confederation lie in an exposed situation, and the events of 193859 should have convinced Czechoslovakia of her need for the maximum possible support from her smaller neighbours.

8. If only in Czechoslovakia's interest, therefore, everything possible ought to be done to include her in a union containing other Danubian members. Fortunately—in view of the uncertain prospects of the Polish-Czechoslovak agreement—it is possible to make plans which could be applied, with only slight modifications, whether Poland became (or remained) a member or not. For, except in the single case of Teschen,[60] the claims of Poland and the Danubian States do not greatly clash or mingle. They lie against each other like flat surfaces, with little dovetailing. The interests and claims of the Danubian peoples, on the other hand, are closely interlocked. If they could be fitted together correctly, they could give a compact and solid result; if not, the outcome is a hopeless pattern of gaps and protuberances.

9. Czechoslovakia is thus the starting-point of the proposed union. The component parts of the pre-1938 Czechoslovak Republic would necessarily be included in the union, and the union's existence might indeed help towards the solution of some of the internal problems of Czechoslovakia. It is necessary to reckon with the possibility of a Slovak national movement, and there are certainly economic interests particular to Slovakia and not identical with those of the Czechs. Membership of the union would make it easier to satisfy these interests, and even make it easier for the Czechs to allow the Slovaks a degree of autonomy which they would feel they could not safely grant to Slovakia if the union did not exist. These considerations also apply to Sub-Carpathian Ruthenia, where the interests and perhaps the wishes of the population are not exclusively in favour of Czechoslovakia. If a close form of union were achieved, Slovakia and Ruthenia might even ultimately become member States within the Danubian union themselves, though this prospect might not appeal to Czechs. (On Slovakia and Sub-Carpathian Ruthenia cf. C.E.E., paras. 90–94.)

10. Hungary.—Without Hungary, no satisfactory Danubian

union is possible. If she were excluded there could be only a revived Little Entente, with the possible addition of Austria, which would be an entirely different association and which would leave Hungary with the opportunity, and indeed the strongest possible incentive, to become again a point d'appui for German penetration. Because of Hungary's central position her exclusion from a Danubian union would leave it in every respect—geographic, economic, political and strategic—a collection of limbs with no body.

11. To have Hungary as a partner instead of as a potential enemy would obviously contribute to the security of Czechoslovakia. If Poland is a member (cf. paras. 62–69) she will also desire Hungary to be included. On her side, Hungary might hope that her own inclusion would make it easier for her to obtain equitable treatment at a peace settlement. The existence of a union might also make it possible to meet certain of her wider wishes and interests in the Danubian area.

12. This would be particularly the case in Sub-Carpathian Ruthenia. The USSR, which might have claimed an interest in the Ruthenes on the grounds that they are Ukrainian-speaking people, has acquiesced in their inclusion in Czechoslovakia. Hungary fears the extension of USSR influence over this area (an influence the USSR might exercise indirectly through an association with Czechoslovakia), and thus across the Carpathians. Hungary has also strong economic interests in the area, in relation to irrigation and flood control in the Hungarian plain and to timber supply. Her fears might be allayed and her interests met if she and Czechoslovakia were in the same union, even if Ruthenia belonged within that union to the sub-unit Czechoslovakia.

13. There are also strong economic links between Hungary and Slovakia, the rupture of which after 1919 was disadvantageous to both parties. If Hungary and Czechoslovakia are sovereign States it is particularly difficult, in the case of both the Hungaro-Slovak and the Hungaro-Ruthene frontiers, to combine ethnic considerations with those of economic practicability and strategic security.

14. At the same time, the antagonism between Magyars and Czechs is so considerable that a union consisting only of

Czechoslovakia and Hungary would be impossible. This antagonism is too deep-rooted to vanish quickly, even in the event,
which is not perhaps very likely, of revolutionary sentiment at
the end of the war sweeping away the representatives of
extreme nationalism on both sides. Even if Poland were also a
member of the union (cf. below paras. 62–69) this would not
necessarily ease the position of the Czechs, who might fear,
with some reason, that they would be permanently placed at a
disadvantage by a Magyar-Polish combination. They would be
unlikely to join any union which did not include either
Yugoslavia or Roumania. For these reasons it is necessary (and
for many others desirable) that the membership should be
planned from the start to include some, or all, of the countries
dealt with below, although the membership of none of them is
so essential to a Danubian union as that of Hungary and
Czechoslovakia.

15. Roumania.—The culture and traditions of Roumania, including in particular those derived from the religion of
the great majority of Roumanians, are still in many respects
Balkan rather than Central European. To this extent the inclusion of Roumania would introduce into the union an area representing a different civilisation and way of life. This factor
should not, however, be over-emphasised. It derives partly from
past conditions, now no longer operative. The present-day
Roumanians prefer to think of themselves as a Danubian
rather than a Balkan people; and, in the nineteenth and even
in the early twentieth centuries, there were serious suggestions
both in Austria-Hungary and in Roumania that the then
Roumania should be incorporated in the Monarchy.

16. The Roumanian population of Transylvania also
links Roumania very closely with Central Europe. The
Transylvanian problem is discussed in greater detail in an
accompanying paper. Here only the conclusions of that discussion need be repeated. These are as follows: In view of the
strong claims and interests of both Roumania and Hungary in
Transylvania, the award of the whole area to the complete possession of one party is likely to produce lasting discontent and
hostility, open or covert, in the other. If Transylvania is given,
entire and under her full sovereignty, to Roumania, it is impos-

sible to conceive of Hungary co-operating in one unit with Roumania. In that case it is not likely that Czechoslovakia and Yugoslavia would co-operate with Hungary over such a conflict of interest against Roumania, and this would make a Danubian union impossible. If the whole of Transylvania were given to Hungary the same results would follow. Roumania would refuse to join the union and the other States would be unwilling to unite with Hungary against her.

17. The best hope of a permanent solution lies in sharing the prize, either geographically by partition or by constituting Transylvania as a separate political unit, not under the sovereignty either of Roumania or of Hungary. The rival merits of these two solutions are discussed elsewhere. In either case, the solution requires that Roumania should be a member of the Danubian union. In both cases, but especially in that of partition, this is necessary for the economic well-being of Transylvania itself, and desirable in the interests of Hungary and Roumania. In both cases also it is desirable in the interests of the Magyars and Roumanians in Transylvania. Above all, and particularly if Transylvania is constituted as a separate unit, it is necessary in order to prevent Hungary and Roumania from intriguing against the settlement. In the same union each would have less need for intrigue, since its own interests and those of its relatives in Transylvania could be better protected.

18. It is possible that the USSR might oppose Roumanian membership of a Danubian union even if her claims at Roumania's expense had been fully satisfied (cf. Document 7).

19. Austria.—The Austrian problem, again, is discussed in a separate memorandum. The inclusion of Austria in a Danubian union would be of advantage to the union in many respects. It would protect the southern frontier of the Czech area and the western frontier of Hungary, neither of which has any natural defences. It would improve communications and the possibilities of internal trade within the union, and would help to preserve the union from excessive economic dependence on Germany. It would give to the union the great cosmopolitan city and cultural centre of Vienna, in which intolerant nationalism has never been strong and in whose mixed pop-

ulation all the Danubian peoples are represented. It would give Italy a strong interest in the maintenance of the union, since Italy would wish to keep Germany from extending her influence to the Brenner.

20. On the other hand, there is the danger that Austria might become a spearhead of disruptive German influence. The inclusion of Austria in the union might give Germany a grievance, which would appear legitimate in the eyes of many Germans, against the very existence of the union. This grievance would be very widely felt if the inclusion of Austria was brought about without the most scrupulous care to ensure that it not only corresponded but had been shown to correspond with the wishes of a considerable majority of the population. Yet consultation of the Austrian people may not be possible until after an interval for recovery from Nazi domination. During this time it might be necessary to treat Austria as a separate unit under a provisional Government with Allied support.

21. Without Austria, the union would be economically and militarily weaker. This would not, however, be a reason for giving up altogether the plan for a union. It would still be capable of contributing to security in this area especially if it were so constructed as to have the goodwill of the USSR.

22. Yugoslavia.—If Yugoslavia remains a united State, her inclusion in a Danubian union would be welcomed by Croatia and Slovenia. It would ease the access of Czech and Austrian trade to Trieste and of Hungarian trade to Fiume and would provide Yugoslavia with extended markets for her agricultural products. The Danube Valley gives Serbia economic connexions with her northern neighbours; but the other links of the Serbs, cultural and historical, as well as political, are to-day rather with the east and south, and they would be unlikely to cut loose from the Balkans. Thus, if Yugoslavia retains her unity, it is very doubtful whether she would join a Danubian union unless it were enlarged to cover all Eastern Europe. Such an enlargement would result in a very loose confederation, which might not seem worth while to the other partners (see para. 28). Yugoslavia should therefore not be counted on as a member of the union, though, as suggested below (para. 83), links should be forged between the union and the Balkan areas

which might bring about a closer association between them at a later stage. The absence of Yugoslavia, as a whole, would be a serious loss to a Danubian union. It might cause the Czechs to reject all proposal for such a union (cf. para. 14).

23. It is necessary also to consider how the possibility of a break-up of Yugoslavia would affect the prospects of a Danubian union (cf. Memorandum 5 of this series, paras. 5–8). In this case Croatia and Slovenia would probably wish to join a Danubian union and should be encouraged to do so. (But see para. 28 below on the difficulty of including small units in a loose confederation). The possibility of a break-up of Yugoslavia is related to the prospects of a Danubian union in two further ways. If Roumania is not included in the union (and even perhaps to a large extent if she is) Czechoslovakia would feel her position was a weak one over against Hungary and Austria. She would therefore hesitate to join the union unless she had a counterweight to her ex-enemies. It would obviously be difficult for the victor Powers to impose on one of the United Nations a grouping in which she felt herself at a permanent disadvantage. In this respect the accession of Croatia and Slovenia might give to Czechoslovakia just the reassurance necessary; for the present legal position of the Croats as allies of Germany would not be likely to cause the Czechs to regard them, after the war, as ex-enemies. It is also probable that the existence of definite arrangements for a Danubian union would exercise so great an attraction on Croats and Slovenes as to be an additional force disruptive of the unity of Yugoslavia. For this reason such plans may be strongly resisted by champions of Yugoslav unity.

24. Bulgaria, Albania, Greece.—None of these States could well join a Danubian union unless Yugoslavia did so. For Greece and Albania, membership would be entirely impossible and for Bulgaria practically so, if Yugoslavia were not included.

III. The Form of a Danubian Union

25. The possible forms of union between States in this area were examined in a previous memorandum (C. E. E., paras. 36–69) in relation to the Polish-Czechoslovak and Greek-Yugoslav Confederations. The arguments advanced in that con-

text are all applicable equally to a Danubian union and are therefore not restated here. Some of their implications may, however, be noted.

26. Many of the ends suggested as desirable (cf. paras. 1–4 above and 29–42 below) could be effectively achieved only if there was considerable central control, though in each case even a loose confederation would make some, though perhaps only a slight, contribution to their achievement. Claims to territory which are based on economic or strategic security in relation to another member of the union clearly lose their validity proportionately with the closeness of the relations between the member-States. Only in a close union could the full military and economic value of union be attained, or minorities effectively protected.

27. Yet even in a loose confederation some added degree of security and economic efficiency would be achieved and the external fomentation of minority problems might be diminished.

28. If a loose confederation were the maximum possible, this would affect the problem of membership in two different ways. It would be difficult for small units such as Slovenia or Slovakia to be separate members of such a confederation. The cost to them of maintaining a State machine, their weakness, and in some cases their backwardness, would handicap them very greatly (cf. C. E. E., paras. 25–29, 56). It may also be suggested that, if the confederation is to be a very loose one anyhow, there is no point in limiting it to the Danubian States. It would be better in many respects if it included all the States between the Baltic and the Aegean Seas (cf. below, paras. 30, 41, 82).

IV. The Desirability of a Danubian Confederation

29. Some of the arguments in favour of a Danubian Confederation would be valid also in support of other groupings of States in the area between Germany and the USSR. Some may be adduced in favour of this particular grouping as contrasted with others.

30. Strategically the object of any grouping would be to

create a unit capable of deterring an aggressor and serving as a safeguard against the piecemeal destruction of the independence of its constituent States. For this purpose a single union stretching from the Baltic to the Aegean would naturally be the most adequate solution if it were practicable. The only special advantage of a Danubian union in this field might be that it should be easier to get four or five States to collaborate effectively than eight or nine. Yet when the four or five include countries hostile to each other this argument is not necessarily conclusive. The addition of countries which have no bones of contention with all or most States in the area might even make collaboration easier. This is especially true in the case of Poland, whose inclusion from the standpoint of military strength is, in any case, desirable not only in Poland's own interest, but also in that of the union itself (cf. paras. 62–69).

31. The special field in which a Danubian union has a case stronger than that for other groupings is the social and political field. In Danubia populations are so intermingled and the difficulties of separating them by adequate frontiers so great that genuine union in this area should greatly diminish the dangers arising from frontier disputes, irredentas, and potentially subversive minorities. Except in the case of Teschen, where the dispute affects a relatively small population, Poland has no such difficulties in relation to Danubian States. Moreover, among the various frontiers which might bound a Danubian union on the south there are at least three (the Austro-Yugoslav, Roumano-Yugoslav and Roumano-Bulgarian) which raise no serious problems.

32. Irredentism and minority problems would still remain on some of the external frontiers of the union and the position of German and Jewish minorities would not necessarily be alleviated by the union's existence. But the inherently greater strength of such a union would make its German minorities less of a danger and would make to opportunities for them or their kinsmen in Germany to play off one people against another less than they would be if the area were divided into independent States. The existence of a union might also ultimately reduce the spirit of nationalism which is the

principal menace to minorities of all kinds.

33. If a Danubian grouping were adopted, the chances of political co-operation and social progress should be increased by the fact that the peoples have inherited from the Habsburg Empire some degree of common civilisation and a common way of life (though this would not extend to the same degree to the old kingdoms of Roumania and Serbia, if they were to be included).

34. The economic aspects of union are dealt with in a separate memorandum and need only summary treatment here. In general, three types of advantage might be expected: Areas producing similar products might have a combined selling policy. Areas producing different products might increase their exchange of goods. There might be possibilities for planned development in transport, industry and agriculture.

35. The first advantage would be slight. It is in relation to agricultural produce that the problem of export outlets has in the past had most serious consequences. The additional bargaining power to be gained by joint export marketing plans for Danubia would do little to strengthen its position, since its main competitors in grain lie outside the area and start with great advantages. Even Germany, the nearest and most natural single market for such exports, would be able in peace time to draw supplies from overseas if combinations in Danubia attempted to raise prices against her. If, however, Germany wished to revive her practice of paying prices above world levels for Danubian exports, there would be nothing in the existence of a Danubian union to prevent this.

36. It is also suggested by some authorities that the problem of Danubian exports may diminish after the war. It is argued that, on any reasonable standards of nutrition, the Danubian area could consume much more of its own food production, especially if the cereal areas were reduced and agriculture were diversified and supplemented by local food-finishing industries. It is suggested that these industries, and others newly developed in the area, might produce alternative exports which would enable the area to maintain its imports of the goods previously exchanged for cereal exports. These reasonable standards could, however, be attained only if Danubia's

production as a whole was greatly increased. This could be achieved either by substituting home-produced goods for former imports (provided that agricultural production was not decreased to an equivalent extent) or by developing new commodities for export.

37. The manufacturing industries of Austria and Czechoslovakia should find a broader basis of demand if they had free entry to the markets of the other members of a Danubian union, and could thus develop more beneficial trading relations with other States in the area than have existed hitherto. This would not, however, dispense altogether with the need for the markets outside the Danubian area which have been developed in the past and might be further developed in the future.

38. It is said against this that the proposed trading relations would have no welcome anywhere. Czechoslovakia and Austria had both developed their own agricultural production before the war, and the "agricultural" countries had developed industries producing just those consumer goods in which Czechoslovakia and Austria had been pre-eminent. It would also be difficult to disentangle Czech and Austrian industry from German control, though in the case of Czech industry this will have to be done in any case.

39. In reply to these objections it may, however, be said that in Austria the development of agriculture was an artificial policy forced on her by circumstances; and in Czechoslovakia a policy of self-sufficiency was made possible largely by the inclusion of the Magyar-inhabited areas on the southern fringe of Slovakia and Ruthenia. It is also important that the consumer-goods industries of Austria and Czechoslovakia have been greatly curtailed during the war, and their factories have fallen derelict or been switched over to heavy industry, to serve German war-production policy. If this last tendency were prolonged into the post-war period, these areas might become suppliers of machinery, machine tools, (c., to Danubia. A certain revival in the production of the fine quality consumer-goods, for which Austria especially was noted, would not involve serious competition with industries producing consumer-goods of lower quality more recently established in Hungary or Roumania.

40. It is clear, however, that the intensification of economic relations and co-operation in Danubia would not be an automatic process. It will depend on the policies adopted outside the area, e.g., by the United States, Great Britain and Germany, on the policies, industrial and agricultural, adopted or encouraged in the various countries of the union, and on the location of different types of industry surviving or planned after the war. But the direction of all these plans and policies should from the start be such as to facilitate co-operation in the area and to bring about conditions which would make political union more practicable.

41. In the economic field, however, the special case for a Danubian Union, as contrasted with other groupings, is not strong. The economic benefits to be hoped for from it would be still more probable if there could be economic co-operation between all the States from the Baltic to the Aegean. If economic measures alone are practicable (cf. below, paras. 61, 80–82) this wider area should be taken as their basis. In particular there is a strong economic argument for including Poland with the Danubian States in one economic unit (cf. below para. 68).

42. An indirect advantage of economic collaboration is that it encourages a habit which might spread into the political field or make the difficulties arising there easier to surmount. This effect might be of considerable importance even if the purely economic gains were slight.

V. The Practicability of a Danubian Confederation

43. The creation of the union sketched above would necessarily involve severer birth-pangs than the foundation of either the Polish-Czechoslovak or the Greek-Yugoslav Confederation. These two unions are being negotiated between allies and partners in misfortune, who have, moreover, comparatively few bones of contention between them. Once it is proposed to unite peoples with large conflicting claims, such as Magyars and Roumanians, or long-standing mutual hostility, such as Magyars and Czechs, a much more difficult situation arises. It is particularly difficult when the union has to be sponsored by

outside Powers, of whom some of the peoples concerned are friends and allies, while others are declared enemies.

44. Nevertheless, it is clear that no stability for the future can be expected unless all parties to the union enter it on an equal footing. So far, therefore, as permanent arrangements are concerned, there is no possible principle other than that of strict equality in planning for the future, e.g., in the assessment of economic needs. The first consideration must be the future, not the past (though this does not exclude specific measures of redress for specific acts committed, e.g., some form of redress by Hungary for her attack on Yugoslavia).[61] While the feelings arising from the past cannot be completely left out of account, it should be recognised that no country can be expected to be a loyal member of a union unless the terms on which she is admitted are such as to leave no permanent sense of irreparable injustice. Thus, as between rival and irreconcilable claims, there would have to be at least some degree of justice for all parties, and therefore also inevitably concessions by all.

45. Besides the difficulties in achieving a union noted above (para. 43), there is a special difficulty in its adoption as an immediate post-war policy. Only some of the peoples concerned are represented by Governments in exile, and with the others no preliminary negotiations are possible before hostilities in Europe end. Even the Governments in exile may be uncertain of their post-war hold over their own peoples, and, therefore, unable or unwilling to negotiate regarding limitations of their post-war sovereignty or concessions to their present enemies.

46. If Danubian union is to be achieved, it would, therefore, be essential that outside Powers should take the first steps. It would be necessary for Great Britain to reach provisional agreement with the United States and the USSR on the desirability of such a union, on the areas to be included in it, and on the order of procedure in bringing it about. Without such prior agreement the whole project would be unworkable.

47. Agreement with the USSR at this early stage would be essential for many reasons. The peoples in this area are divided in their attitude to the USSR, and if the plan had not got her goodwill the area might easily be disrupted into pro-Soviet and anti-Soviet elements, and the USSR might intervene in the

internal politics of States whose régimes she disliked. The co-
operation of the USSR, in the construction of any union in this
area would be desirable in order to disarm the suspicion with
which she appears to regard all confederations. Otherwise,
Britain and the United States might be forced into a choice
between giving up their plans for union here and pushing them
through against Soviet opposition.

48. The inclusion of these preliminary discussions of the
Allied Governments in exile would be necessary, both because
secrecy would be impossible and because exclusion would antag-
onise them. It would, however, be impossible (in view of the difficulties noted in para. 45 above) for these Governments to enter
into any formal commitments, through they might make agreements to be subsequently ratified by their Parliaments.

49. At the conclusion of hostilities in Europe, forces of
the United Nations would presumably be in occupation (partial
or complete) of the Danubian area. At this time the Governments of Great Britain, the United States and the USSR should
send forces, in the name of the United Nations, to occupy and
administer areas within the Danubian region lying between the
pre-1938 frontiers and the frontiers most recently in operation.
This is particularly important in the interests of the inhabitants
of these debated areas. These forces should not include representatives of any State directly interested in the fate of the territory occupied. Since some Danubian peoples will regard Soviet
forces as coming within this category (owing to Soviet partiality
for some of the competing claimants), they will be strongly hostile to their use as occupation forces. Their presence will, however, presumably be inevitable, if the USSR is to co-operate fully
in the plan. The most that the objectors could possibly hope for
is that the forces in each area should be mixed, that the Soviet
element might be reduced to token dimensions where USSR is
impartial as between the contesting claimants.

50. At the same time a United Nation Commission
would have to take the economic measures necessary for relief
and reconstruction.

51. Meantime, as soon as any Government is so firmly
established in its own country that it and the other Powers can
feel confident of its stability, direct negotiations should be

opened between it and the major Allies on the bases of the plans which the latter have provisionally agreed. These negotiations should continue until Governments in all the States proposed for membership of the union have been approached.

52. In this context there is likely to be a special problem. It would probably be generally agreed that negotiations could not be opened with those same Governments which have committed their States to policies of alliance with the Axis or aggression against their neighbours. Nor are such Governments likely to survive an Allied victory. But when successor Governments are established, the question will arise whether the three major Allies should negotiate with all of them or only with such of them as are held by their neighbours or the USSR to be "non-Fascist" in character. This type of limitation has already been put forward in Czechoslovak circles and is likely to be supported by the USSR. While precautions are obviously needed against the premature recognition of new Governments differing only in outward show from their aggressive or pro-Axis predecessors, it is also clear that a refusal to negotiate which operated as a veto on successive Governments until one sufficiently "co-operative" (or subservient) was installed would be unlikely to bring about stable conditions allowing of a satisfactory settlement. This is a general problem beyond the scope of the present paper, but it is again one on which failure to reach some prior understanding with the USSR would be likely to destroy plans for union.

53. The final stage, if negotiations with all the several Danubian Governments gave sufficient hopes of success, would be the summoning of their representatives to a conference, before which the plans for union and invitations to enter it would be laid.

54. The most unpredictable factor in the above procedure is the time which would have to elapse between the end of hostilities in Europe and the summoning of the conference. This inevitable interval will raise in any case, besides other questions, the difficult problem of frontiers.

55. Any measure of unification which removes the military menace on frontiers within a union and opens these frontiers to movements of men and goods should greatly affect ter-

ritorial claims which rest on strategic or economic grounds. Accordingly the theoretically ideal time for fixing frontiers would be after it is clear whether such a union is feasible.

56. But if the conference summoned to accept a union is long delayed, this would mean that Allied Powers, with great commitments elsewhere, would have during the whole of this interval to occupy the disputed areas mentioned above (para. 49). They would have to take full responsibility for the method and the ultimate control of justice and administration. While their selection of the law to be enforced and their necessary use of local administrative organs would inevitably bias the situation in favour of one claimant, the grant of full authority over the area to one claimant would prejudice the ultimate position still more, would probably lead to great personal hardship for many of the inhabitants and would be correspondingly resented by the other claimant.

57. The only alternative to a protracted occupation by Allied forces would be the imposition of definitive frontiers before the prospects of union were known, and the authorisation of the States concerned to bring under their complete sovereignty the areas allotted to them. The immediate imposition of definitive frontiers with a view to ultimate union raises the danger that frontiers suitable to partners in a union might prove unpractical if union failed to materialise. Moreover, the satisfaction on any frontier of the full claims of one party would probably make its rival refuse to join with it in a union. Thus, the achievement of a union would involve some concessions by all countries in the area. (Cf. para. 44.) These could be imposed by the United Nations on their ex-enemies, but the Great Powers would also have the difficult task of persuading some of their Allies to abandon territories to which they have claims or even legal rights.

58. It might be suggested that frontiers should be laid down provisionally, subject to revision if and when a union is achieved. But this would not satisfy the rival claimants nor would it make the negotiation of a union easier, since frontier questions are, of all questions, the most difficult to settle by negotiation.

59. A special problem arises over Transylvania. While it

does not, at present, raise the issue of Allies versus enemies, it is otherwise more complex than all the rest. Here it would be particularly difficult to lay down a definitive solution if union were envisaged but its prospects not fully known. For some solutions would so offend either Hungary or Roumania as to make a union including both impossible (cf. paper 3 of this series, paras. 15, 16, 21, 25). Others require such a union if they are to be possible or effective (cf. Document 4, paras. 29, 43). If a plan for union had been provisionally agreed to, it might perhaps be thought desirable, after the cessation of hostilities in Europe, to declare Transylvania an independent State and then later to invite her to the conference with the others. Yet the rival claims are so violently maintained, and the feelings between the various peoples in Transylvania itself are likely to be so embittered, that its frontiers and administration would probably require Allied control. In this case, therefore, the advantage of imposing an immediate solution—the possibility of terminating Allied occupation (cf. para. 57)—would not after all be achieved. There might thus be a special case in Transylvania, even if nowhere else, for maintaining Allied control until the chances of union are sufficiently known.

60. In view of the relations between possible members of the union it is unlikely that anything closer than a confederation of the type envisaged by the Greek-Yugoslav Agreement would be immediately acceptable to the peoples concerned. In this case there might be a case for extending the confederation beyond the Danubian area (cf. paras. 28, 30, 41). It might also seem that the slight value of a loose confederation would make it hardly worth the effort needed to achieve it. This point however, would be less strong if it could be hoped that loose confederation would lead on, as has happened before, to a greater degree of co-operation and central control. It might also be helped to develop into something more effective by the measures suggested in paras. 78–82 below.

61. On a review of all the factors, the possibility must be faced that political union of any kind will be impracticable in the immediate post-war period between peoples divided by so many antagonisms as are the Danubian peoples to-day. The preliminary discussions and negotiations suggested above (paras.

46–48, 51) might also lead to this result. But, if immediate union is unpracticable, it does not follow that the quest for it should be abandoned. On the contrary, the end of the war will provide a unique opportunity to pave the way for eventual union by creating conditions which might later make it both desirable and practicable. By these means its peoples might be led into the reality of union without its name. Some of the conditions which could thus be created are indicated below (paras. 78–82).

VI. The Northern and Southern Neighbours of The Confederation

62. Poland.—As is said above (para. 8), all these plans can and should be made on the assumption that Poland can be included or not, according to her own wishes. The present Polish Government appears to favour Poland's inclusion in a union with Czechoslovakia, Hungary and Roumania. Poland would add to the military strength of the confederation and she might help to mediate between the Czechoslovaks (with whom she has a tradition of friendship). Czechoslovakia in her turn might help to improve relations between Poland and the USSR. Poland is also linked to the Danubian region by her Catholic religion and by the fact that the one area where Poles shared in their own Government before 1914 was that included in the Austro-Hungarian Empire. Seeing that active pressure for confederation has recently come more from the Poles than from any other people, it would be a poor recompense for their foresight if they could not ultimately be included.

63. On the other hand, there are elements in Poland's geographical position and in her previous economic contacts which have placed her rather apart from the Danubian area. She is a large State compared with the others and has better prospects than most of them of achieving ultimately a stable economy. Moreover, the present negotiations with the Czechoslovaks seem to be encountering great difficulties, and the USSR (which seems generally suspicious of all confederations) might view a Danubian union with less aversion if it did not include Poland. This suspicion might be lessened if the USSR

got a frontier with the new Poland lying far to the west of the pre-1939 line. Any plans to include in a new Poland purely German territories (even East Prussia) would certainly subject her, even more than before, to lasting German resentment. If she belonged to a union, the whole union would be involved in this quarrel.

64. The main issue is that of security. Placed as she is with open frontiers between Germany and the USSR, Poland would be weak in isolation and liable to fall either under German or under Russian domination. This would be a serious threat not only to her own independence but also to the security of a union to the south of her. It was characteristic of Polish-Czechoslovak relations before the present war that the Poles felt relieved when aggressive German designs were directed against Czechoslovakia; and even in the latter State, though its Government always interpreted German aims more realistically, some degree of relief was felt when Germany's designs appeared to be directed against Poland. A union which included them both would signalise the abandonment of this attitude and prevent its recurrence.

65. Poland might be strengthened by a general security system; but, apart from this, only her southern neighbours can give her support. It is unlikely that she can hope to have the Baltic States as partners or even Lithuania only, nor would they be of much value to her. If her confederation with Czechoslovakia becomes a reality worth counting on, it should therefore be used as a foundation for any plans for union in the Danubian area.

66. One obstacle to its achievement (apart from the attitude of the USSR) has been a tariff difficulty, which might be diminished in a wider union. If, however, close economic co-operation remained unattainable, a security association between Poland and the Danubian union might be possible, perhaps by the implementation of the military clauses of the Polish-Czechoslovak Agreement. A mere alliance between Poland and Danubia would be open to outside disruptive influences, which a more thorough "mixing up" might be more easily able to resist. This could include pooled and standardised munitions manufacture, a joint general staff, joint manoeuvres and

defence plans and shared aerodromes and naval bases. The United States-Canadian Defence Board and the present arrangements between the United States and Great Britain show the value of such machinery, even when the partners remain politically only allies and are not confederated.

67. If even this limited form of co-operation could not be achieved and if the first steps towards union were economic (cf. paras. 80–82), Poland and Danubia might in the first instance be treated separately. Poland will probably acquire Western aid on a far greater scale than other areas. Moreover, transport and communications will be the sphere first requiring unified control; and, in this sphere, it would be essential to treat Danubia as a unit but quite natural for Poland to be organised separately.

68. Yet, on the longer view, there is one strong economic argument for including Poland in a Danubian union. There seem to be good reasons for a rather complex division of functions between Upper Silesia and Bohemia-Moravia (not unlike that between the Ruhr and Saxony), an arrangement which policies of economic nationalism would prevent.

69. If in course of time economic links in Danubia developed into political union, it might also by then have become clear how far Poland's strategic position could be remedied by a general security system or by alliances, or whether confederation with Danubia was a vital necessity for her. The attitude and intentions of the USSR might also by then have been so clarified as to help the solution of this problem.

70. The Southern Neighbours.—[Note. The future of the Balkan area is not directly relevant to this paper and has not yet been fully discussed by the Foreign Research and Press Service. The following sections are therefore put forward tentatively, and include only a few points, general and specific, on which the existence of a Danubian union might have repercussions further south.]

71. In general, it is clear that strategically the existence of a Danubian union would help to protect its southern neighbours from attack by Germany. Politically, it might accentuate some of their difficulties. Economically, the Balkan area should be included along with the Danubian area in future plans for economic co-operation.

72. The southern neighbours of the Danubian union might unite in a Balkan Confederation based on the Greek-Yugoslav agreement. But the necessary inclusion of Roumania or of all or part of Yugoslavia in a Danubian union (cf. paras. 14, 22) would considerably weaken a Balkan Confederation, while the absence from it of both Yugoslavia and Roumania would reduce the possible members to Turkey, Bulgaria, Greece and Albania, and would prevent the confederation from helping to solve the Macedonian problem.

73. If Roumania is included neither in a Danubian nor in a Balkan Confederation, the probability of her falling under Soviet domination is very greatly increased. In this case also the Transylvanian problem becomes much more difficult, and partition might be the only possible solution of it (cf. document (4) of this series, paras. 18–29). The creation of a completely independent buffer State of Transylvania would not be a promising solution (cf. document (4), para. 43).

74. If Yugoslavia remained outside the Danubian union, and if there were no Balkan confederation, Yugoslavia would be likely to co-operate either with Greece to the detriment of Bulgaria or with Bulgaria to the detriment of Greece. The latter alternative would be rendered more probable if Yugoslavia broke up and the Croats and Slovenes joined the Danubian union. In this case Serbs and Bulgars might well unite, even in a single State (cf. document 5 of this series, paras. 15, 16); and Greece would then be isolated and would regard her northern frontier as in serious danger.

75. As with Poland in the north, so with Greece in the south, the main problem would be one of security. Unless she feels safe within her frontiers and in no danger from irredentism in Thrace and Macedonia, she must regard any plan which might tend to leave her isolated with apprehension. So far as the plan for a Danubian union may well tend to detach the Croats and the Slovenes from the Serbs (cf. para. 23) and thus to bring together the Serbs and the Bulgars, this would be its effect.

76. Great Britain will have to give special attention to the fate of Greece, always our friend and tied to us by common maritime interests. If she were left in a position of isolation, she

would have to be included in a Mediterranean security system organised by the United Nations. She might also find special support from Turkey, who would probably regard a Serb-Bulgar union with equal suspicion, especially as it might become a field of Soviet influence.

77. The weakest position of all would be that of Albania. Even in a Balkan Confederation she would be a weak unit; and if she were a member of no union it would seem likely that only some special form of Western aid would save her from partition between her neighbours.

VII. Steps towards Danubian Union

78. It has been suggested above (para. 61) that even if no form of political union is immediately possible, conditions which might ultimately make it practicable could nevertheless be established at once.

79. A political settlement could be achieved which eliminated as far as possible the seeds of permanent and irremediable hostility between Danubian peoples. This would involve concessions by all of them (cf. paras. 44, 57), and could not be built on the principle of the maximum satisfaction of the claims of particular States.

80. It might also be considered whether closer union could not be achieved by machinery specially devised to meet the immediate economic needs of the Danubian area, rather than by too close an attachment to constitutional forms of the traditional type. If economic assistance is granted by the United States and Great Britain they might well promote the establishment of some central body with temporary powers over the whole area. The administrative organs necessary for reconstruction and relief would function much better if there were some central political authority also responsible for local order, tariffs and communications. It might be possible to secure the creation of such a body with the consent of the several States to which administrative boards might report. If this scheme were put forward as temporary but necessary to secure adequate outside assistance, it might subsequently develop into a more permanent form. Clearly no such end could be achieved without

considerable pressure and persuasion from outside.

81. If such a single central body were not practicable, the maximum number of common economic administrative organs, cutting across political frontiers, should be created, revived or encouraged. These also would have to be subject to the control of the Great Powers in the first period after hostilities, but they might conceivably develop into common organs maintained by Danubian co-operation and leading on the Danubian union.

82. These economic plans might, however, be more effective in many cases if they extended beyond the Danubian area; and in that case the political union to which they led need not necessarily be Danubian. So long as nothing more than loose confederation is possible in the area, a single unit reaching from the Baltic to the Aegean might be the best goal, and a Danubian Confederation would have few special advantages over the Northern and Southern confederations examined in the previous memorandum. But if close union is ever in sight, its application to the whole area would be the most remote possibility; and there are ethnic and political issues which would benefit more from close union in Danubia than in the two confederations previously examined. As an ultimate possibility, even if not as an immediate goal of policy, therefore, a close Danubian union remains worthy of consideration.

Foreign Research and Press Service,
Balliol College, Oxford,
January 1, 1943.

DOCUMENT 7

The Attitude of the USSR

I. Introduction

1. The attitude which the USSR may take up towards the future of East-Central Europe i.e., of the lands between its own western frontiers and the eastern borders of the future Germany and Italy, presents a series of problems on which only mere flickers of light have been thrown from Soviet sources, either in public statements or in privately-conveyed hints. At the present stage all that can be done is to set down some factors which, since they will affect the Soviet approach to East-Central Europe in the post-war period, must be kept in mind in any plans elaborated for the settlement of the area.

2. In the present paper an attempts is made to estimate the possible interests of the USSR in the area, and then to consider how far these interests would be affected by schemes for confederation in the area and how far they could be met in such schemes.

3. It is imaginable that the USSR might look to a coalition with Germany after the war as the best way to secure her interests in Europe. This policy would be a more obvious one if Germany became Communist and its adoption would give the USSR a motive to turn the German revolution in a Communist direction. But under these circumstances East-Central Europe would be engulfed by the German-Soviet coalition, and it would be useless to consider, from the point of view of British policy, how Soviet interests in the area could be met. This possibility is, therefore, excluded from the discussion in the present paper.

II. USSR Interests in East-Central Europe

4. USSR interests may be classed as strategic economic, and political; but in view of the great difficulty, especially in discussing USSR policy, of distinguishing economic and strategic interests from political interests, the terms "strategic" and "economic" will be used below in a narrow and strict sense. "Strategic" will be used to cover only security from the threat of actual military, naval or air attack; "economic" to cover security of standard of living, markets, supplies, and trade routes. All other interests will be classed together as political.

Strategic Interests

5. The only strategic threat to the USSR that can come from the west is one from Germany, either acting alone or in combination with the Western Powers. In either case the USSR will have a strategic interest in the protection of her western land frontier. To meet a possible attack by Germany alone, she will have a further strategic interest in maintaining her lines of contact, round Germany's flanks, with the outer world to the west of Germany.

6. The course of the present war has shown the relative unimportance of the actual strength of land frontiers and the vulnerable nature of advanced bases not capable of immediate and massive support. It is, therefore, possible that the USSR will not make a special point of acquiring western frontiers having intrinsic natural strength (such as the Carpathian Mountains) or wish to establish bases for land warfare on the territory of its western neighbours. But the value of maintaining a land frontier far removed from vital centres of production and communication has been, on the whole, confirmed by events; and it is therefore probable that the USSR will wish to retain such "glacis" territories as would shelter Leningrad, Moscow and the Donetz region from immediate attack. This would involve a claim to substantial territory from Finland and to the retention of the Baltic States, of most of the Polish territory occupied in 1939, and of Bessarabia.

7. Apart from these territorial claims, the USSR is likely to have a strategic interest in the future of East Prussia

(always the advanced base for German attacks on Russia) and in the mouths of the Danube. In neither case, however, is this interest likely to involve further territorial claims. The USSR would probably support Polish annexation of East Prussia and insist on Soviet representation on any international Danube River authority.

8. The routes from the Soviet Union to the outside world in the west are the northern route round (or across) Norway, the Baltic route, and the Black Sea-Mediterranean route. Sections of these routes nearest its own territory, such as the Gulf of Finland and the Black Sea, may be regarded by the USSR as "home waters" over which it is entitled to claim effective control. This might require Soviet bases on the eastern shore of the Baltic, in Finnish, Estonian, Latvian and/or Lithuanian territory, and on the western shore of the Black Sea, in Roumanian and/or Bulgarian territory. At more remote points, where contact with the west is made (such as the North Cape, Narvik, the Baltic entrance and the Eastern Mediterranean), the Soviet Government might be satisfied by a system of joint bases under Anglo-Saxon-Soviet control, as a security measure against Germany. For (as suggested above, para. 5) these routes would be of value to the Soviet Union only if Germany's attack upon it had not got the support of the Western Powers.

Economic Interests

9. The USSR is likely to have few purely economic interests in East-Central Europe. The area is of little importance to the Soviet Union for material supplies, for markets, or for trade routes. Nor would alterations in the standard of living of the area have economic repercussion in the USSR. But the economic structure and development of East-Central Europe might well have political implications for the Soviet Union. These are dealt with below (paras. 15, 16).

Political Interests

10. It might be supposed that the USSR would have an interest in the extension of the Communist revolution to her western neighbours, on ideological grounds. The Comintern idea has, however, dropped into the background of Soviet policy in recent years; and internal developments in the USSR (especially the emergence of Russian nationalism) suggest that this tendency may be permanent. Yet the Comintern policy is too useful a weapon ever to be renounced outright, and an appearance of Anglo-Saxon economic domination of East-Central Europe might bring about its revival (cf. paras. 3, 15, 35).

11. The Soviet Government would be likely, in any case, to lend its support to extreme radical ("people's") régimes, which, without leading their countries into membership of the Soviet Union, might yet be counted upon to regard it as their protector.

12. It is certainly a political interest of the USSR that East-Central Europe, as a whole, should not fall under German political domination, and that individual States in the area should not again serve as points d'appui for German pressure or aggression.

13. While, however, the fear of Germany will remain as a long-term pre-occupation, it is likely that, in the period immediately after the war, the USSR will demand, and will participate in, such reduction of German power that it can relegate this particular menace to a distant future. This tendency will be strengthened by the recognition that few of the liberated peoples of East-Central Europe will be likely to look to Germany for support soon after the war, and that any who do could probably be kept in order by their violently anti-German neighbours.

14. Under these circumstances, with the German danger removed, the USSR might conceivably regard Anglo-Saxon political influence in East-Central Europe as a danger more immediate than German domination of the area. The legacy of past suspicion may cause this fear to take two different forms.

15. The USSR may suspect that (short of armed invasion) the Western Powers might use their economic hold on East-Central Europe to threaten the internal system of the

Soviet Union. But, if Soviet information on Anglo-Saxon opinion
is at all adequate, it should be possible to convince the Soviet
Government that neither in Britain nor in the United States
are there any ideas or intentions that would give any such fear
a real basis. In both countries there will be powerful movements
to withdraw from positive intervention in East-Central Europe
altogether. In any case, an attempts to upset the internal system of the Soviet Union could succeed only by armed invasion.
For the USSR is too powerful and too self-sufficient for German
methods of peaceful penetration by economic pressure or by
"tourists and technicians" to have any hope of success.

    16. Perhaps the most plausible form of Soviet suspicion
might be a fear that the existence of an area, revived and flourishing through Western aid, just across the Soviet border, would
bring the Soviet people into too close proximity to an effective
non-Communist economy, and thus cause internal unrest in the
Union itself, even though this result was no part of the aim of
the Western Powers. The justification for this fear would
depend on the sharpness of the contrast between the two
economies. In so far as Western capitalism, when applied to the
reconstruction of East-Central Europe, lost some of its features
most obnoxious to Communist critics (such as control by private
enterprise primarily in the interests of Western shareholders),
and in so far as Soviet institutions involved less restriction on
the Soviet people after the war, the danger would be lessened.
While it is likely that the contrast between peasant ownership
and collective farming would remain to give the fear some sub-
stance, it may also be recalled that the Soviet Government has
been able so far to preserve its peoples to a remarkable degree
from the infiltration of knowledge even about contiguous peoples.

III. Confederations and Soviet Interests

    17. It is now possible to consider how far the existence
of confederations in East-Central Europe would further or
would threaten the interests of the Soviet Union suggested
above.

Confederations and Strategic Interests

18. The strategic demands of the Soviet Union (cf. paras. 5–8 above) will remain completely unaffected by the existence of combinations of States in East-Central Europe.

19. Bases for control of the essential routes to the outside world (whether under joint occupation or exclusively Soviet authority) will be demanded whether or not the States within whose territory they lie belong to such combinations. The demand for Soviet bases on the western Black Sea coast is likely to be made easier to satisfy because of the probable pro-Soviet attitude of Bulgaria after the war.

20. Similarly, territorial demands (or claims to bases for land warfare situated on the territory of neighbouring States) are likely to be made equally strongly whether or not the States against whom these demands are directed belong to confederations.

Confederations and Economic Interests

21. Since purely economic developments in East-Central Europe would affect hardly at all any economic interest of the USSR, it follows that the Soviet Government need find no difficulty in accepting plans for economic unification in this area, so far as markets, material supplies and trade routes are concerned. The possible political implications of such unification are considered below (paras. 33–37).

Confederations and Political Interests

22. While it thus appears that plans for confederation in East-Central Europe would leave unaffected the strictly strategic or economic interests of the USSR the political field presents difficult problems.

23. If the Comintern policy were to be revived (cf. para. 10), it would obviously be easier for the Soviet Union to develop this policy if the States in East-Central Europe were disunited and could be dealt with one by one, or played off one against another. Since, however, it seems more probable that this policy

would remain in abeyance, and be revived only if some other political interest of the USSR seemed threatened, measures to minimise its dangers are most likely to succeed if they are indirect and are devised to remove fears and suspicions arising out of the other political interests examined below.

24. For security against Germany, unification in East-Central Europe is the best possible safeguard for the USSR, however difficult it may be to persuade the Soviet Government to recognise this. For the alternative policy it might adopt would be that of creating satellite States on its own Western frontiers, bound to it by military alliances and also perhaps by the characteristics of their internal political régimes (cf. para. 11). But this is a game at which Germany can also play; and it is a dangerous game for the USSR because the number of peoples who could be expected to welcome the role. of Soviet satellite is probably less than that of those who would reject such a role. In the former group only Czechs, Serbs and Bulgars can be included with any probability; while among Poles, Croats, Slovenes, Magyars, Roumanians, and even Slovaks there are likely to be dominant elements of resistance to Soviet control. In the absence of any political unification in the area, this latter group of peoples would then tend to fall in the long run under German influence, if Soviet protection were their only alternative.

25. The majority of the peoples in the area would not wish to fall either under German or Soviet control. If there were unions among these peoples, this desire to avoid dependence on either great neighbour, reinforced by the existing balance of anti-German feeling, should be enough to guarantee the USSR that no such union would fall as a whole under German control.

26. Thus, with the aim of resisting German domination of the area, the USSR would find its best safeguard in solid combinations of the States included in the area. But it is likely that, if the USSR attempted to bring any such unit directly under its own influence, the solidity of the unit would be disrupted into pro-Soviet and anti-Soviet elements and the danger from Germany greatly increased (cf. para. 24 above). The protection afforded to the USSR by such solid combinations, independent both of German and of USSR control, would be further strengthened by any general security system which would offer

the USSR or any confederation guarantees against renewed
German aggression.

27. While it might be possible to convince the USSR that
any confederation would be unlikely to become a tool of German
aggression, there would remain the possible suspicion that such
confederations might operate as solid units under the control of
Britain or the United States.

28. In the past, Soviet policy has followed lines laid
down by centuries of Russian history and by the geographical
relationship between the main centres of Russian life and those
of other powerful neighbours. Up to the 18th century the power-
relationship in Eastern Europe was dominated by the balance of
forces between Russia, Sweden, Turkey and Poland; later
between Russia, Prussia, Turkey and Austria-Hungary; and
from the later years of the 19th century between Russia and the
two Central Empires. Soviet statesmen may fear that after the
present war the place of Germany will be taken by the Anglo-
Saxon Powers; and any proposed combination of the smaller
States in East-Central Europe, launched under the aegis of
those Powers, may well appear designed as a check on Soviet
influence in that area, if not as a direct threat to Soviet security.

29. The position of the USSR vis-a-vis Britain and the
United States will be influenced by the fact that the greater part
of the money, material and personnel needed for reconstruction
in East-Central Europe will have to be supplied by the Anglo-
Saxon Powers. Soviet Russia, owing to its own internal needs
and its relatively lower standard of development will be unable
to help much in this field and will reap little of the prestige that
the rendering of such services will create.

30. Soviet fears of Anglo-Saxon dominance over this
area may be met in two different ways: by detailed adjustments
in the constitution and membership of the proposed confederations, or by reducing the general suspicions of the Western
Powers which lie behind these special fears concerning East-
Central Europe.

31. The first detailed point on which the Soviet
Government might wish to influence plans for confederations is
the question of the membership of Poland. Any solution of the
Polish-Soviet frontier issue which satisfies the Soviet Union is

likely to leave strong anti-Soviet feeling widespread among certain circles in Poland, though the influence of these circles may prove to be a diminishing factor in the situation. If there were unions elsewhere in East-Central Europe, excluding Poland and including no State likely to harbour lasting grievances against the USSR, the Soviet Government might view with equanimity the survival of anti-Soviet feeling in Poland. For a Poland thus isolated would have to depend for support on a general security system in which the USSR itself would play a leading part; or, if such a general security system were ineffective (or believed to be so by Poland), she could turn only to Germany for support, and this alternative would be unlikely, at least for several generations, to be welcomed by Poles. Soviet coolness towards the Polish-Czechoslovak Confederation seems due mainly to a fear that the Czechs might support Poland in her frontier dispute with the USSR (though Czechoslovak representatives have repeatedly affirmed their own neutrality on this issue); and there is also evidence that the Poles themselves reckon that they are likely to get a better deal if they are members of a bloc than if they negotiate alone.

32. A second detailed point on which the USSR might have preferences is that of the distribution of the peoples of East-Central Europe in various possible combinations. On the whole, it is probable that the plan for two unions—a Central Confederation excluding Poland and a Balkan confederation—would be less unwelcome to the USSR than any possible alternative. For a single union covering the whole area would appear in itself a greater menace than two smaller units; and in such a single union pro-Soviet elements would be unlikely to be dominant. The latter point would also be true of a Danubian Union. But if there were two unions, the USSR might have good prospects of exerting a dominating influence at least in the Balkan Confederation through her relations with the Serbs and Bulgars (and it is in the Balkan area that she is mainly interested), while she might hope to retain through the Czechs at least a foothold in the Central confederation.

33. The USSR is likely also, for political reasons, to wish to be represented alongside the Western Powers on any international organs established to deal with the special problems of

East-Central Europe.

34. It is clearly desirable from all points of view that, at any rate before the end of the war, the USSR and its Allies should reach an agreed policy, or al least an agreement on general principles, concerning the future of East-Central Europe. But attempts to meet the views of the Soviet Government on such details as membership and structure of confederations are of less importance than the task of removing the general fears and suspicions from which Soviet interest in such details would arise.

35. Neither by themselves nor as possible tools of Germany is it likely that such confederations can be directed against the USSR. It is only as possible tools of Anglo-Saxon "Imperialism" or "Western capitalism" that they can be suspect. But the latter suspicion is one which no precautions in the selection of members or the forms of unification in the area can remove.

36. It is only if the Soviet Government can be convinced that the British policies of intervention and then of rebuff in the period 1918–39 have been completely abandoned that it will regard Anglo-Saxon influence in East-Central Europe as no longer a menace. This can be achieved only through the full implementation of the Anglo-Soviet Treaty by associating the USSR not only with any plans for East-Central Europe but with all planning for peace. The Soviet Government must somehow be convinced that its own suspension of the Comintern policy will be irrevocably matched by an equal determination on the part of the Anglo-Saxon Powers to give up any attempt, direct or indirect, to destroy or weaken the hold of communism within the Soviet Union.

37. It is probable that, if only the Soviet government could feel secure on these general issues, it would turn with relief from the attempt to pursue an independent forward policy of intervention in East-Central Europe to that co-operation for general security with the Western Powers which it showed itself ready to adopt after 1934, and to its pre-1939 detachment from the detailed affairs of its smaller Western neighbours.

38. The temporary material weakness of the Soviet Union, its tasks of internal reconstruction, the urgent need for

demobilisation of its armies, its preoccupations on its own eastern borders, and the temper of its people, may all combine to make a strong, independent policy in East-Central Europe difficult for it to pursue.

39. Two factors may help to promote this result. The USSR no less than East-Central Europe, will require Anglo-Saxon economic aid. If this aid can be given in such a way that it does not injure Soviet susceptibilities, and that its technical and humanitarian aspects are kept always in the foreground, the similar aid which goes to East-Central Europe may appear in a less menacing light. Secondly, if the European war ends before the Far Eastern war, the much closer co-operation with Russian arms which might come about in the course of the final reckoning with Japan could serve to break down some existing barriers and lead from a genuinely combined war strategy to co-operation for peace.

Foreign Research and Press Service,
Balliol College, Oxford,
2 February 1943.

Notes to Introduction

1. See Ignác Romsics' basic study, "A brit külpolitika és a 'magyar kérdés' 1914–1916" [British foreign policy and the "Hungarian Question," 1941–1946], *Századok* (February, 1966): 273–339.

2. E. L. Woodward and Rohan Butler, eds., *Documents on British Foreign Policy* (London: His Majesty's Stationary Office, 1956), Second Series, vol. 5, 328.

3. Romsics, "A brit külpolitika," 302–303.

4. György Barcza, *Diplomata emlékeim* [My memoirs as a diplomat] (Budapest, Európa, 1994), vol. 1, 384–385.

5. Winston Spencer Churchill, *The Second World War*, vol. 1, *The Gathering Storm* (Boston: Houghton Mifflin, 1948), 223.

6. John Lukacs, *The Duel* (New York: Ticknor and Fields, 1991), 216.

7. Eduard Beneš, "The Organisation of Postwar Europe," *Foreign Affairs* (January 1942): 226–242.

8. Gyula Juhász, ed., *Diplomáciai iratok Magyarország külpolitikájához 1936–1945*, IV kötet, *Magyarország külpolitikája a második világháború kitörésének időszakában 1939–1940*. [Diplomatic documents relating to the foreign policy of Hungary 1936–1945, vol. 4, Hungary's foreign policy during the time of the outbreak of World War II 1939–1940] (Budapest: Akadémiai Kiadó, 1962), 743–761; Ignác Romsics, *István Bethlen: A Great Conservative Statesman of Hungary, 1874–1946* (Highland Lakes, NJ: Atlantic Research and Publications; distributed by Columbia University Press, New York, 1995), 355–356.

9. Károly Urbán and István Vida, eds., "Hexagonálé Bethlen módra. Gróf Bethlen István emlékirata a Duna-federációról"

[Hexagonal cooperation in the Bethlen fashion, memorandum of Count István Bethlen on the Danubian confederation], *Kritika* (November 1991): 32–38.

10. Otto of Austria, "Danubian Reconstruction," *Foreign Affairs* (January 1942): 243–252.

11. Oszkár Jászi, "Federációs tervek" [Federative plans], *Magyar Fórum* (New York) (April, May, August 1942): 9–14, 31–33, 79–80. For the federative concepts by Beneš, Otto von Habsburg, Bethlen, Pelényi, Eckhardt and Jászi, see Ignác Romsics, ed., *Wartime American Plans for a New Hungary, Documents from the U.S. Department of State, 1942–1944* (Highland Lakes, NJ: Atlantic Research and Publications; distributed by Columbia University Press, New York, 1992), 5–14.

12. Gyula Juhász, ed., *Magyar-brit titkos tárgyalások 1943-ban* [Hungarian and British secret negotiations in 1943] (Budapest: Kossuth, 1978), 43.

13. András Rónai, *Térképezett történelem* [Mapped-out history] (Budapest: Magvető, 1989).

14. Winston Spencer Churchill, *The Second World War,* vol. 6, *Triumph and Tragedy* (Boston: Houghton Miffin, 1953), 73.

15. Graham Ross, ed., *The Foreign Office and the Kremlin. British Documents on Anglo-Soviet Relations 1941–1945* (Cambridge: Cambridge University Press, 1984), 46–47, 180–181.

16. John Lukacs, *1945: Year Zero* (New York: Doubleday, 1978), 66.

Notes to Documents

1. Sargent, Sir Harold Orme Garton (1884–1962). British diplomat, and Foreign Office official. Head of the Central European Department of the Foreign Office since 1926. Since 1939 second under secretary of the Foreign Office.

2. According to the agreement of 23 January 1942, the signatories agreed to bring about common customs and tax systems, and to coordinate their foreign, military, and social policies.

3. The forced unification of Austria and Germany took place after the resignation of Austrian Chancellor Kurt von Schuschnigg (1897–1977); the German military occupied Austria on 12 March 1938 and the Anschluss was officially declared a day later.

4. Roosevelt and Churchill made the declaration on 14 August 1941, which was joined by the Soviet Union and other nations on September 24. The Atlantic Charter, which became a document of war aims, specified the Allies' respect of every nation's right of self-determination.

5. The representatives of the exiled Yugoslav and Greek governments signed an agreement on 15 January 1942. They announced plans for the establishment of a Balkan union which would aim to have a common customs union, stabilized currencies, and a coordinated foreign policy; any third country could join it.

6. In December 1935, British Foreign Secretary Samuel Hoare and French Prime Minister Pierre Laval came to an agreement to resolve the Ethiopian crisis. According to the Hoare-Laval Agreement, Italy were to receive two-thirds of the territory of Ethiopia; independent Ethiopia were to receive, as a form of compensation, part of Eritrea. The deal expressed

223

Franco-British acquiescence to Italian expensionism. When the plan was published in the press, there was such a public outcry against it in England and in France, that it could not be put into effect. Hoare, was forced to resign.

7. Principle two of the Atlantic Charter stated that the governments of the United States and Great Britain "desire to see no territorial changes that do not accord with the freely expressed wishes of the peoples concerned."

8. The eighth principle expressed the following: [Roosevelt and Churchill] "believe that all of the nations of the world, for realistic as well as spiritual reasons, must come to the abandonment of the use of force. Since no future peace can be maintained if land, sea or air armaments continue to be employed by nations which threaten, or may threaten, aggression outside of their frontiers, they believe, pending the establishment of a wider and permanent system of general security, that the disarmament of such nations is essential. They will likewise aid and encourage all other practicable measures which will lighten for peace-loving peoples the crushing burden of armaments."

9. Masaryk, Tomáš Garrigue (1850–1937). Czech sociologist and university professor; he championed the Czech national movement and the idea of Czech statehood. He was the president of Czechoslovakia between 1918 and 1935.

10. The Slovakian People's Party was led by the Roman Catholic priest, Father Andrej Hlinka (1864–1935). In the years between the two world wars, it was almost always the opposition party.

11. A reference to the pro-German Slovak puppet regime between 1939 and 1945.

12. The Prague National Assembly ratified the law concerning the autonomy of Ruthenia only on 19 November 1938.

13. On 15 March 1939 the units of the Hungarian army retook Ruthenia which declared its independence from Slovakia the previous day.

14. The date is wrong; the year was 1939, not 1938.

15. On 10 April 1941, German troops occupied Zagreb, and the Independent Croatian state was established; the head of the fascist Ustasha movement, Ante Pavelić was declared its "Poglavnik" (leader).

16. On 7 September 1940, under German pressure Romania returned the territory to Bulgaria.

17. It refers to the agreement of 29 September 1938 between Germany, Italy, Great Britain and France. As the result of the decisions, the Sudeten region was handed over to Germany.

18. In line of to the Munich Agreement, the decision of the German and Italian arbitrators of 2 November 1938 accorded Hungary 11,927 square kilometers of Czechoslovak territory. According to the Czechoslovak census of 1930, there were 1,027,000 people living in the area (of whom 587,000 were Hungarians). The Hungarian census of 1941, counted 1,062,000 people of whom 892,000 were Hungarians.

19. This account is not correct; see note 18.

20. The Peace Treaty of Neuilly was signed by the Allies and defeated Bulgaria on 27 November 1919. According to this treaty, North Dobrudja was ceded to Romania and a smaller stretch along the sea coast to the river Marica was given to Greece; in addition, there was some minor border rectification in favor of Yugoslavia.

21. On 7 April 1939 Italy attacked Albania and began the occupation of the country.

22. Reference made to the Second Vienna Award. According to the decision of the arbitrators, the German and Italian foreign ministers, North Transylvania and the Székelyföld (the three counties where the Székelys lived) were given to Hungary (43,591 square kilometers, 2,185,546 people, of whom Hungarians were 54.5% and Romanians 42.1%).

23. Wrong time frame; obviously, it has to do with the borders before 30 August 1940.

24. Atatürk, Kemal (1881–1938). Turkish statesman; the founder of the Turkish Republic and its first president (1922–1938).

25. Hitler, Adolf (1889–1945). German politician; the leader of the National Socialist Workers' Party since 1921; German chancellor between 30 January 1933–29 April 1945; head of the government since 2 August 1934 (its leader and chancellor); the Commander in Chief of the German military since 1935; committed suicide.

26. Heydrich, Reinhard (1904–1942). SS general, assistant Reich governor of the Czech-Moravian Protectorate since 1941 was assassinated by Czech resistance fighters.

27. Mabbott, J. D., an associate at the Foreign Research and Press Service.

28. Historic German territorial aspirations toward the east.

29. Jebb, Hubert Miles Gladwyn. Private secretary (Dec. 1937–Aug. 1940) of Sir Robert Vansittart, chief diplomatic adviser in the Foreign Office; after August 1940, under secretary at the Ministry of Economic Warfare. Head of the Economic and Reconstruction Department 1942–1945.

30. Ripka, Hubert (1895–1958). Czech politician, historian and journalist; state secretary for foreign affairs. Information minister of the Czechoslovak government-in-exile in London.

31. Seton-Watson, Robert William (1879–1951). Scottish historian; university professor; writer under the pen name Scotus Viator; before and during World War I, he was the most prominent English advocate of the realignment of the East Central European political order. He was an expert of European renown, concentrating on the relations between the minorities in the East Central European region.

32. Allen, William Dennis. Secretary at the British Embassy in China (Jan. 1938–Oct. 1941). At the time of writing the document, he was an official in charge of Far Eastern Affairs.

33. Zimmern, Sir Alfred Eckhard (1879–1957). Montague Burton professor of international relations at Oxford University. An associate working in a subdivision of the Foreign Research and Press Service that was focusing on the British empire. At the end of the war he was briefly the executive director of UNESCO.

34. Welles, Sumner (1892–1961). American politician, diplomat, under secretary of state between 1937–1943. At the beginning of 1940, he flew to Europe as the personal representative of President Roosevelt and undertook negotiations with the representatives of the concerned governments about the possibilities of ceasing military hostilities.

35. Fisher, A. G. B. An associate of a subdivision of the Foreign Research and Press Service that focused on economic issues.

36. Maisky, Ivan Mikhailovich (1884–1975). Soviet diplomat, ambassador to Great Britain between 1932–1943, under secretary of the Foreign Ministry between 1943–1946.

37. The alliance of Yugoslavia, Romania and Czechoslovakia was based upon the pact that was concluded on 14 August 1920 between Yugoslavia and Czechoslovakia. This was complemented by the pact of Romania and Czechoslovakia on 23 April 1921 and that of Romania and Yugoslavia on 7 June 1921. The Little Entente was founded against the revisionist policy of Hungary, against the reunification of Austria and Hungary and against the reestablishment of the Habsburg monarchy; from the beginning it enjoyed France's support.

38. Beneš, Eduard (1884–1948). Czech politician. A founder of Czechoslovakia, minister of foreign affairs (1918–1935), president of the republic between 1935–1938 and between 1946–1948.

39. This agreement was signed by the Czechoslovak government-in-exile in London and by the representatives of the Soviet government on 18 July 1941.

40. Roberts, Frank Kenyon (1907–) official in the British Foreign Office; diplomat; since 1938 he was the chief administrator of the Foreign Office's Central European Department. He became its assistant head at the time of writing the document, and from 1943 to 1945 served as its head. After World War II, he was twice (1945–1947 and 1960–1962) British ambassador to Moscow.

41. Dixon, Pierson John (1904–1965). Secretary at the

British Embassy, Rome (Feb. 1938–Jan. 1940). He was a member of the Southern Department of the British Foreign Office. Appointed principal private secretary to Eden in November 1943.

42. This rejected demarcation line was recommended as the eastern border for Poland by Lord Curzon of Kedleston (1859–1925), British foreign secretary from 1919 to 1924. At the Yalta Conference, which was held from 4 to 11 February 1945, Churchill, Roosevelt and Stalin agreed that Poland's eastern borders have to follow the Curzon line; at certain stretches it deviated between 5–8 kilometers in depth, favoring Poland. The Polish border of 1945 corresponds loosely to the Curzon line that went through the center stretch of Suwałki, Grodno, Brest-Litovsk and Przemyśl.

43. Ronald, Nigel Bruce. At the time the document was written, he was a consultant to the Foreign Office.

44. Seyss-Inquart, Arthur (1892–1946). Austrian politician, the minister of interior for the Schuschnigg government from February 16, 1938. Austrian chancellor from 12 March 1938 to 24 May of the same year. It was he who proclaimed the unification of Austria with Germany, the Anschluss. He remained Reich governor of the Ostmark (Austria) from 24 May 1938 to 30 April 1939 and was Reich commissioner for the Netherlands from 1 May 1940 to 30 April 1945. He was condemned to death as a war criminal at the Nuremberg trials and was executed.

45. Bürckel, Josef (1894–1944). Was Austria's Reich commissioner of Austria from 23 April 1938 to 1 May 1939, then Reich commissioner for Saarland-Lorraine.

46. Ostmark. The name for annexed Austria after the Anschluss.

47. Lightning war, representing German military strategy of World War II.

48. Reference to Schuschnigg's government (1934–1938), which was forced to make compromises with Germany from 1935 on.

49. Reference to the 1 December 1918 decision made by the national assembly that was called by the Romanian National

Committee; the assembly met in Alba Iulia. The delegates accepted Transylvania's accession to Romania with the remarks: "Our unique institutions make the maintenance of a provisional autonomy necessary. This will not alter the achievement of an unconditional union."

50. The Romanian land reform was carried out in 1921, and, as a result, the importance of the dwarf holdings and small holdings increased.

51. The correct date for the Second Vienna Award is 30 August 1940.

52. See the previous footnote.

53. Reference to the pact of 18 May 1941 between Italy and Croatia in which Dalmatia and most Dalmatian islands were attached to Italy.

54. Radić, Stepan (1871–1928). Founded the Croatian Peasant Party with his brother Ante Radić (1868–1919) in 1904. He was the victim of an assassination. Maček, Vlatko Vladimir (1879–1964). Became the leader of the Croatian Peasant Party after the murder of Radić.

55. Wilson, Thomas Woodrow (1856–1924). American politician; President of the United States (1913–1921). His message of January 8, 1918 to Congress contained his famous Fourteen Points. In it, he outlined his ideas for peace.

56. In the Secret Treaty of London, Italy joined the Allies on 20 April 1915, then on 23 May it declared war on the Austro-Hungarian Monarchy.

57. See note 54.

58. Reference to the treaty signed in London on 26 May 1942, a treaty of alliance and mutual assistance.

59. Reference to the Munich Conference of September 1938 (See note 17) and to the events in its wake that led to the dismemberment of Czechoslovakia, the resignation of President Beneš, and the First Vienna Award.

60. After 1918 the contested Czechoslovak sovereignty over

Teschen (Cieszyn, Těšín) and vicinity constituted a constant element of friction between Poland and Czechoslovakia.

61. On 11 April 1941, in the wake of Germany's attack on Yugoslavia, Hungarian troops occupied the formerly Hungarian areas.

Maps

231

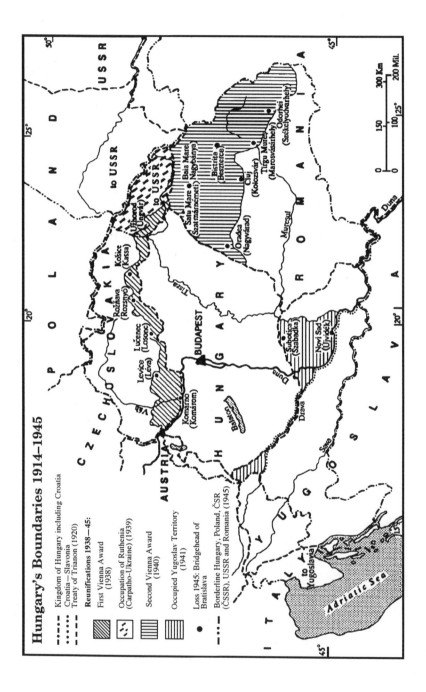

Hungary's Boundaries 1914–1945

Kingdom of Hungary including Croatia
Croatia – Slavonia
Treaty of Trianon (1920)

Reunifications 1938—45:

First Vienna Award
(1938)

Occupation of Ruthenia
(Carpatho-Ukraine) (1939)

Second Vienna Award
(1940)

Occupied Yugoslav Territory
(1941)

Loss 1945: Bridgehead of
Bratislava

Borderline Hungary, Poland, ČSR
(ČSSR), USSR and Romania (1945)

Map 233

Territorial Changes in Central Europe after World War I

LEGEND
Postwar Losses of Territory by

RUSSIA
GERMANY
AUSTRIA & HUNGARY
BULGARIA

Name Index

Place Index

Volumes Published in
"Atlantic Studies on Society in Change"

No. 1 *Tolerance and Movements of Religious Dissent in Eastern Europe.* Edited by B. K. Király. 1977.

No. 2 *The Habsburg Empire in World War I.* Edited by R. A. Kann. 1978.

No. 3 *The Mutual Effects of the Islamic and Judeo-Christian Worlds: The East European Pattern.* Edited by A. Ascher, T. Halasi-Kun, B. K. Király. 1979.

No. 4 *Before Watergate: Problems of Corruption in American Society.* Edited by A. S. Eisenstadt, A. Hoogenboom, H. L. Trefousse. 1979.

No. 5 *East Central European Perceptions of Early America.* Edited by B. K. Király and. G. Bárány. 1977.

No. 6 *The Hungarian Revolution of 1956 in Retrospect.* Edited by B. K. Király and Paul Jonas. 1978.

No. 7 *Brooklyn U.S.A.: Fourth Largest City in America.* Edited by Rita S. Miller. 1979.

No. 8 *Prime Minister Gyula Andrássy's Influence on Habsburg Foreign Policy.* János Decsy. 1979.

No. 9 *The Great Impeacher: A Political Biography of James M. Ashley.* Robert F. Horowitz. 1979.

No. 10
Vol. I* *Special Topics and Generalizations on the Eighteenth and Nineteenth Century.* Edited by B. K. Király and Gunther E. Rothenberg. 1979

* Volumes no. I through XXXVI refer to the series War and Society in East Central Europe.

No. 11
Vol. II
East Central European Society and War in the Pre-Revolutionary 18th Century. Edited by Gunther E. Rothenberg, B. K. Király, and Peter F. Sugar. 1982.

No. 12
Vol. III
From Hunyadi to Rákóczi: War and Society in Late Medieval and Early Modern Hungary. Edited by János M. Bak and B. K. Király. 1982.

No. 13
Vol. IV
East Central European Society and War in the Era of Revolutions: 1775–1856. Edited by B. K. Király. 1984.

No. 14
Vol. V
Essays on World War I: Origins and Prisoners of War. Edited by Samuel R. Williamson, Jr. and Peter Pastor. 1983.

No. 15
Vol. VI
Essays on World War I: Total War and Peacemaking, A Case Study on Trianon. Edited by B. K. Király, Peter Pastor and Ivan Sanders. 1982.

No. 16
Vol. VII
Army, Aristocracy, Monarchy: War, Society and Government in Austria, 1618–1780. Edited by Thomas M. Baker. 1982.

No. 17
Vol. VIII
The First Serbian Uprising 1804–1813. Edited by Wayne S. Vucinich. 1982.

No. 18
Vol. IX
Czechoslovak Policy and the Hungarian Minority 1945–1948. Kálmán Janics. Edited by Stephen Borsody. 1982.

No. 19
Vol. X
At the Brink of War and Peace: The Tito-Stalin Split in a Historic Perspective. Edited by Wayne S. Vucinich. 1982.

No. 20
Inflation Through the Ages: Economic, Social, Psychological and Historical Aspects. Edited by Edward Marcus and Nathan Schmuckler. 1981.

No. 21   *Germany and America: Essays on Problem of International Relations and Immigration.* Edited by Hans L. Trefousse. 1980.

No. 22   *Brooklyn College: The First Half Century.* Murray M. Horovitz. 1981.

No. 23   *A New Deal for the World: Eleanor Roosevelt and American Foreign Policy.* Jason Berger. 1981.

No. 24   *The Legacy of Jewish Migration: 1881 and Its Impact.* Edited by David Berger. 1982.

No. 25   *The Road to Bellapais: Cypriot Exodus to Northern Cyprus.* Pierre Oberling. 1982.

No. 26   *New Hungarian Peasants: An East Central European Experience with Collectivization.* Edited by Marida Hollos and Béla C. Maday. 1983.

No. 27   *Germans in America: Aspects of German-American Relations in the Nineteenth Century.* Edited by Allen McCormick. 1983.

No. 28   *A Question of Empire. Leopold I and the War of Spanish Succession, 1701–1705.* Linda and Marsha Frey. 1983.

No. 29   *The Beginning of Cyrillic Printing—Cracow, 1491. From the Orthodox Past in Poland.* Szczepan K. Zimmer. Edited by L. Krzyżanowski and I. Nagurski. 1983.

No. 29a   *A Grand Ecole for the Grand Corps: The Recruitment and Training of the French Administration.* Thomas R. Osborne. 1983.

No. 30
Vol. XI
The First War between Socialist States: The Hungarian Revolution of 1956 and Its Impact. Edited by B. K. Király, Barbara Lotze, Nandor Dreisziger. 1984.

No. 31
Vol. XII
The Effects of World War I, The Uprooted: Hungarian Refugees and Their Impact on Hungary's Domestic Politics. István Mócsy. 1983.

No. 32
Vol. XIII
The Effects of World War I: The Class War after the Great War: The Rise of Communist Parties in East Central Europe, 1918–1921. Edited by Ivo Banac. 1983.

No. 33
Vol. XIV
The Crucial Decade: East Central European Society and National Defense, 1859–1870. Edited by B. K. Király. 1984.

No. 35
Vol. XVI
Effects of World War I: War Communism in Hungary, 1919. György Péteri. 1984.

No. 36
Vol. XVII
Insurrections, Wars, and the Eastern Crisis in the 1870s. Edited by B. K. Király and Gale Stokes. 1985.

No. 37
Vol. XVIII
East Central European Society and the Balkan Wars, 1912–1913. Edited by Béla K. Király and Dimitrije Djordjevic. 1986.

No. 38
Vol. XIX
East Central European Society in World War I. Edited by B. K. Király and N. F. Dreisziger, Assistant Editor Albert A. Nofi. 1985.

No. 39
Vol. XX
Revolutions and Interventions in Hungary and Its Neighbor States, 1918–1919. Edited by Peter Pastor. 1988.

No. 41
Vol. XXII
Essays on East Central European Society and War, 1740–1920. Edited by Stephen Fischer-Galati and B. K. Király. 1988.

No. 42   *East Central European Maritime Commerce and*
Vol. XXIII *Naval Policies, 1789–1913.* Edited by Apostolos E.
            Vacalopoulos, Constantinos D. Svolopoulos, and B.
            K. Király. 1988.

No. 43   *Selections, Social Origins, Education and Training*
Vol. XXIV   *of East Central European Officers Corps.* Edited by
            B. K. Király and Walter Scott Dillard. 1988.

No. 44   *East Central European War Leaders: Civilian and*
Vol. XXV   *Military.* Edited by B. K. Király and Albert Nofi. 1988.

No. 46   *Germany's International Monetary Policy and the*
            European Monetary System. Hugo Kaufmann. 1985.

No. 47   *Iran Since the Revolution—Internal Dynamics, Region-*
            al Conflicts and the Superpowers. Edited by Barry
            M. Rosen. 1985.

No. 48   *The Press during the Hungarian Revolution of 1848–*
Vol. XXVII *1849.* Domokos Kosáry. 1986.

No. 49   *The Spanish Inquisition and the Inquisitional Mind.*
            Edited by Angel Alcala. 1987.

No. 50   *Catholics, the State and the European Radical Right,*
            1919–1945. Edited by Richard Wolff and Jorg K.
            Hoensch.   1987.

No. 51   *The Boer War and Military Reforms.* Jay Stone and
Vol. XXVIII Erwin A. Schmidl. 1987.

No. 52   *Baron Joseph Eötvös, A Literary Biography.* Steven
            B. Várdy. 1987.

No. 53   *Towards the Renaissance of Puerto Rican Studies:*
            Ethnic and Area Studies in University Education.
            Maria Sanchez and Antonio M. Stevens. 1987.

No. 54   *The Brazilian Diamonds in Contracts, Contraband and Capital*. Harry Bernstein. 1987.

No. 55   *Christians, Jews and Other Worlds: Patterns of Conflict and Accommodation*. Edited by Philip F. Galagher. 1988.

No. 56   *The Fall of the Medieval Kingdom of Hungary:*
Vol. XXVI *Mohács, 1526, Buda, 1541*. Géza Perjés. 1989.

No. 57   *The Lord Mayor of Lisbon: The Portuguese Tribune of the People and His 24 Guilds*. Harry Bernstein. 1989.

No. 58   *Hungarian Statesmen of Destiny: 1860–1960*. Edited by Paul Bődy. 1989.

No. 59   *For China: The Memoirs of T. G. Li, Former Major General in the Chinese Nationalist Army*. T. G. Li. Written in collaboration with Roman Rome. 1989.

No. 60   *Politics in Hungary: For a Democratic Alternative*. János Kis, with an Introduction by Timothy Garton Ash. 1989.

No. 61   *Hungarian Worker's Councils in 1956*. Edited by Bill Lomax. 1990.

No. 62   *Essays on the Structure and Reform of Centrally Planned Economic Systems*. Paul Jonas. A joint publication with Corvina Kiadó, Budapest. 1990.

No. 63   *Kossuth as a Journalist in England*. Éva H. Haraszti. A joint publication with Akadémiai Kiadó, Budapest. 1990.

No. 64   *From Padua to the Trianon, 1918–1920*. Mária Ormos. A joint publication with Akadémiai Kiadó, Budapest. 1990.

No. 65   *Towns in Medieval Hungary.* Edited by László Gerevich. A joint publication with Akadémiai Kiadó, Budapest. 1990.

No. 66   *The Nationalities Problem in Transylvania, 1867–1940.* Sándor Bíró. 1992.

No. 67   *Hungarian Exiles and the Romanian National Movement, 1849–1867.* Béla Borsi-Kálmán. 1991.

No. 68   *The Hungarian Minority's Situation in Ceauescu's Romania.* Edited by Rudolf Joó and Andrew Ludanyi. 1994.

No. 69   *Democracy, Revolution, Self-Determination. Selected Writings.* István Bibó. Edited by Károly Nagy. 1991.

No. 70   *Trianon and the Protection of Minorities.* József Galántai. A joint publication with Corvina Kiadó, Budapest. 1991.

No. 71   *King Saint Stephen of Hungary.* György Györffy. 1994.

No. 72   *Dynasty, Politics and Culture. Selected Essays.* Robert A. Kann. Edited by Stanley B. Winters. 1991.

No. 73   *Jadwiga of Anjou and the Rise of East Central Europe.* Oscar Halecki. Edited by Thaddeus V. Gromada. A joint publication with the Polish Institute of Arts and Sciences of America. New York. 1991.

No. 74   *Hungarian Economy and Society during World War*
Vol. XXIX   *Two.* Edited by György Lengyel. 1993.

No. 75   *The Life of a Communist Revolutionary, Béla Kun.* György Borsányi. 1993.

No. 76   *Yugoslavia: The Process of Disintegration.* Laslo
              Sekelj. 1993.

No. 77   *Wartime American Plans for a New Hungary. Docu-*
Vol. XXX   *ments from the U.S. Department of State, 1942–1944.*
              Edited by Ignác Romsics. 1992.

No. 78   *Planning for War against Russia and Serbia. Austro-*
Vol. XXXI   *Hungarian and German Military Strategies, 1871–1914.*
              Graydon A. Tunstall, Jr. 1993.

No. 79   *American Effects on Hungarian Imagination and*
              Political Thought, 1559–1848. Géza Závodszky. 1995.

No. 80   *Trianon and East Central Europe: Antecedents and*
Vol. XXXII   *Repercussions.* Edited by B. K. Király and L. Veszprémy.
              1995.

No. 81   *Hungarians and Their Neighbors in Modern Times,*
              1867–1950. Edited by Ferenc Glatz. 1995.

No. 82   *István Bethlen: A Great Conservative Statesman of*
              Hungary, 1874–1946. Ignác Romsics. 1995.

No. 83   *20th Century Hungary and the Great Powers.* Edited
Vol. XXXIII   by Ignác Romsics. 1995.

No. 84   *Lawful Revolution in Hungary, 1989–1994.* Edited
              by B. K. Király and András Bozóki. 1995.

No. 85   *The Demography of Contemporary Hungarian Society.*
              Edited by Pál Péter Tóth and Emil Valkovics. 1996.

No. 86   *Budapest, A History from Its Beginnings to 1996.*
              Edited by András Gerő and János Poór. 1996.

No. 87   *The Dominant Ideas of the Nineteenth Century and*
              Their Impact on the State. Volume 1. *Diagnosis.* József

Eötvös. Translated, edited, annotated and indexed
with an introductory essay by D. Mervyn Jones. 1996.

No. 88   *The Dominant Ideas of the Nineteenth Century and
Their Impact on the State.* Volume 2. *Remedy.* József
Eötvös. Translated, edited, annotated and indexed
with an introductory essay by D. Mervyn Jones. 1997.

No. 89   *The Social History of the Hungarian Intelligentsia
in the "Long Nineteenth Century," 1825–1914.* János
Mazsu. 1996.

No. 90   *Pax Britannica: Wartime Foreign Office Documents
Vol. XXXIV Regarding Plans for a Postbellum East Central Europe.*
Edited by András D. Bán. 1997.

No. 91   *National Identity in Contemporary Hungary.* György
Csepeli. 1996.

No. 92   *The Hungarian Parliament, 1867–1918: A Mirage of
Power.* András Gerő. 1997.

No. 93   *The Hungarian Revolution and War for Independence
Vol. XXXV 1848–1849. A Military History.* Edited by Gábor Bona.
1997.

No. 94   *The End of Assimilation: "The Jewish Question" in
Hungary.* Tamás Ungvári. 1997.

No. 95   *Academia and State Socialism: Essays on the Political
History of Academic Life in Post-1945 Hungary and
East Central Europe.* György Péteri. 1997.

No. 96   *Through the Prism of the Habsburg Monarchy:
Vol. XXXVI Hungary in American Diplomacy and Public Opinion
during World War I.* Tibor Glant. 1997.